RAIDERS
FROM OAKLAND TO LOS ANGELES

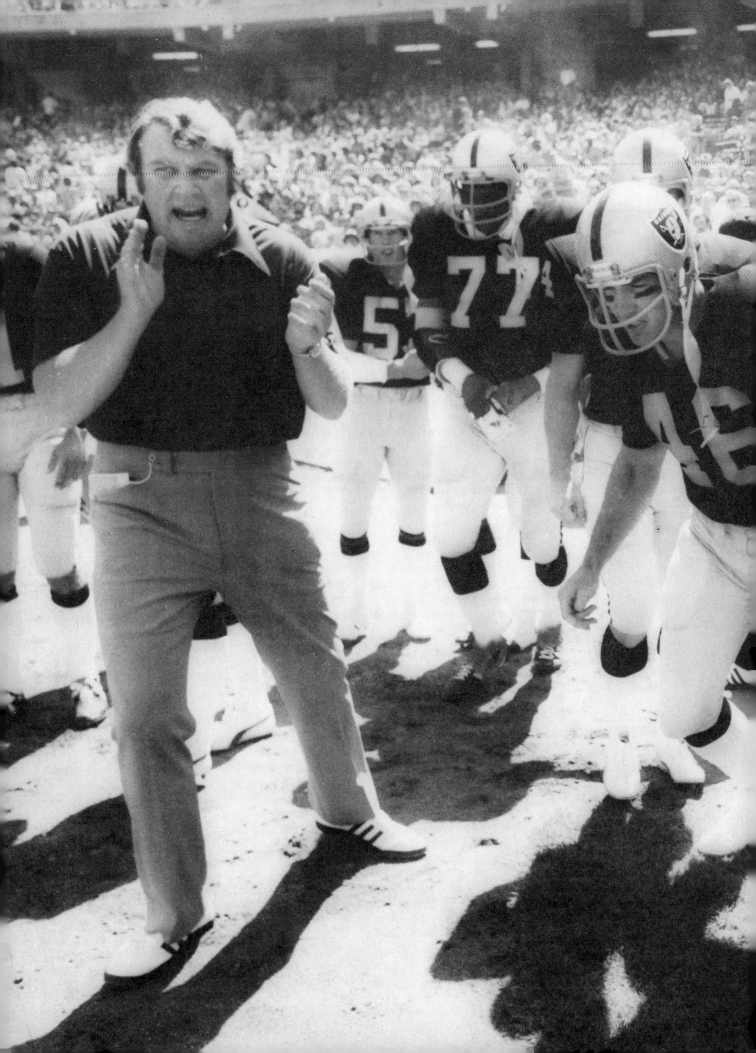

RAIDERS
FROM OAKLAND TO LOS ANGELES

BY JOSEPH HESSION
& STEVE CASSADY

FOGHORN PRESS
SAN FRANCISCO

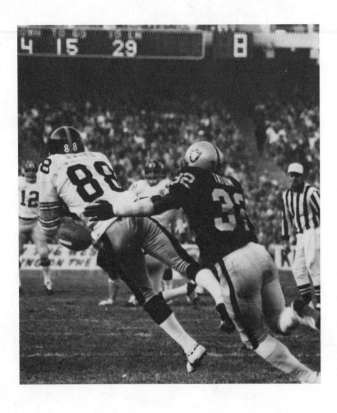

ISBN 0-935701-35-4
Printed in the United States of America

CONTENTS

FOREWORD

I had a long and satisfying NFL career but my 10 seasons with the Oakland Raiders were something special. I have vivid memories of those years. When I played with the Raiders they were the team people loved to hate. I don't know if that was a reflection on the cast of characters we had there or if it all started with Al Davis. I do know that Oakland was a blue collar town that appreciated our brand of football.

We always had a huge and loyal following in Oakland. Everything seemed to fit together there. The team had an incredible amount of camaraderie. Guys like Jack Tatum, Marv Hubbard and Otis Sistrunk all played through intimidation. My receivers, Cliff Branch, Fred Biletnikoff and Dave Casper, were some of the most exciting players to ever step on a football field. They all helped make the Raiders a perennial winner. They also entertained people both on and off the field.

One of the things that made the Raiders unique was the club's uncanny ability to pull out wins in the last minute of a ball game. We will always be remembered for that. The Raiders were involved in some of the most dramatic games in NFL history, like the Immaculate Reception game and the Heidi game. It was that kind of excitement that ultimately gave John Madden ulcers and drove him to the broadcast booth.

The one moment in my career that really stands out is Super Bowl XI. After coming so close so many times we finally won it all by beating the Minnesota Vikings. My good friend, Freddy Biletnikoff was the game's Most Valuable Player. His clutch receptions set up three scores. I'll always remember the scene in the locker room after the game; the elation of all the players and everyone hugging one another. We didn't want that feeling to end.

The Raiders are starting a new tradition in Los Angeles. The club's legacy will continue to thrive there. As always, Al Davis has assembled a great cast of characters centered around an intimidating defense. Hopefully that cast can lead the silver and black to another Super Bowl soon. Like all my former teammates, I'm looking forward to that day.

KEN STABLER

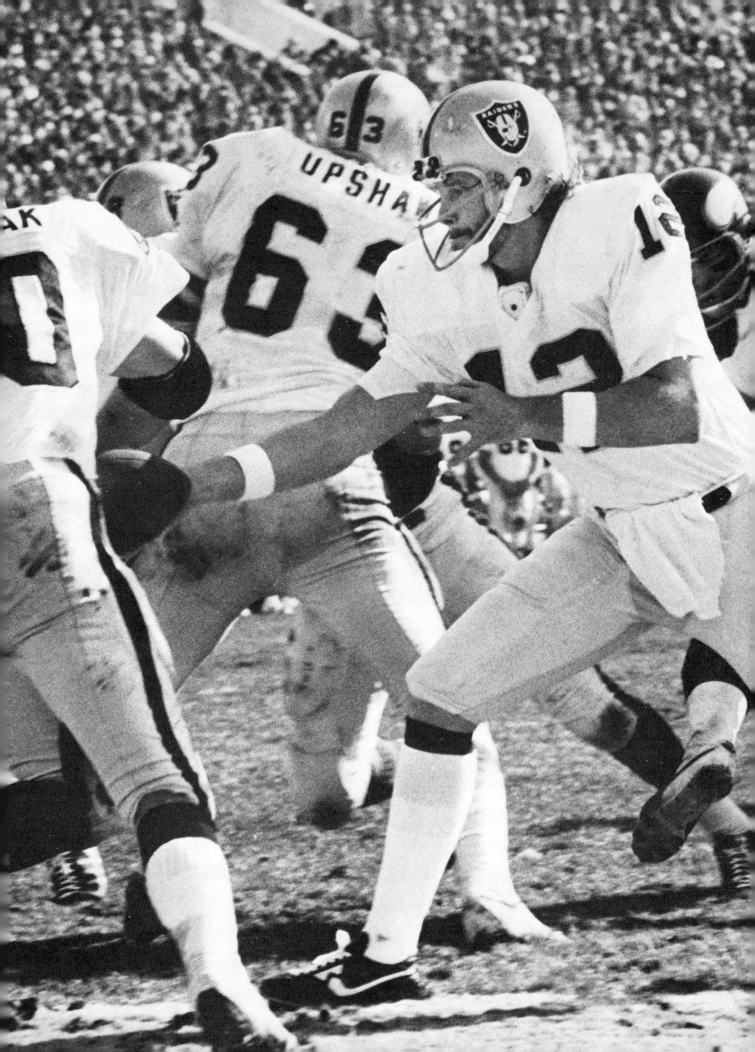

INTRODUCTION

The picture will be forever engraved in my mind. Ken Stabler rolling left with 31 seconds to play and the 1974 AFC playoff game on the line. He was closely pursued by Vern Den Herder, the Miami Dolphin's 6'6" defensive end.

The scene had been set only 73 seconds earlier when the Miami Dolphins scored to take a 26-21 lead. Stabler calmly led his men back onto the field with just under two minutes to play. Guard Gene Upshaw recalled the atmosphere as he joined the huddle. "Ken gave us confidence. He was so cool, so calm. He said, 'Just give me a little time and we'll get the job done.'"

Stabler was good on his word. He quickly marched the Raiders to the Miami eight-yard line. With 31 seconds remaining on the clock, he dropped back and was chased out of the pocket by Den Herder. The All-Pro defensive end finally caught Stabler and hurled him to the Oakland Coliseum turf. As Stabler was being tackled, he was able to hurl a desperation pass in the direction of running back Clarence Davis. Davis was in the end zone surrounded by three Dolphin defenders. He outmanuevered the trio and made a spectacular catch.

The Coliseum crowd sat momentarily stunned, then erupted like a neutron bomb. Fans swarmed from their seats and onto the field, screaming like Banshees. The sudden victory sparked a common emotion among Raider fans. They had to touch and congratulate their team. I found myself swept along by the crowd then looking up at Otis Sistrunk, Oakland's mountainous defensive tackle. Sistrunk was slapping hands with anyone he could find, including the fans gathered around him.

Once the spontaneous celebration subsided, the stadium security guards moved in and attempted to clear the field. Twenty seconds still remained on the clock. Miami had one last shot, but the Raiders held and advanced to the AFC Championship Game.

That victory proved once again the Raiders were not an average football team. For years prior to that 1974 playoff game I had seen the Raiders pull off remarkable last minute wins. There was Daryl Lamonica's "Mad Bomber" attacks in the late 1960s, the "Heidi" game in 1968, George Blanda's heroics in five consecutive contests in 1970, and Stabler's constant success with two minutes to play. But nothing had ever rivaled the Miami game for sheer drama.

Of course, the Raiders always had a flair for the dramatic but there was something else that became painfully obvious about the club that day. It was embodied in Stabler's style, the way he swaggered onto the field, oozing confidence, as the clock continued to tick away. He moved the offense toward the Miami goal line with the efficiency of a well-oiled steam roller. There was no hint of worry or nervousness. Stabler acted as though it was his divine right to win that game and nothing could stop him.

Such arrogance has become a Raider trademark, what Al Davis calls "Pride and Poise." For 22 years, from 1960 to 1981, the Raider legacy grew in Northern California. During that time some of the country's finest football players called Oakland their home. Men like Jim Otto, George Blanda, Willie Brown, Fred Biletnikoff and Art Shell helped transform the Raiders from a rag-tag band of losers into the winningest franchise in sports history. Indeed, since Al Davis joined the Raiders in 1963, the club has won over 70 percent of its football games and has the best winning percentage in the NFL.

The Raiders' rich history is just now beginning to take hold in Los Angeles. Since moving south in 1982, the club has continued its winning ways with a new generation of stars. Marcus Allen, Dokie Williams, Howie Long, Don Mosebar and Greg Townsend are just a few of the talented players who have carried on the Raider tradition of excellence.

That tradition is sure to continue.

—Joseph Hession

Pages 2-3: John Madden stirs up his troops prior to the 1976 home opener against the Super Bowl champion Pittsburgh Steelers. **Page 4:** Waiting on the sidelines for the next series. **Page 6:** Jack Tatum (32), also known as ''the Assassin,'' prepares to crush Lynn Swann in the secondary. **Pages 6-7:** Steeler running back Rocky Bleir (20) is gang tackled by Art Thoms (80), Gerald Irons (86) and Nemiah Wilson (48). **Pages 8-9:** Clarence Davis (28) makes one of the most dramatic catches in Raider history to beat the Miami Dolphins with 20 seconds remaining in the 1974 AFC conference playoffs. **Pages 10-11:** The Raider offensive line clears a hole in the Minnesota defense for running back Pete Banaszak (40). Quarterback Ken Stabler (12) makes the hand off. **Pages 12-13:** The Raider offense prepares to begin a drive from their own one-yard line against the Green Bay Packers. **Page 14:** Wide receiver Cliff Branch makes a spectacular catch to set up a Raider touchdown. Branch is second on the club's all-time receiving list behind Fred Biletnikoff. **Page 18:** Tight end Billy Cannon (33) juggles a pass as two New York players close in. Cannon won the Heisman Trophy at LSU in 1959.

1960–1969

CHAPTER ONE

THE FORMATIVE YEARS

O akland was a sleepy town in 1959. The city had no professional sport franchises. The California Bears, with Joe Kapp at quarterback, were the closest thing to big time football in the area. Kapp led Cal to the Rose Bowl that year.

In the summer of 1959 a group of football enthusiasts with large bankrolls got together to form a new league, something to rival the National Football League. They called it the American Football League and chose wealthy Texas oilman Lamar Hunt as its president. Franchises were awarded to businessmen from the cities of Boston, Buffalo, Dallas, Denver, Houston, Los Angeles, Minneapolis and New York. They agreed to begin operation in the fall of 1960. Once again, Oakland was left in the cold.

Not long afterward the owners selected former South Dakota governor Joe Foss as the league's first commissioner and retained Lamar Hunt, owner of the Dallas franchise, as the league's president. They ran into a crisis almost immediately.

Barely six months before the AFL season was to begin, Minneapolis was offered an NFL franchise. The Minneapolis club owners decided to sever their relationship with the AFL in order to join the NFL in 1961. Meanwhile, the AFL team owners were determined to find another city that could support a franchise before the season began.

After several days of discussion, the AFL's management was prepared to award the Minneapolis franchise to the city of Atlanta. However, Barron Hilton, owner of the Los Angeles Chargers, refused to endorse Atlanta's bid for a team. Hilton wanted a companion franchise on the west coast, a team that would serve as a natural rival for his Chargers. Hilton's negative vote opened the door for a group of Bay Area businessmen.

Most of the league's team owners expressed concern about the San Francisco Bay Area's ability to support two franchises since the 49ers were already firmly entrenched there. Nevertheless, on January 30, 1960, AFL management voted to award Oakland a football team. Hilton got want he wanted, a team that would later become one of the Chargers most bitter rivals.

Among the group responsible for bringing football to Oakland were the team's co-owners Ed McGah, Harvey Binns, Wayne Valley, Chet Soda, Robert Osborne, Charles Harney and Don Blessing. Soda was named the club's first general manager.

Ed Erdelatz was appointed head coach of the Oakland Raiders. Erdelatz was a local product, raised in Berkeley and educated at nearby St. Joseph's grammar school. He later attended St. Mary's College in Moraga.

General Manager Chet Soda said of Erdelatz at the time of his signing, "As far as we are concerned we have the best football coach in the Ameri

can Football League. When we go into New York or Boston or Dallas, we won't have to introduce Eddie Erdelatz. He is a nationally known figure."

Erdelatz began to gain recognition as the line coach of the San Francisco 49ers in 1948-49. Both years the 49ers led the NFL in rushing, largely because of the team's tough line play. He moved on to become head coach at the U.S. Naval Academy in 1950. It was with the Middies that he really made his mark. In his first season at the helm he directed the Academy to one of college football's greatest upsets, a 14-2 win over an Army team that was favored by 20 points. In nine seasons at Annapolis, he guided the Middies to a 50-26-8 record, including a victory over Rice in the 1958 Cotton Bowl. The Raiders signed him to a three-year contract at a reported $25,000 per season.

Oakland's next move was to acquire a playing field and 40 respectable football players. It wasn't easy. The Berkeley City Council turned down a request for temporary use of the University of California's Memorial Stadium. Soda then approached San Francisco's Recreation and Parks Department and got permission to share Kezar Stadium with the San Francisco 49ers.

Meanwhile, Soda began work on a long range plan to build a stadium in Oakland. With the help of Robert Osborne, an Oakland city councilman and co-owner of the team, and Oakland Mayor Clifford Rishell, a stadium bond issue was eventually placed on the ballot.

Erdelatz spent his time weeding through the available football talent. For the most part, the AFL honored existing NFL contracts and did not attempt to lure players away from the established league. Instead, the new clubs concentrated on free agents, unknown rookies, ancient NFL stars and players from the Canadian League. Some AFL teams went all out to sign top-notch rookies. Heisman Trophy winner Billy Cannon, who signed with Houston, was the most notable.

Since Oakland was the last city to be awarded a franchise, the club had a hard time locating tal-

Daryle Lamonica (3) eludes the rush of San Francisco 49er defensive tackle Charlie Krueger. Lamonica set a team record in 1969 by throwing six touchdown passes in a single game against the Houston Oilers.

ented players. Erdelatz did his best. He sifted through dozens of marginal players and was able to field a surprisingly respectable team. Among the athletes signed by Oakland were quarterbacks Babe Parilli and Tom Flores, running backs Tony Teresa, Billy Lott and James "Jetstream" Smith, and a pair of rookie linemen named Jim Otto and Wayne Hawkins.

The 30-year-old Parilli brought needed experience to the club. He had spent four years with the Green Bay Packers and one year with the Cleveland Browns before joining the Raiders. Tom Flores, a rookie from College of Pacific, challenged Parilli for the starting quarterback job. Their main targets would be receivers Gene Prebola, Charley Hardy and Al Goldstein.

The Raiders' biggest problem was in attracting fans to San Francisco to watch an Oakland-based team. Only 1,500 season tickets were sold that first year. Kezar Stadium, located near San Francisco's Golden Gate Park, held over 61,000. Nevertheless, when Oakland played its first game, a preseason affair on July 31, 1960 against the Dallas Texans, nearly 12,000 curious spectators turned out at Kezar.

Tom Flores got the starting call at quarterback. Early in the opening quarter, Oakland recovered a fumble at the Dallas 34. The Raiders took just four plays to put the ball in the end zone. Flores completed two passes to Billy Lott covering 32 yards. On first down from the two-yard line, fullback Buddy Allen blasted off left tackle to score the first touchdown in Raider history. Larry Barnes kicked the extra point.

Dallas scored 14 straight points and took a 14-7 lead into the fourth quarter when Flores began to march the Raiders downfield again. He tossed short passes to receiver Charley Hardy and halfback Tony Teresa while Billy Lott picked up yardage on the ground. From the one-yard line, Buddy Allen banged over to score his second touchdown of the day.

Down 14-13, Oakland decided to play for the win and went for the two-point PAT. Flores gave the ball to Lott on an off-tackle play. He was stopped short of the goal line and Dallas held on to win.

Flores ended the day with 14 completions in 25 attempts for 151 yards. Buddy Allen was the leading ball carrier, gaining 37 yards on 16 tries. Despite scoring two touchdowns, including the

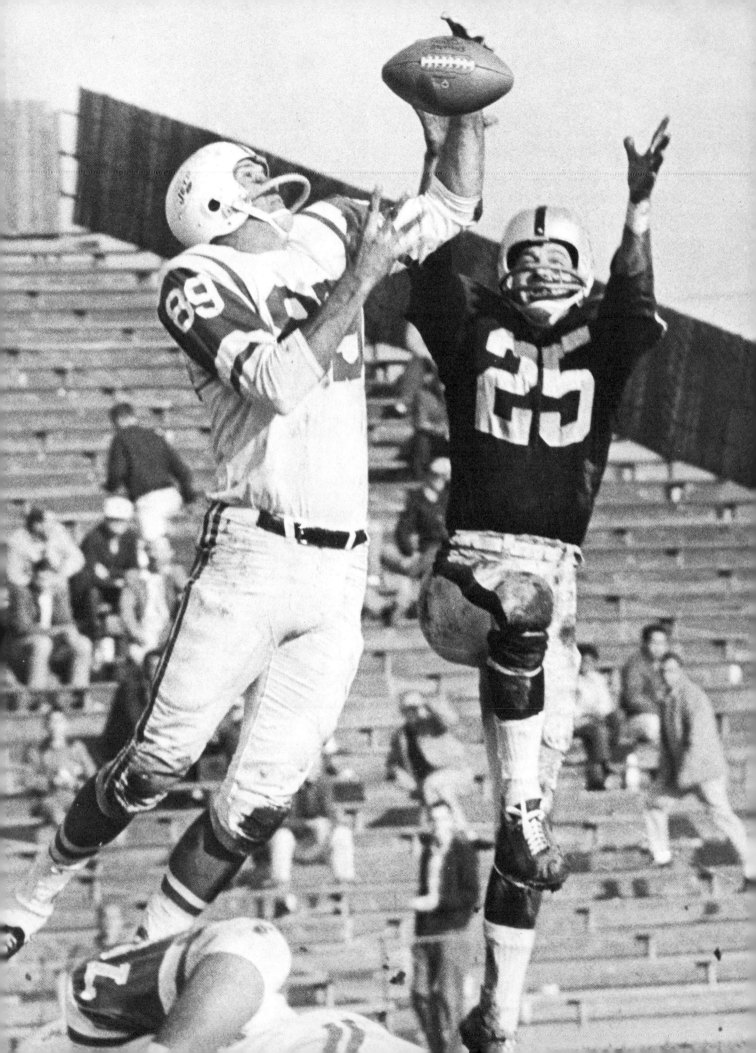

first in Raider history, Allen failed to make the team and is not mentioned on the club's all-time roster.

Although Oakland lost to Dallas, the local media had high hopes for the Raiders. Bill Leiser, sports editor of the San Francisco Chronicle, wrote, "They don't have anything approaching real running power, nor breakaway strength. They have no big, tall, fast pass receivers. But they do have at least one real passer, and they have a game . . . Their fight is terrific. They actually ran from one end of the field to the other during the time out shift from third quarter to fourth. We have never seen a team—college or professional—so anxious to play."

The Raiders got their first win a week later by whipping the New York Titans, 23-17, at Sacramento's Hughes Stadium before 9,551 spectators. The Titans, coached by Sammy Baugh, had one of the best young receivers in the league in speedy Don Maynard. Maynard caught nine passes for 135 yards, almost half of New York's total offensive output.

Oakland's defense began to show some potential against the Titans. The line, anchored by 6-4, 245-pound Carmen Cavalli and defensive end Charley Powell, held the Titans to just 101 yards rushing. Titan quarterback Dick Jamieson was sacked four times by the Raider front four.

Oakland finished the preseason with a 2-3 record after defeating the Buffalo Bills, 26-21, and losing to the Los Angeles Chargers and the Boston Patriots. The club's first opponent in regular season competition would be the powerful Houston Oilers.

Houston was one of the class teams in the new league. Starting at quarterback for the Oilers was George Blanda, a veteran of 10 NFL seasons with the Chicago Bears. Blanda teamed in the backfield with Heisman Trophy winning halfback Billy Cannon and rugged fullback Dave Smith.

Nearly 13,000 fans showed up at Kezar Stadium to watch Oakland's first league contest. The Raiders played tough football for nearly three quarters. They tied the Oilers, 7-7, in the second quarter on a 13-yard pass from Tom Flores to Tony Teresa. It was the Raiders' first touchdown ever in league play.

Midway through the third period the Raiders took a 14-7 lead when defensive back Eddie Macon intercepted a Blanda pass and returned it 42

Above: Raider fullback Billy Cannon (33) explodes around right end against Houston. **Page 22:** Defensive back Claude Gibson (25) goes high in the air to break up a pass intended for New York Jet receiver Dee Mackey. Gibson was the Raider's most effective punt returner between 1963-65. He averaged 12.6 yards per return, a Raider record, and scored three touchdowns.

yards. The interception seemed to do nothing more than irritate Blanda. After that, the 32-year-old veteran took matters into his own hands. He threw four touchdown passes and kicked one field goal enroute to a 37-22 Houston victory.

The Dallas Texans were next on Oakland's schedule. A slightly smaller crowd of 8,020 fans at Kezar Stadium watched the Texans intercept five passes as they posted a 34-16 win. League president Lamar Hunt, who was in attendance at the game, expressed disappointment at the crowd.

"Oakland was the last team in the league and got the leftovers as we realized they would," Hunt said. "But the other teams helped provide them with players. I knew it would take time to create fan interest but I never expected the first season to be this poor."

Babe Parilli went most of the way at quarterback for Oakland. He completed 16 of 28 passes for 174 yards and two touchdowns. Two of his passes were picked off. Flores also threw two interceptions. Teresa was the team's leading receiver with five catches for 94 yards. He scored in the second period on a 36-yard pass from Parilli.

In the third week of the season, Oakland got its first AFL victory by defeating Houston, 14-13. It was a thrilling win for Oakland. Tom Flores marched the Raiders 52 yards in the fourth quarter and capped it with a 14-yard pass to end Gene Prebola for the game-winning touchdown.

Houston had one last chance to score late in the game. The Oilers recovered a Raider fumble on the Oakland 28 with less than a minute to go. After picking up seven yards on two plays, Houston's George Blanda came in to attempt a 28-yard field goal. The kick was wide and Oakland had its first league victory.

One of Oakland's most satisfying wins in 1960 came against the New York Titans at the Polo Grounds in New York. The Raiders started the game with a 3-4 record. New York was 4-3.

The game was played in a steady drizzle and biting wind. For nearly four quarters the Titans dominated the game behind the passing of Al Dorow and receptions of Don Maynard and Art Powell. In the fourth period, with New York clinging to a 24-14 lead, the Raiders finally got a break. Oakland cornerback Eddie Macon stopped a Titan drive by intercepting a pass at his own nine-yard line.

Quarterback Babe Parilli took over and guided Oakland the length of the field. "Jetstream" Smith finished off the 91-yard drive by blasting three yards for the touchdown. But Oakland still trailed, 24-21. New York kicker Bill Shockley added a field goal and with five minutes left, the game was in quarterback Babe Parilli's hands.

After the kickoff, Parilli went to work. He kept the ball on the ground, sending Tony Teresa on

Top: New York Jet quarterback Joe Namath (12) is brought down from behind by defensive tackle Tom Keating (74).
Bottom: Ben Davidson (83) and Tom Keating sack San Francisco 49er quarterback John Brodie (12) as the ball bounces away.

Fred Biletnikoff 1965-78

Every now and then, a player will come along who teaches the coaches themselves a little about football.

When George Blanda and Ray Guy played in Oakland, for instance, special teams assistant Joe Scannella used to laugh at the idea he was "coaching" them.

"I don't coach them," Scannella scoffed. "I take film of what they're doing when they're in a groove. Then when they fall out of that groove, I take them in and show them the film. But coaching, no. Those guys teach themselves how to kick and punt."

Flanker Fred Biletnikoff was another one from whom the coaches could learn. After watching Biletnikoff catch passes, John Madden worked out his definition of "hands".

" 'Hands,' " said Madden, "are more than having a gift for catching the ball. The true definition of 'hands' in football is where both hands work as one. No matter where the receiver is, how off balance he might be, it's both hands going for the ball as though they were one. I learned that from watching Freddy."

Fred Biletnikoff from Erie, Pennsylvania, was the son of a national AAU boxing champion. He was named All-American in college in 1964, ranking fourth in the nation with 57 catches. He set records at Florida State for receptions, touchdowns and points scored.

Biletnikoff eventually would have the same impact on the record book as a professional in Oakland. Al Davis drafted him in the second round in 1965, during the player talent wars just before the AFL-NFL merger. Davis outbid the Detroit Lions, and in doing so brought one of the all-time greats to the Oakland Coliseum for a career that lasted 14 seasons, 1965 to 1978.

Freddy was at his best during big games, a technician without speed, a student of the science of pass receiving. Number 25, worked free in the zones and beat cornerbacks with a dazzling array of ins, outs, hooks, comebacks and occasionally ups.

He started, however, with less than a bang. His first game as a rookie, a preseason match against Denver in Salt Lake City, he dropped five passes before catching an 80-yard scoring toss from Lee Grosscup.

The touchdown was an omen of things to come, but on the long bus ride to the airport that day, Biletnikoff sat alone, staring at his hands. Then and later, he was thoroughly impatient with substandard performance, always feverish to improve and excel.

As a rookie, he saw how different the professional game was from college. He said, "When I was at FSU, we played against the types of defenses where all I had to do was run straight downfield, go either in or out, and I was clear. But when I got to Oakland in 1965, I had to beat somebody really good to get open each time.

"I tended to get so hung up trying to beat my man, I had trouble catching the football."

Freddy had the natural hands that John Madden marveled at. And his answer to the other part, getting open, was to study pass receiving as though it were a science to be applied on Sunday in the secondary.

"Running a pattern is not as easy as it looks," he said. "Unless you've worked hard on the difficult steps in a route, it gets awkward when you try it in a game."

Every year in training camp, Biletnikoff broke down each of his patterns into a series of individual moves. He practiced each step until it was fluid and in stride. Only when each one had been mastered in turn would he run the pattern as one continuous route.

He created a rhythm of acceleration, momentum and body control, such that he was rarely distracted when his hands flicked out for the ball.

He perfected all the Raiders' routes, especially the comebacks. He brought variations into every one, and he studied defensive backs until he was confident of their reactions in a given situation.

"In any pattern," he said, "I took into consideration the four men on my side—the cornerback, the safety, the outside and middle linebackers.

"Having an idea where those guys were really helped. I had to know not only how they would cover me but how the entire coverage would be influenced by our other receivers. If you know what's involved in a pattern, you can get open."

Most will remember the 1974 playoff classic—Oakland Raiders versus Miami Dolphins—for the eight-yard touchdown pass Kenny Stabler threw from his knees to Clarence Davis in the last 26 seconds of play.

But to have reached the eight-yard line in the first place, to be in position to pull out a 28-26 victory against the favored Dolphins in the most intense pressure sports can produce, that depended on the execution of a classic Raider drive.

Stabler had to take the offense 60 yards in 95 seconds against the Dolphins' "No-Name Defense" which had won consecutive Super Bowls the two previous seasons. In that drive, Biletnikoff caught two passes for critical first downs, one a hook, the other an out, for a combined total of 38 yards.

He caught them with no Dolphin close enough to stop him because he had read the coverage and beaten the zones. Those catches in combination were as crucial to victory as what Stabler and Davis did. They stand in testimony to Biletnikoff's artistry.

And as an artist, he was a bundle of temperament. He routinely threw up from tension before every Raider game. It got to be a clubhouse joke. Some players would get ready by staring blankly ahead. Others by talking out their nerve ends, by religiously strapping on equipment, or by repeating meaningless gestures.

Freddy would smoke cigarettes, drink coffee, then vomit. "When we heard Freddy in the bathroom calling for Earl," recalls Madden, "we knew he was ready."

One muggy summer night in 1975, the Raiders held a night scrimmage at a lighted high school field near training camp in Santa Rosa. The field was open. High-fence security of the type the Raiders liked was impossible, so the public was invited.

Spectators fringed the sidelines, including a couple of nuns from a nearby church. One fan leaned over and told his teenage son, "There's number 25, Fred Biletnikoff. Watch everything he does."

At that moment, Biletnikoff reached up on a crossing pattern and saw the ball carom off his hands. With the nuns and the kid now rapt in attention, he ran over to the offending oval, kicked it 35 yards, and cussed it loudly for not staying in his grasp.

It was a rich moment of Raider excess, bad public relations, but indicative of the man's intensity. He wasn't in camp to work on his social graces. He was there to practice catching the football.

Freddy was that way. He always was in violation of the commissioner's uniform code, hair hanging out the back of his helmet, pants rolled up above his knees (allowed by a doctor's bogus claim he had some kind of skin infection), his forearms and calves splotched with orange-yellow globs of Stickum.

But appearance aside, he could get open and catch the football. That was his genius. He was the reverse of the speedy receivers, such as Warren Wells and Cliff Branch, who would terrorize cornerbacks with the deep threat, then break it off short and catch the ball underneath. Biletnikoff did it the other way. He made the secondary so conscious of his short and intermediate routes, he could often sucker them in tight while he sped past for the touchdown catch.

He made three big receptions in the Raiders 31-14 win over Minnesota in Super Bowl XI. None was for a touchdown, but the performance earned him the Most Valuable Player trophy. Typically, he cried in nervous appreciation over his award in such a big game.

Biletnikoff retired after the 1978 season, a legend in Oakland. He caught 589 passes in his career, putting him in the top ten in NFL history. He still holds most of the Raider receiving records.

He was the ultimate receiver for a team that then and now has chosen to live by the pass. A player whose every performance seemed to conduct a coaching clinic.

Clem Daniels (36) picks up yardage against the Denver Broncos in a night game at Sacramento, California.

sweeps and fullback ''Jetstream'' Smith barreling through the middle. The Raiders moved the ball 62 yards on eight plays to the nine-yard line. Then Smith went off left tackle and bulled his way into the end zone to tie the game at 27-27. Kicker Larry Barnes added the extra point to give Oakland the win.

With a 4-4 record, the Raiders were the surprise of the league. The club's late start and lack of quality players almost destined it to finish near the bottom of the AFL's Western Division. In the second half of the season the team's late start became evident. Oakland dropped four of its next five games. The club's lone win during that stretch was a 20-7 victory over the Buffalo Bills at Kezar Stadium.

The Raiders played the final game of their inaugural season at Candlestick Park against the Denver Broncos. Oakland was forced to move the game from Kezar to Candlestick due to a scheduling conflict with the San Francisco 49ers.

Oakland had a 5-8 record, while Denver had a 4-8-1 mark. The Broncos were six-point favorites.

The Raiders needed a win to stay out of the western division cellar and they put together their finest game of the season to do so. Before just 5,159 fans, the Raiders demolished Denver, 48-10.

Oakland didn't score its first touchdown until four minutes remained in the half. The Raiders marched 45 yards on five plays at that point with Tom Flores scoring on a one-yard run to break a 3-3 tie.

The Raiders put their offense in high gear in the fourth quarter when they posted 31 unanswered points. Quarterbacks Babe Parilli and Tom Flores alternated and skillfully engineered five scoring drives in that period. Oakland ended the day with 532 offensive yards.

Fullback Billy Lott was the team's leading ground gainer. He picked up 87 yards in nine carries while Tony Teresa packed the ball 23 times for 75 yards. Parilli connected on 10 of 20 passes for 167 yards and two touchdowns. Flores was nine of 14 for 145 yards.

The defense was just as spectacular as the offense. Raider linebackers Riley Morris and Tom Louderback stuffed the run at every opportunity.

27

The Broncos were held to 5 yards rushing and just 206 total yards.

Tom Flores ended the year as the team's leading passer. He completed 136 of 252 passes for 1,738 yards. His 54-percent completion rate was the best in the AFL. Twelve of his passes were for touchdowns. Billy Lott was his favorite receiver. Lott's 49 receptions led the club. Tony Teresa was the club's top rusher with 608 yards in 139 carries. He also led the team in scoring with 10 touchdowns.

Center Jim Otto was selected to the AFL's first all-league team. He was the only Raider selected to the squad in 1960.

Oakland's 6-8 record was good enough for third place in the four-team AFL Western Division. Despite the club's respectable record, Oakland attracted only 53,537 fans to its seven home games. Average attendance at Kezar Stadium and Candlestick Park was a disappointing 7,648.

The Los Angeles Chargers won the western division crown with a 10-4 record. They faced the Houston Oilers in the league championship game. Houston quarterback George Blanda led his club to a 24-16 win.

Running back Abner Haynes of the Dallas Texans gained 875 yards in 156 carries to lead the league in rushing. He was voted AFL Rookie of the Year and Player of the Year.

1961 Prior to the 1961 season E.W. McGah was named president of the Oakland Raiders. Changes were made on the roster as well. Oakland acquired free agent halfback Clem Daniels and signed former Pittsburgh Steeler defensive back Fred "the hammer" Williamson. Wayne Crow, a starting defensive back in 1960, was switched to running back and became the Raiders' leading rusher. And quarterback Tom Flores was handed the starting job after Babe Parilli was traded to the Boston Patriots.

The Raiders had a new home at Candlestick Park in 1961. Season ticket sales were up to

Cleveland's Leroy Kelly (44) tries to leap over the Raider defensive line in a vain attempt to score.

nearly 2,000 and team management was confident of a successful season on the playing field.

The Raiders began their second season of professional football at Honolulu, Hawaii for an exhibition game with the AFL champion Houston Oilers. Houston quarterback George Blanda paced his club to a 35-17 win before 12,500 fans. Oakland lost two more preseason games before getting a win over the Denver Broncos, 49-12, at Candlestick Park.

Despite the Raiders' preseason optimism, the year went bad in a hurry. Oakland traveled to Houston for its first league game and was rudely greeted by the Oilers. George Blanda threw three touchdown passes for Houston and added two field goals and six extra points as the Oilers whipped Oakland, 55-0.

The Raiders were shut out again the following week at San Diego. The Chargers, who relocated from Los Angeles, destroyed Oakland, 44-0. General Manager Chet Soda had seen enough. Coach Eddie Erdelatz was fired after the game and replaced by his assistant, Marty Feldman.

Feldman didn't fare much better. In his first game as the head man, Oakland lost its home opener to the Dallas Texans, 42-35. Only 6,737 fans were in attendance at Candlestick.

The Raiders finally got a win a week later when they beat the Denver Broncos at home, 33-19. Oakland posted a 33-3 lead in that game before Denver was able to find the end zone in the fourth quarter.

Oakland halfback Wayne Crow was the workhorse against Denver. He gained 107 yards in 16 carries and got the scoring started in the opening period on a one-yard plunge.

Raider place kicker George Fleming booted a 54-yard field goal in the second quarter to set a club record. It was also the longest field goal in AFL history at that point.

Oakland could manage only one more win in 1961, a 31-22 victory over the Bills at Buffalo. Tom Flores was the hero in that game as he threw touchdown passes of 85, 30 and 55 yards. His first pass of the day was an 85-yard scoring heave to halfback Charlie Fuller. He ended the day with

Hewritt Dixon (35) takes the handoff from Daryle Lamonica (3) and follows behind lead blocker Jim Harvey (70).

31

15 completions in 28 tries for 256 yards.

Oakland ended the disappointing season with a 47-16 loss to Houston. Running back Billy Cannon paced the Oiler attack with 145 yards on 21 carries. George Blanda passed for 350 yards and four touchdowns. The loss left Oakland with a 2-12 mark, worst in the AFL. They scored the fewest points in the league and allowed the most. Average attendance at the team's six league games was just 7,655.

Flores was the main cog in the Raider offense all season. He completed 52 percent of his 366 passes for 2,176 yards and 15 touchdowns. End Doug Asad and fullback Alan Miller each caught 36 passes to lead the club. Wayne Crow was the team's top ground gainer with 490 yards. Center Jim Otto was selected to the all-league team for the second straight year. He was the only Raider to make the club.

Once again, the Houston Oilers met the Chargers for the AFL title. Houston won its second consecutive league crown, 10-3.

1962 The Raiders ran into trouble before the 1962 season even began when starting quarterback Tom Flores contracted a lung infection and was lost for the season. Don Heinrich and M.C. Reynolds, a pair of journeymen signal callers, were brought in to lead the offense. Chon Gallegos, a rookie quarterback from San Jose State, provided backup help.

Two rookies who were expected to strengthen the defensive unit were Dan Birdwell, a 6-4, 235-pound defensive end from Houston, and defensive back Tom Morrow of Mississippi Southern.

For the third year in a row, the Raiders found themselves playing their home games in a new stadium. Frank Youell Field, a 23,000-seat stadium near downtown Oakland was their new residence. Playing in Oakland for the first time, season ticket sales increased nearly three-fold over 1961 to 5,400.

The Raiders opened the exhibition season on the road against the Dallas Texans at Atlanta. The offense must have remained in Oakland because Dallas defeated the Raiders, 13-3.

Quarterback Don Heinrich finally got the offense moving a week later in a 21-20 win over the Boston Patriots. Nevertheless, Coach Feld-

man decided to go shopping for another signal caller. He eventually purchased veteran Cotton Davidson from the Dallas Texans.

The Raiders played their first game at Youell Field on August 26, 1962. Over 17,000 fans turned out to see Oakland play the San Diego Chargers. At that point it was the largest home crowd in the club's short history. San Diego defeated Oakland, 33-27.

After posting a 1-4 exhibition mark, the Raiders opened the regular season at Youell Field against the New York Titans. Nearly 13,000 fans were on hand to see the Titans down Oakland, 28-17. It was the first in a series of disheartening losses for Oakland. The club went on to lose 13 consecutive games in 1962. Added to the six consecutive defeats Oakland suffered at the tail end of 1961, the Raiders had 19 straight regular season losses. After the club's fifth straight loss in 1962, Feldman was replaced by assistant coach William "Red" Conkright.

The Raiders salvaged the season in their final game when they met the Boston Patriots at Youell Field. Nearly 6,000 loyal fans braved a driving rainstorm to see Oakland shut out Boston, 20-0. The Raiders capitalized on eight turnovers. The big offensive play was supplied by Cotton Davidson, who tossed a 74-yard touchdown pass to Clem Daniels. Davidson completed nine passes for 230 yards.

For the second straight year, Oakland scored the fewest points in the league. The Raiders went through five quarterbacks during the course of the season without much luck. Davidson had his moments at quarterback, but he was ineffective most of the time. He completed just 37 percent of his 321 passes and threw 23 interceptions. Only seven of his passes were for touchdowns.

The lone bright spots on offense were center Jim Otto and running back Clem Daniels. Daniels gained 766 yards on 161 carries for a 4.7-yard average. He also caught 24 passes for 318 yards and scored eight touchdowns. Otto was selected all-league for the third straight season.

The defensive secondary was another area of optimism. Oakland allowed the fewest pass completions in the AFL and the least passing yardage. Defensive back Tom Morrow intercepted 10 passes and Fred Williamson had eight. Williamson also was selected to the all-league team.

George Blanda 1967-75

George Blanda was 31 years old in 1958 when pro football phased him out the first time. He was a 10-year veteran with the Chicago Bears, and Bears' owner and head coach George Halas had just given him three unpalatable options. Blanda could make the team as a quarterback (which Halas said he wouldn't be able to do), stay with the Bears only as a kicker, or retire.

Blanda said bitterly, "I won't play for anybody just as a kicker," so he retired.

He was phased out again eight years later, in March of 1967, when the Houston Oilers of the AFL put him on waivers. He was 40-years-old, replaced by a "Texas quarterback with peach fuzz on his chin."

Over in Oakland, Al Davis remembered Blanda well. In one game in 1960, when Davis was an assistant coach with the Los Angeles Chargers, Houston had beaten L.A. Blanda had thrown 55 times, completing 31, for 366 yards and three touchdowns. In the league championship game that same year, Houston beat the Charters, 24-16, with Blanda accounting for all the scoring. He threw three touchdown passes and kicked a field goal.

Now managing general partner of the Raiders, Davis had this idea. He liked to season his roster with veterans who had winning attitudes, who didn't wilt under big game pressure. He liked what it did for team chemistry, liked the role model it provided.

For his part, Blanda still believed he was a quarterback and kicker who could win in professional football. "Experience has taught me optimism," he said, "Or maybe I'm just dumb." Either way, Davis paid the $100 waiver fee, gave up "the player to be named later," and George Blanda entered his third life in pro football, this one as an Oakland Raider.

His first coach in Oakland was John Rauch, whom he had played against in college. He was installed as the number two quarterback, behind newly acquired Daryle Lamonica, and the number one kicker. That year, the Raiders were 13-1. They won the AFL championship and played the Green Bay Packers in Super Bowl II.

John Madden replaced Rauch in 1969, and right away the rookie head coach knew he had the ideal quarterback situation — Daryle Lamonica the starter, with Blanda the veteran behind him. "When Daryle went down," explained Madden, "It wasn't, 'Oh God, now we're dead.' It was, 'Okay, here comes George, now lets go.' "

Behind Lamonica and Blanda, of course, was the future star the Raiders were developing, Kenny "Snake" Stabler. Blanda did his part there as well. He studied films with Stabler. They watched games from the sidelines in concert, Blanda probing the defense for ways to exploit it, passing along his insights.

Blanda was a crusty Slav from the hard-scrabble coal country of western Pennsylvania. During his Hall of Fame induction speech in 1981, he thanked George Halas for giving him the chance to play for a real league. He had fought with Halas in Chicago and spent an angry year in exile after Halas released him. He had started strong in Houston as a charter member of the AFL. But at the end, he was playing second fiddle to home grown quarter-backs on a team that one year had no offensive playbook, nor a game plan for any one week.

In Oakland at age 39, Blanda finally found a happy football home. From the moment Al Davis claimed him on waivers in 1967, to his last game in the AFC playoffs of 1975, he was integral to the Raiders' success.

Through it all, he defied the aging process. His feats during one year in particular, 1970, will stand as an all-time monument to positive thinking. As one writer in Kansas City said at the time, Blanda had become menace to everyone in his forties, because he had "robbed them of the alibi of age."

Blanda was 43-years-old in 1970. The Raiders had started slow. They were 2-2-1, playing their sixth game in Pittsburgh against the Steelers.

Blanda was down on one knee, as always, away from the crowd around the bench. He was riveted on Pitts-burgh's defense, figuring ways it could be attacked and talking about it with Stabler.

Still in the first quarter, he saw Pitts-burgh was leaving the middle wide open, that it probably was weak against deep patterns on the left, and that it red-dogged predictably by down and yardage.

Madden interrupted him, yelling, "George, you're going in." Blanda looked up. The score was tied at seven. Lamonica was coming out injured.

Madden had several reasons for liking Blanda as the backup. He set up two steps shorter than Lamonica, he called different patterns and he threw to different receivers. Blanda could change the tempo of a game, and it might be three series before the defense caught up.

Blanda trotted to the huddle and went right to work. He threw two touchdowns, one to wide receiver Warren Wells deep on the left, the other to tight end Raymond Chester over the middle. He also kicked a field goal. The Raiders beat Pittsburgh that day, 31-14. Their record jumped to 3-2-1.

The following week at Kansas City, the Chiefs were ahead 17-14 with only seconds left to play.

Blanda was jogging through the cold air behind the Raider bench, knowing victory was riding on a long field goal against the wind. Madden sent him in. Daryle Lamonica spotted the ball on the Chiefs' 48. Blanda hit it low, for an early trajectory, to offset the Chiefs' 6'7" Buck Buchanan, who had lined up over the middle. The kick was good, the game ended in a tie and George Blanda had given the Raiders the momentum to regain first place.

Blanda was getting telegrams from over-40 clubs all across America. The next week, against the Browns in Cleveland, he did it again, this time replacing Lamonica with more than four minutes to play, and the Raiders behind, 17-13. He threw a fast interception that netted the Browns three more points, then he got untracked. He hit Warren Wells for a touchdown that tied the game. Then, after a Kent McCloughan interception, he lined up for a 52-yard field goal attempt. He put it through with three seconds showing.

Madden sent him in the next week in Denver, with four minutes to play and the Raiders behind, 19-17. Blanda moved the team right up the field, hitting Fred Biletnikoff in the end zone for the winning score. There was a little more than two minutes remaining.

He did it again the next week in Oakland against the San Diego Chargers, kicking a 16-

yard field goal in the last seven seconds. The streak ended the following Thursday, Thanksgiving day in Detroit, when the Lions beat the Raiders, 28-14. But for five weeks in 1970, no player in NFL history, certainly none his age, had accomplished so many last minute heroics.

Blanda's playing time at quarterback diminished after his protege, Kenny Stabler, was named the starter in the fourth week of the 1973 season. He kicked his last field goal for Oakland in the 1975 AFC Championship Game in Pittsburgh, a 16-10 Raider loss.

It wasn't majestic, not a strong kick, but it lifted off through the snow at icy Three Rivers Stadium. It traveled 41 yards, clearing the crossbar for three points that left his team within striking distance of a victory they never quite got.

He was gone the next year, cut without ceremony (he wouldn't have wanted any) in training camp. He railed to the last he had been denied the chance to compete against the rookies brought in to take his job. He left with a resentment that later would ebb, certainly by the time he was in-ducted into the Hall of Fame in 1981, the first year he was eligible. Notably, he would ask Al Davis to present him.

But at the time, he left believing, even at 49, he still could play quar-terback and kick in the NFL.

Above: Linebacker Gus Otto (34) and defensive back Dave Grayson (45) close in on Boston Patriot receiver Larry Garron (40). **Pages 36-37:** George Blanda (16) kicks a field goal against the Kansas City Chiefs as Daryle Lamonica holds. During a career that spanned 26 years, Blanda missed just 15 extra point attempts. **Pages 38-39:** Oakland's Ben Davidson (83), Dave Grayson (45) and Bill Laskey swarm to Buffalo fullback Wray Carlton.

The Dallas Texans, led by Len Dawson and Abner Haynes, won the western division crown. They met the Houston Oilers in the AFL title game. After two overtime periods, Dallas defeated Houston, 20-17.

1963
Several changes took place in the AFL in 1963. The New York Titans were sold to a group headed by Sonny Werblin. Werblin changed the club's name to the New York Jets. Dallas Texans owner Lamar Hunt packed up his team and moved to Kansas City. His club was renamed the Chiefs.

Meanwhile, the Oakland Raiders lured Al Davis away from the San Diego Chargers. Davis was made head coach of the Raiders after serving the

Chargers as an assistant coach for three seasons.

Davis went to work acquiring the players he needed to develop a winning ball club. He signed receiver Art Powell, who played out his option with the New York Titans, linebacker Archie Matsos, who came over from Buffalo, and rookie defensive end Dave Costa.

Quarterback Tom Flores gingerly worked his way back into the starting lineup after sitting out the 1962 season with tuberculosis. Cotton Davidson, 30, was his backup.

Al Davis got a victory in his first game as head coach, beating the Boston Patriots, 24-17, in pre-season. Oakland's passing game looked unstoppable as Flores and Davidson ran up 334 yards through the air. Flores completed four of six passes for 83 yards before losing a contact lens and leaving the game. Cotton Davidson took over and completed 16 of 37 attempts for 251 yards. Powell caught nine passes for 123 yards and one touchdown.

Oakland finished the exhibition season with a 3-2 record including wins over the Denver Broncos and the New York Jets at Youell Field. In the season opener the Raiders were matched with the Houston Oilers, the defending eastern division champions. Oakland took the field in new

silver and black uniforms replacing the club's old orange and black colors.

After a sluggish first half, Tom Flores had a spectacular second half. On the Raiders' first possession he led the club on a 54-yard drive. Clem Daniels capped it with a three-yard run to put Oakland in front, 7-6. Flores continued his torrid passing on the club's next possession when he threw an 85-yard touchdown pass to Art Powell. Oakland went on to post 17 unanswered points enroute to a 24-13 win.

Oakland returned home to face the Buffalo Bills at Youell Field. Before 17,568 elated fans, the Raiders jumped out to a 7-0 lead as Cotton Davidson directed the offense magnificently. He drove the club 61 yards in 10 plays on the club's first drive and capped it with a five-yard pass to Art Powell. Later in the period, Davidson tossed a 73-yard scoring pass to Clem Daniels. And midway through the third quarter he scored on a five-yard run to give Oakland a 28-10 lead.

Buffalo quarterback Jack Kemp rallied the Bills for a score in the final quarter, but the Oakland defense shut down Buffalo the rest of the way. The Bills' potent running attack, featuring Cookie Gilchrist, was held to just 90 yards. Gilchrist, the AFL's leading rusher in 1962, gained just 19 yards in 10 carries.

Clem Daniels rushed for 76 yards on 13 carries for Oakland and Cotton Davidson completed 14 of 29 passes for 315 yards. Daniels also had three receptions for 173 yards, an average of 57 yards per catch.

The Raiders found themselves tied for first place in the AFL's Western Division after two games. It was the first time Oakland had ever been in first place. But the club then lost its next four games. Included in that string was a heartbreaking 20-14 loss to the Boston Patriots at Fenway Park.

In that game the Raiders led, 14-3, late in the third period. Then Boston quarterback Babe Parilli connected on a 53-yard scoring toss to flanker Jim Colclough. Boston recovered a fumble on the next series and closed the gap to 14-13 when Gino Cappelletti booted a 32-yard field goal. On the very next kickoff, Oakland return man Bo Roberson fumbled and Boston recovered again. Two plays later Parilli tossed a 15-yard scoring pass. It was enough to beat the Raiders, 20-14.

Oakland rebounded and put together an eight-game winning streak. The Raiders started with a 49-26 win over the New York Jets, then went on to win seven more times to close out the season with 10-4 record.

Included in the winning streak was a dramatic 34-33 victory over the San Diego Chargers before 30,182 at Balboa Park. Cotton Davidson was the hero of the day, throwing three touchdown passes in the second half. The clincher was a 10-yard pass to running back Glenn Shaw with 1:52 left on the clock. Ironically, Shaw had been activated by the Raiders just hours before the game.

Running backs Clem Daniels of Oakland and Keith Lincoln of the Chargers put on a show for the fans in San Diego. Daniels ended the day with 125 yards in 19 carries. Lincoln had 130 yards on 15 carries. The Chargers' Paul Lowe added 82 yards on 12 attempts.

On the final day of the season Oakland beat the Houston Oilers, 52-49, to finish in second place in the western division. It was the highest scoring game in AFL history at that time. The win gave Oakland a 10-4 record. The San Diego Chargers retained their western division crown with an 11-3 mark.

Several records fell in the game. Oakland's 588 total yards broke the previous single-game mark held by Houston (582). Clem Daniels gained 158 yards and finished the season with 1098 yards, breaking Cookie Gilchrist's single-season rushing mark. And Art Powell caught four touchdown passes to break the AFL's previous one-game record of three.

Tom Flores threw six touchdown passes in the game to set a club record. He finished the season as the league's third-ranked passer.

Clem Daniels was voted the AFL Player of the Year. He was joined on the all-league squad by end Art Powell, center Jim Otto, cornerback Fred Williamson and linebacker Archie Matsos.

1964 Oakland opened training camp at Santa Rosa in 1964 with high expectations. After finishing the 1963 season with eight straight wins it looked like the Raiders had the nucleus of a contending team. Coach Al Davis strengthened the offense by obtaining from Houston fullback Billy Cannon, the AFL rushing leader in 1961, and converting him into a tight end. He also signed 6-8, 270-pound defensive

Willie Brown 1967-1978

The Oakland Raider franchise turned toward respectability in 1963, the year Al Davis was hired as head coach and general manager. It turned toward briliance in 1967, when Davis hired 30-year-old John Madden as an assistant coach. That same year he drafted Gene Upshaw in the first round, traded for Daryle Lamonica, and claimed George Blanda off the waiver wire.

Those moves, plus one other, laid the cornerstone for Oakland's division titles during nine of the next ten years. The other was acquiring a cornerback named Willie Brown, who had been laboring in obscurity in Denver. Davis had Kent McCloughan at one corner. He wanted to move the other, Dave Grayson, to free safety.

Before he could, he needed a replacement for Grayson. Lou Saban had just taken over in Denver, a team that had won only 12 games in the past four years. Saban wanted to sweep out the veterans. He gave the Raiders Brown and quarterback Mickey Slaughter for defensive linemen Rex Mirich and a draft choice.

Felons have gotten 10 to 20 years for less flagrant thefts. Rex Mirisch and the draft choice failed to distinguish in Denver. But Willie Brown showcased himself in Oakland as the consummate cornerback. He played 13 all-star seasons for the Raiders, and in 1984 was named to the Pro Football Hall of Fame.

John Madden used to say, ''The fastest place to get beat is on the corner. If a receiver gets behind a cornerback, it's just God and grass between him and a touchdown.'' Cornerback is a special position played by special men who thrive on that solitary challenge.

Such a man was Willie Brown. ''To play a receiver all day, man-to-man,'' said Brown, ''knowing that any pass could be seven points for him or seven for me, that's something a good cornerback really loves.''

Part of it is technique, part athletic ability— footwork, skill and instinct. The corner backpedals reacting to every variation in the route—release, glide, plant, break. When he's right, he mirrors every move the receiver makes but the false ones.

But so much more of it is mental. A cornerback is not always on. Quarterbacks complete in the neighborhood of 50 percent of their passes. Defensive backs are going to get beat. The cornerbacks, the good ones, develop an almost arrogant disregard for error. They scorn the fear of failure, not submit to it.

''That's the most important thing,'' said Brown. ''If a guy caught a pass on me, I didn't worry about it, he just caught a pass. If he caught a touchdown, he just caught a touchdown. You have to forget it. If you couldn't

forget you wouldn't be around long.''

Willie Brown's eyes used to light up when he talked about receivers. He got excited by the mano-a-mano challenge of going against Lance Alworth or Paul Warfield. He wanted to intimidate the receivers physically and psycho-logically. He wanted to own them. In every respect he was a cornerback, though he reached that position, and Oakland, almost by accident.

Brown was always a natural athlete, growing up in Yazoo City, Mississippi, population 11,000. He went to Grambling and played for Coach Eddie Robinson.

He was a tight end on offense, an end and linebacker on defense. He ran track, a 9.6 hundred, so he was fast enough. But he was overlooked in the 1963 draft after his senior season. At 6'2'' and right around 200 pounds, he was too small for any of the positions he had played so well in college.

He tried out as a free agent with Houston in training camp in 1963. The Oilers were desperate for defensive backs, and the coach, Frank Ivy, converted the rookie from Grambling. ''It was a new position,'' Brown said. ''I had to learn to run backwards.''

Brown stayed after practice, working against AFL all-stars— quarterback George Blanda throwing to end Charley Hennigan. He was learning his new position, but not fast enough to avoid the ax. Ivy waived him after the last exhibition game. He was claimed right away by Denver, then a franchise without much direction.

In fact, the Broncos were bad enough to give anyone a long look. It was all Brown needed. His skills at the corner improved rapidly. He ended up making All-AFL in 1964, his second season, after intercepting nine passes.

Al Davis liked him, among other reasons, for his pure cornerback talent, his size, speed, quickness and agility. Brown also proved he was tough enough to be a near perfect executioner of the bump-and-run, which Davis was installing as a way to control receivers.

''I would play a receiver nose up all day,'' recalled Brown, explaining the Raiders' early use of the bump. ''I'd hit him as many times as possible, even knock him down if I could. I would go at his throat with my hand, then to the side of his head, then to the chest. That would sting him for at least two or three seconds, and he'd be easier to follow on patterns.''

The bump rules were changed in 1974, outlawing unlimited contact until the ball was airborne. By then the Raiders were playing less man and more zone anyway.

Brown also changed, adjusting his technique. One memorable instance came in a playoff game in 1973, against the Pittsburgh Steelers at the Oakland Coliseum.

It was late in the third quarter with the Raiders ahead, 16-7. From his own territory, Steeler quarterback Terry Bradshaw play-faked and dropped back to pass. Covering the sideline as the underneath man in the zone, Brown bumped the wide receiver and let him go. He saw the running back coming toward him.

He held off until Bradshaw cocked his arm, then he swooped in, reaching over the running back's shoulder, slapping the ball into the air and catching it on the dead run. It was a 54-yard return for a touchdown that sealed a Raider victory, 33-14.

Brown had an attitude about his position and a set of skills that raised him above the level of normal pro football player. John Madden once put together a short training film from a play Brown had made earlier that season, 1973. The subject was why you never quit.

The game was in Houston against an awful Oiler team, and the Raiders were flat on a day they could not afford to be. Even one loss at that point would have crippled their chances for the playoffs. It was late in the fourth quarter, with Oakland ahead only 10-6.

Houston had the ball around midfield. An Oiler running back named Lewis Jolley took a screen pass through the middle of the Raider defense and broke through for what looked to be a 52-yard touchdown.

Near the sideline where he had been covering a wideout, Brown saw the play, reacted, spun and pursued. He overtook the surprised Jolley at the two and dropped him with a low tackle. Two plays later, Oakland recovered a fumble, and the win was theirs.

''I didn't think about it, I just took out,'' Brown said at the time. ''You don't think about it. If you do, it's already too late. You just do it.''

Brown ''just did it'' for so many of Oakland's glory years. He played alongside superior talent—George Atkinson, Jack Tatum, Dave Grayson, Nemiah Wilson, Skip Thomas— but he was always the leader. ''Willie held the group together,'' said his secondary coach Bob Zeman.

In 1969, just before the merger, the Pro Football Hall of Fame announced its all-time AFL team. Willie Brown, of course, was one of the cornerbacks.

That same year, the New York Times polled several AFL coaches, asking them to name the five players they'd choose for building a winner in 1970. Brown tied for first place with San Diego Charger wide receiver Lance Alworth. Each received five votes.

''To coaches, the glamor position is cornerback,'' said John Madden, unsurprised by the results. ''Not running backs and wide receivers.''

Indeed, Willie Brown of the Oakland Raiders was one of the most glamorous of all time.

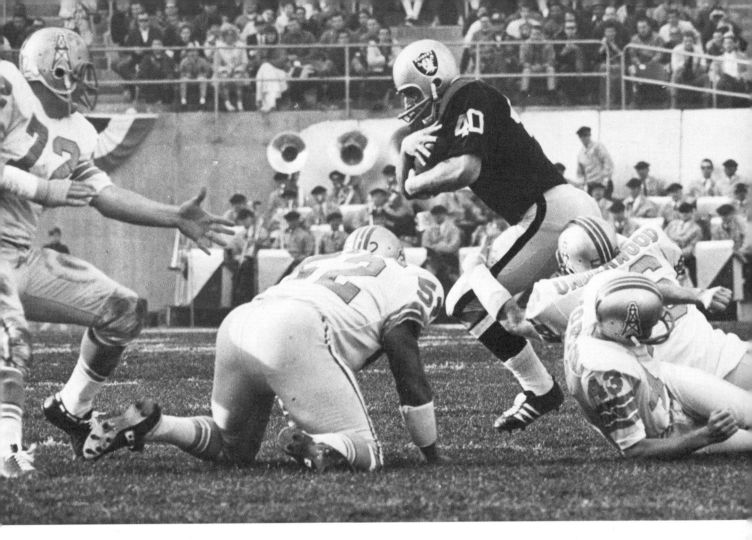

Running back Pete Banaszak (40) drives through the Houston Oiler line in the 1967 AFL Championship Game at Oakland. The Raiders destroyed Houston, 40-7, to advance to their first Super Bowl.

end Ben Davidson, a former Washington Redskin, and second-round draft pick Dan Conners. Conners was expected to beef up the linebacking corps.

The season didn't go as Davis had hoped. In the preseason the Raiders looked sluggish. After dropping their exhibition opener to the Kansas City Chiefs, 21-14, the Raiders traveled to Denver for their second preseason game. Oakland showed some spark in that contest winning, 20-7, in a game that featured several fights. Most prominent was a brawl that erupted in the fourth period. On that play, Denver quarterback Mickey Slaughter was sacked and the play was whistled dead. The Raider defense relaxed after the whistle, thinking the play was over. But Denver center Jerry Sturm wanted to get in one more lick. He flattened Raider linebacker Clancy Osborne with a forearm and both benches emptied onto the field. The referees restored order after several minutes then ejected Sturm from the game.

The regular season started disastrously. Oakland was matched with the Boston Patriots before a record crowd of 21,226 at Youell Field. The Raiders trailed just 17-14 late in the fourth period and were threatening to score. Oakland ad-

vanced to the Boston four-yard line where halfback Clem Daniels fumbled a handoff. The Patriots recovered to preserve the win.

Things went downhill from there as Oakland lost its first five games of the season before salvaging a tie with the Boston Patriots. Oakland kicker Mike Mercer saved the day in that one. His 32-yard field goal with five seconds to play tied the game.

The Raiders got a victory the following week with a 40-7 rout of Denver. Oakland piled up 628 yards of total offense. Quarterback Cotton Davidson set a club record with 25 completions in 34 attempts for 419 yards. Five of his passes were for touchdowns. Clem Daniels gained 167 yards rushing and had an additional 55-yard run called back because of a penalty.

Oakland finished the year strongly with four wins and a tie. In the final game of the season the Raiders came from behind to beat the western di-

vision champion San Diego Chargers before 20,214 at Youell Field. Tom Flores, who took over for the injured Cotton Davidson, was 21 of 39 and threw touchdown passes to Gene Mingo, Billy Cannon and Art Powell. Clem Daniels added 144 yards on the ground, including 120 in the fourth quarter.

The victory ended a frustrating season for the Raiders. They finished with a 5-7-2 record for third place in the western division. Despite their record the Raiders continued to show promise. Receiver Art Powell developed into one of the league's best. He ended the year with 76 catches for 1,361 yards. Running back Clem Daniels also continued to blossom. He picked up 824 yards in 173 attempts for a 4.8-yard average. Once again, center Jim Otto was awarded all-league honors.

The defense was another bright spot for Oakland, allowing just 21 touchdowns in 14 games, the lowest in the AFL. Dave Costa, Dan Birdwell and Ben Davidson anchored a tough defensive line. They were supported by rookie linebacker Dan Conners and an excellent defensive backfield that included Fred Williamson, Warren Powers and Tom Morrow. Williamson was selected all-league for the second year in a row.

The Buffalo Bills, behind quarterback Jack Kemp and running back Cookie Gilchrist, went on to win the AFL title with a 20-17 win over the San Diego Chargers.

1965 The Raiders strengthened their defense in 1965 by acquiring all-league defensive back Dave Grayson from the Kansas City Chiefs and 280-pound defensive end Ike Lassiter from the Denver Broncos. They also signed several promising rookie prospects including Nebraska defensive back Kent McCloughan, Missouri linebacker Gus Otto and defensive tackle Carlton Oats from Florida A&M. Fred Biletnikoff, a rookie from Florida State, won a starting wide receiver spot, while tackle Harry

Fullback Hewritt Dixon (35) eludes a Cleveland Brown tackler as center Jim Otto looks on. Dixon was named to the All-AFL team three times as a member of the Raiders. He averaged 4.0 yards rushing and caught 263 passes during his NFL career.

45

Schuh, from Memphis State, added depth on the offensive line.

The defense looked unbeatable in the club's preseason opener against the San Diego Chargers. San Diego sported one of the most explosive offenses in pro football, with quarterback John Hadl and All-Pro receiver Lance Alworth. Yet Oakland held the Chargers to just one field goal in a 10-3 victory. The defense also proved to be Oakland's best weapon. Cornerback Kent McCloughan scored the game's only touchdown after intercepting a pass and returning it 42 yards.

With Tom Flores firmly entrenched as the Raiders' starting signal caller, Dick Wood and journeyman quarterback Lee Grosscup battled for the backup spot. Grosscup, acquired by the Raiders in the offseason, started the second preseason game against the Denver Broncos at Ute Stadium in Salt Lake City, Utah. He was unimpressive, completing just two of eight passes. One of his completions was an 80-yard scoring strike to Fred Biletnikoff. It was Biletnikoff's first catch as a professional.

Wood won a spot on the roster behind starting quarterback Tom Flores. He proved to be a valuable replacement when Flores was knocked senseless in the second quarter of the opener against the powerful Kansas City Chiefs. Wood came off the bench to throw two touchdown passes and run for another in a 37-10 Oakland win. He ended the day with 12 completions in 25 attempts.

Oakland lost two of its next three contests before meeting the Boston Patriots in a night game at Fenway Park. Tom Flores put together one of his best passing efforts of the season, completing 20 of 34 passes for 261 yards enroute to a 24-10 win over the Pats. The win sparked the Raiders. They won six of their last nine games and finished the season with an 8-5-1 record.

The Raiders played their last game at Youell Field on December 12, 1965. The club was scheduled to move into the newly constructed Oakland Coliseum for the 1966 season. Over 19,000 fans were on hand that day to see the Raiders take on Joe Namath and the New York Jets. It was Namath's first visit to Oakland and the Raiders proved to be less than gracious hosts. He was sacked three times and forced into throwing three interceptions as the Raiders defeated the Jets, 24-14. Namath completed 19 of 36 passes for 280 yards. Raider quarterback Tom Flores connected on 12 of 29 passes for 219 yards.

Flores was the team's leading passer in 1965, completing 122 of 269 passes for 1,593 yards. Art Powell led the club in receptions again, hauling in 52 passes for 800 yards and 12 touchdowns. Clem Daniels had 953 yards on the ground to pace the running backs. Powell, center Jim Otto and defensive back Dave Grayson made the all-league squad.

Oakland finished second to the San Diego Chargers in the western division, but more importantly they were beginning to attract fans. Attendance had gradually risen each season despite playing at tiny Youell Field. At the start of the 1965 season, the Raiders sold 13,300 season tickets and average attendance had jumped to 19,500 per game.

1966 The year 1966 was a turning point for the Oakland Raiders and the American Football League. In early April, Raider coach and general manager Al Davis was named AFL commissioner. He was elected to the post by a unanimous 9-0 vote of AFL executives. Davis launched an all-out effort to recruit NFL players after the New York Giants signed kicker Pete Gogolak away from the Buffalo Bills. Among the AFL's targets were quarterbacks Roman Gabriel of the Los Angeles Rams and John Brodie of the San Francisco 49ers.

By June, the two leagues decided to put an end to the bidding war and a merger was reached. Among the items provided for in the agreement was a common draft and a championship game, later dubbed the Super Bowl, to be played between the winners of both leagues. NFL Commissioner Pete Rozelle was appointed commissioner of football.

While Davis headed the AFL, John Rauch was appointed the Raiders new head coach. Oakland

Fred Biletnikoff (25) prepares to run a pattern against the New England Patriots in 1975. Biletnikoff had 76 touchdown catches during his 14 seasons with the Raiders, a club record.

public relations director Scotty Stirling was promoted to general manager.

In July, after serving as AFL commissioner for just three months, Davis resigned his position and rejoined the Raiders as a general partner along with Wayne Valley and Ed McGah.

The Raiders began to put all the pieces together in 1966. They acquired bruising fullback Hewritt Dixon from the Denver Broncos and selected University of Miami running back Pete Banaszak in the college draft. Defensive tackle Tom Keating was acquired from Buffalo and joined Dan Birdwell, Ike Lassiter, Carleton Oats and Ben Davidson on the defensive line. Rodger Bird, another rookie, won a starting spot in the defensive backfield.

Oakland opened the exhibition season against the Houston Oilers at Rice Stadium. The club was without the services of receiver Art Powell and halfback Clem Daniels. Both men were holding out while contract negotiations were settled. Without that pair the Oakland offense was stagnant. The Raiders put just 17 points on the board and lost to the Oilers, 26-17.

Oakland posted a 2-2 record in exhibition play, then opened the regular season on the road against the league's newest entry, the Miami Dolphins. Miami was owned by entertainer Danny Thomas. Cotton Davidson got the starting call at quarterback after engineering a convincing, 52-21, win over Denver in the Raider's final preseason game. He was backed by Tom Flores. Holdouts Art Powell and Clem Daniels were back in uniform for the game.

The new franchise got off to a fantastic start when Miami's Joe Auer returned the opening kickoff 95 yards for a touchdown. Oakland came back to take a 10-7 lead at halftime after Hewritt Dixon scored on a two-yard run. The Raiders never relinquished the lead.

Tom Flores took over for Davidson in the second half. He completed 11 of 20 passes for 161 yards and two touchdowns as Oakland defeated Miami, 23-14.

After being shut out, 31-0, in the second game of the season at Houston, the Raiders came home to play their inaugural game at the newly constructed Oakland-Alameda County Coliseum. An exuberant crowd of 50,746 was on hand to see the Raiders take on the Kansas City Chiefs.

The game was tied, 10-10, late in the third period when the game quickly turned around. Raider punter Mike Eischeid was set to kick from his own 40, but it was blocked by Kansas City defensive end Chuck Hurston. The Chiefs recovered at their own six and scored two plays later to take a 17-10 lead.

On the next series, Oakland moved to the Kansas City 33 in six plays. This time Eischeid came on to attempt a field goal, but Buck Buchanan, the Chiefs' 6-8, 290-pound defensive tackle, got a hand on the ball and knocked it away. Three plays later Kansas City was in the end zone again when Mike Garrett scampered 42 yards to score. Kansas City went on to win, 32-10.

After losing its third consecutive game, 29-20, to the San Diego Chargers, Oakland posted six wins in its next seven games. The Raiders ended the disappointing season at home against the Denver Broncos. Oakland had a 7-5-1 record, while Denver was 4-9. Kansas City had already clinched the western division title.

The Raiders ended the year on a victorious note. Tom Flores connected on a 46-yard touchdown pass to Art Powell in the first period, then added two more touchdown passes as the Raiders beat Denver, 28-10. The win gave Oakland an 8-5-1 record and for the third time in four years the club finished second in the western division.

Flores set a new Raider record during the season by throwing 24 touchdown passes. He completed 49 percent of his 306 tosses for 2,638 yards. Art Powell's 53 receptions for 1,026 yards led the club. He also scored 11 touchdowns. Clem Daniels rushed for 801 yards in 204 carries. Daniels was named to the all-league team along with center Jim Otto, guard Wayne Hawkins and defensive back Kent McCloughan.

Oakland's defense continued to be one of the best in the AFL. The Raiders allowed just 2,118 yards, fewest in the league. The defensive line was largely responsible for that figure, leading the AFL with 36 sacks.

The new Oakland Coliseum proved to be a blessing for the Raider franchise. In their first season at the Coliseum, the club's average home attendance nearly doubled from 19,500 per game in 1965 to 36,215 in 1966.

Kansas City met Buffalo for the 1966 AFL title. The Chiefs, with Len Dawson at quarterback, beat the Bills, 31-7. They earned the right to play in the first Super Bowl against the Green Bay

Tom Flores 1960-66 1972-

The Raider front office likes to mark the ballclub's origins with the advent of Al Davis in 1963. That was when Davis was hired as Oakland's head coach and general manager and given a blank charter.

In fact, the Raiders began play three years earlier, a sorry band of orphans who practiced on playgrounds and changed fields every season. From 1960 through 1962, they drew poorly and played worse. They had records of 6-8, 2-12, and 1-13. Few of the early Raiders remained in football, let alone stayed with the team. But one man has, and conspicuously so. He was the quarterback then and is the current head coach, Tom Flores.

Flores came out of the College of Pacific in 1959 with an injured shoulder needing surgery that killed off any chance of him being drafted by the NFL.

But early in 1960, the Raiders were hastily thrown together with Eddie Erdelatz of Navy as head coach. One of Erdelatz's assistants was Ernie George, a former coach at COP. Eddie LeBaron, a COP graduate and former NFL quarterback, recommended Flores to George, and in May of 1960, Flores signed with Oakland for $10,000. Camp began that summer in Santa Cruz. The players trained at Santa Cruz High and stayed at a pensioners' hotel in the downtown area, The Palomar.

"The only people in the hotel were the old folks and us," Flores said. "Sometimes I don't know who felt worse."

The Raiders brought in bodies wholesale that first year. They had more than 100 in camp when it began, including 11 quarterbacks. To keep track, the equipment men printed names on strips of adhesive and taped the strips on the backs of helmets.

"You'd do something good or bad," Flores recalled, "and the coaches would turn you around, see your name, and write it down. They didn't know who was who."

It seems they still didn't know when it came time for cutting players. "With a hundred-odd guys, you had one quick shot and that was it," said Flores. "You blew your one chance, and you were gone.

"The way they cut players, I don't know whether it was on purpose or due to inexperience. But they would start reading off the names at breakfast. One morning I remember they wiped out my whole table. Just one guy at the far end and myself were left. We were in shock. We just looked at each other. After that, not many guys showed up for breakfast on cutdown days."

Flores made the team, of course. He split duties with Babe Parilli in 1960. He was made the starter in 1961 after Parilli was traded. Erdelatz was fired that same year, after losing the first two games of the season 55-0 and 44-0 to Houston and San

Diego. Flores remembers 1960-62 as hard times but good times. The Raiders threw often, all AFL teams did. Defenses were primitive, he recalled, playing mostly man coverage and red dogging all the time.

"They brought linebackers, strong safeties, weak safeties," he said. "Sometimes I swear it looked like the coaches were coming in to make the tackle."

Through it all, the AFL in the early days created an adventure in austerity, what the players came to call the "hamburger-and-roadmap circuit."

"In 1960, we played three games in nine days," Flores says. "Played a game on Friday night in Kezar Stadium when it was so foggy we couldn't see across the field. Then we flew to Buffalo and played the Bills on a Tuesday night. Our next game, that Sunday, was against the Patriots in Amherst, Massachusetts.

"We got on the buses in Buffalo. Our travel agent was in New York, and no one on the buses knew exactly where we were supposed to go. We pulled up in front of a hotel in Holyoke. One of our front office people went in and came back out. He said, 'Okay, they got enough rooms.' So we stayed there.

"The next day, of course, we didn't have any place to practice. But we got our stuff and piled on the buses anyway. We drove around until we found a little league field. We

dressed on the lawn, guys in their jock straps. George Anderson was taping ankles against a tree. We practiced until a cop came and kicked us off. Seems a little league game was scheduled. All the kids and their fathers were standing around. Some of the kids were crying because we wouldn't get off their field—until the cop told us we'd have to leave."

Al Davis took over in 1963 in what Tom Flores calls a "good year for all of us." The orphans at last had a stable parent. Davis brought in new players and new ideas. Flores was his quarterback. The Raiders were picked to finish last, and after a 2-4 start, they rallied to win their final eight games. They finished 10-4, one game behind the San Diego Chargers.

Davis remembers Flores the quarterback. "He had great courage. He's a strong fighter, very, very proud." He had to be. The Raiders from day one under Davis had the quarterback calling the plays and running the huddle. The Raider system demanded that the quarterback stay in the pocket until the receivers made their breaks. It asked the offensive linemen to block until he found the open man, be it three seconds or 13. In such a system, the sacks will come, and the quarterback will get hit as he releases more often than he won't.

For three seasons under Davis and one more under John Rauch, Flores stood up to the

rush, earning his nickname, "Iceman," and performing creditably, if at a few notches below Joe Namath, Johnny Unitas, or Sonny Jurgenson. In 1967, Davis looked ahead at the merger and a chance for a Super Bowl. He made a trade with Buffalo (that same year he also acquired Willie Brown, George Blanda and Gene Upshaw). He sent Flores and receiver Art Powell to the Bills for Daryle Lamonica and receiver Glenn Bass.

It was a good deal for the Raiders. Lamonica, as the starting quarterback in 1967, threw for 30 touchdowns, 3,228 yards and was named AFL Player of the Year. The Raiders won their division. They beat Houston, 40-7, in the championship game before falling to the Green Bay Packers in Super Bowl II, 33-14.

Flores was nearing the end of his playing career by then. Davis had told him, "there would always be something with the Raiders." He played sparingly with the Bills for two seasons and in 1969 found himself backing up Len Dawson and Mike Livingston for the Kansas City Chiefs. The Chiefs finished second to the Raiders that season, but upstaged them in the playoffs, going on to meet and defeat Minnesota in Super Bowl IV. Flores earned the first of four Super Bowl rings.

He returned to Oakland in 1972 as the club's receivers coach. Davis always liked former quarterbacks

coaching receivers, and John Madden concurred. Flores was tutoring the likes of Cliff Branch, Fred Biletnikoff, and Dave Casper when Oakland won Super Bowl XI in 1976. He was head coach himself when the Raiders won Super Bowl XV over Philadelphia in 1980, and again when they won Super Bowl XVII against the Redskins in 1982.

Davis hired Flores in 1979 after Madden retired. He liked Flores' rapport with the players and his feel for another Davis obsession, the vertical passing game. Plus he liked one other thing. "I think you'll find Tom Flores has an inner strength as tough as anyone from any walk of life," Davis said.

The record bears out the judgment. Flores had a rocky first year as the team went 9-7 and missed the playoffs. But in his second year, he was coaching a Super Bowl champion, and he's been in the playoffs every year since. He's been a strong leader. He helped the team stay together during the disruptions surrounding the move to Los Angeles.

Through it all, he's been winning at a pace that would equal that of his predecessor, Madden, and only one other NFL coach, Don Shula. Both scored 100 victories during their first ten years on the job. Tom Flores was a Raider at the beginning and a Raider still going strong.

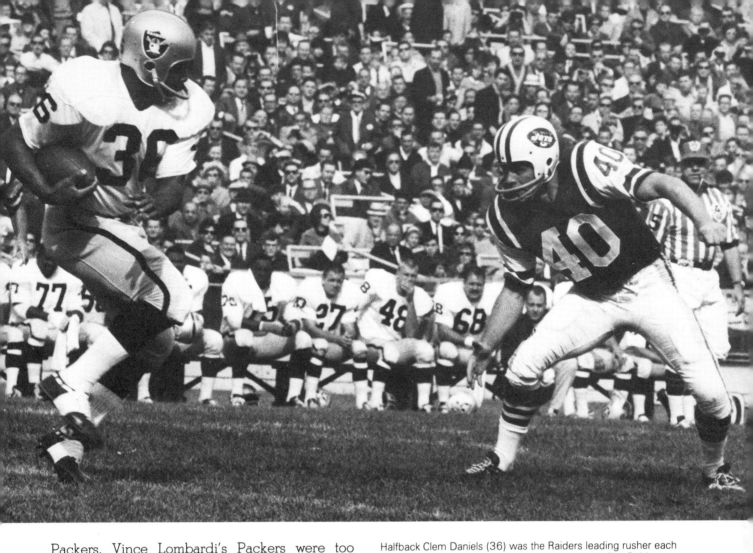

Packers. Vince Lombardi's Packers were too much for the Chiefs. Green Bay took a 14-10 lead into the locker room at halftime then completely outplayed the Chiefs in the second half to win, 35-10.

Halfback Clem Daniels (36) was the Raiders leading rusher each year between 1962-67. In 1963 he became the first Raider to gain over 1,000 yards on the ground. He finished the season with 1,099 yards and a 5.1 yard average.

1967 The Raiders made some daring trades in the offseason. They dealt quarterback Tom Flores and starting receiver Art Powell to Buffalo for quarterback Daryle Lamonica. Willie Brown was acquired from Denver and competed with Dave Grayson for a cornerback spot. George Blanda, who had been released by Houston, was signed as a kicker and backup quarterback to Lamonica. Among the rookies in camp were Gene Upshaw, a guard from Texas A&I, and wide receiver Rod Sherman of USC. Warren Wells, another wide receiver, signed as a free agent.

Lamonica made a spectacular debut with Oakland. In the club's first exhibition game of the season, the San Diego Chargers held a 23-17 lead with two minutes to play. Oakland had the ball on its own 20-yard line. Lamonica took over and drove Oakland 76 yards in nine plays. With 30 seconds left, Oakland had the ball at the four.

Lamonica went to the air and hit running back Roger Hagberg to tie the game, 23-23. Blanda kicked the extra point to win it for Oakland.

The Raiders won two of four exhibition contests, then met the San Francisco 49ers in their last preseason game. It was the first time Oakland faced an NFL team and 53,254 spectators crowded into the Oakland Coliseum to see the matchup. San Francisco was a ten-point favorite.

The game was riddled with errors. San Francisco lost the ball three times on fumbles, while Oakland coughed up three fumbles and had four passes intercepted. Midway through the fourth quarter, San Francisco led just 6-3 when 49er quarterback John Brodie drove his club 81 yards and capped it with a six-yard pass to Dave Parks.

George Blanda took over for Lamonica after the ensuing kickoff. On the first play from scrimmage, he connected on a 41-yard touchdown pass to Fred Biletnikoff. Suddenly, the score was 16-13. Blanda then attempted an onside kick.

51

The ball was recovered by San Francisco and the 49ers ran out the clock to preserve the win.

Oakland opened the season at the Coliseum by thrashing the Denver Broncos, 51-0. It was the largest margin of victory since the club's inception. Rodger Bird set a club record by returning two punts for 143 yards. Hewritt Dixon caught five passes for 78 yards and rushed 11 times for 55 yards. He scored twice. Lamonica completed eight of 14 passes for 118 yards. Blanda also got into the act. He connected on three of seven passes, including a 50-yard touchdown toss to speedster Warren Wells.

The Raiders continued their winning streak, defeating Boston, 35-7, and Kansas City, 23-21, before meeting their match at Shea Stadium against the New York Jets.

Joe Namath guided the Jets to a 17-0 halftime advantage and stretched it to 20-0 before Lamonica got Oakland on the scoreboard in the third period. The Raider quarterback threw touchdown passes of 14 yards to Bill Miller and 24 yards to Warren Wells, but that was all the points Oakland could muster. New York won it, 27-14.

The Raiders went on to win 10 straight games, ending the regular season with a 28-21 triumph over the Buffalo Bills. Hewritt Dixon scored on a one-yard run with just 2:13 left to beat Buffalo. The win gave Oakland a 13-1 record, the best in the AFL. It also gave the Raiders a chance to face the Houston Oilers in the AFL Championship Game. The winner of that game would go on to Super Bowl II.

Lamonica proved to be an excellent quarterback during the regular season. He completed 52 percent of his 425 tosses for 3,228 yards and 30 touchdowns. The former Notre Dame star was named AFL Player of the Year.

Lamonica was helped in the backfield by Hewritt Dixon, who gained 559 yards, and Pete Banaszak with 376 yards. Banaszak took over the halfback slot late in the season when starter Clem Daniels broke his ankle. Daniels gained 575 yards before he was injured. Dixon also led the team in receiving with 59 catches. Fred Biletnikoff caught 40 passes.

The Raiders dominated the AFL's all-league team. Named to the squad were tight end Billy Cannon, tackle Harry Schuh, center Jim Otto, quarterback Daryle Lamonica, defensive end Ben Davidson, defensive tackle Tom Keating and cornerback Kent McCloughan.

The AFL Championship Game was played at the Oakland Coliseum before a record crowd of 53,330. Temperatures hovered in the mid-40s with a chilly, six-mile per hour wind. Oakland's opponent, the Houston Oilers, were the surprise of the league in 1967, finishing with a 9-4-1 record. The offense was led by quarterback Pete Beathard and running backs Hoyle Granger and Woody Campbell.

Both clubs were evenly matched in the first quarter. The only scoring came on George Blanda's 37-yard field goal. Then in the second quarter, Oakland began to open up its offense. Early in the period, on a first down play, Lamonica spotted a hole on the left side of the Oiler defense. He called an audible at the line of scrimmage and handed off to Hewritt Dixon. Dixon swept left, picked up a block from Gene Upshaw, and outran everybody on the way to a 69-yard touchdown.

With 18 seconds left in the half the Raiders lined up to attempt a field goal. Instead, holder Daryle Lamonica threw a 17-yard pass to tight end Dave Kocourek, upping Oakland's lead to 17-0. It was Kocourek's only reception of the season.

The second half was no easier for Houston. Oiler return man Zeke Moore fumbled the kickoff and the Raiders recovered. Seven plays later, Lamonica dove into the end zone from the one-yard line.

The Raider offensive line attacked the Oiler defense in the second half, allowing Dixon and Banaszak to gain steady yardage and run down the clock. Dixon ended the day with 144 yards on the ground. Banaszak picked up 116.

Meanwhile, Blanda added three second-half field goals as Oakland posted a 40-7 victory. The win netted an additional $6,325 for each Raider. The Oilers received $4,994 apiece.

Oakland's next stop was Super Bowl II in Miami where the club was slated to play Vince Lombardi's powerful Green Bay Packers. Green Bay finished the season with a 9-4-1 record, then

Defensive back Dave Grayson (45) tries to stop Chiefs running back Wendell Hayes (38).

beat the Dallas Cowboys, 21-17, in a dramatic NFL Championship Game.

Although Green Bay was a 14-point favorite, the first quarter was fairly even. Green Bay kicker Don Chandler supplied the only points in the period on a 39-yard field goal.

In the second quarter, the Packers began to pick up steam. Boyd Dowler got behind the Raider secondary and caught a 62-yard touchdown pass from Bart Starr. Chandler added two more field goals and Green Bay took a 16-7 lead into the locker room at halftime. The Raiders only score came on a 23-yard pass from Lamonica to end Bill Miller.

Green Bay utilized its ball-control offense throughout the second half to build a commanding 33-7 lead. Chandler kicked his fourth field goal of the game and Packer running back Donny Anderson capped a 62-yard drive with a two-yard run. Green Bay's last score came when Herb Adderly intercepted a pass and returned it 60 yards.

Oakland found the end zone one last time on a 23-yard pass from Lamonica to Miller. It was not enough to beat the overpowering Packers. Vince Lombardi finished his last game as a Green Bay coach with a decisive 33-14 win over Oakland.

The Packers received $15,000 apiece for their Super Bowl victory. The Raiders picked up $7,500 each.

Above: Tight end Billy Cannon makes one of his three touchdown catches in a game against the Miami Dolphins in 1967. **Page 54:** Hewritt Dixon (35) cuts upfield against the Baltimore Colts for a big gain. Dixon was the club's leading receiver in 1967 with 59 catches.

1968

The AFL added another franchise to the western division in 1968 when the Cincinnati Bengals began operation. Paul Brown, a legendary coach with the Cleveland Browns from 1950-1962, was named the Bengals' first head coach.

Among the new faces at the Oakland training camp in 1968 were a trio of rookies that would be instrumental to the club's future success. They were tackle Art Shell of Maryland State, defensive back George Atkinson of Morris Brown and running back Charlie Smith from Utah. Smith replaced veteran Clem Daniels, who was dealt to the San Francisco 49ers in the offseason.

All-league defensive tackle Tom Keating hobbled into camp with an injured achilles tendon suffered during the 1967 AFL Championship Game. He was sidelined for most of the 1968 season.

The Raiders opened the exhibition season against the Baltimore Colts. It was just their third game against an NFL team. Oakland lost its previous two games to San Francisco, during the 1967 preseason, and to the Green Bay Packers in Super Bowl II.

Over 51,000 Oakland rooters filed into the Oakland Coliseum to watch the AFL champions. Colt quarterback Johnny Unitas, the NFL Player of the Year in 1967, led his club to two first-half touchdowns then watched as the Colts cruised to a 14-12 win over Oakland.

Oakland finished the preseason with wins over San Diego, San Francisco and Denver, then began the regular season with three straight games on the road.

The Raiders traveled to Buffalo for the league opener. Rookie defensive back George Atkinson put on an impressive show in his first pro game. He set an AFL single-game record for punt return yardage.

The first time Atkinson fielded a punt in the pro ranks, he scampered 86 yards for a score. Minutes later, while still in the first quarter, he returned another punt 52 yards. Atkinson ended the day with 205 yards on punt returns, shattering the old AFL record of 143 yards set by Oakland's Rodger Bird in 1967.

Oakland easily defeated the Bills, 48-6. The Raider defense dumped Buffalo quarterbacks Dan Darragh and Kay Stephenson eight times for 96 yards in losses. On offense, Hewritt Dixon led the charge with 104 yards in 16 carries. Receiver Warren Wells nabbed three passes for 92 yards and one touchdown.

Oakland added wins over Miami and Houston before returning home to defeat the Boston Patriots, 41-10. In that game, the Raiders spotted Boston a 10-7 lead at the half, then came back to score 21 points in 11 minutes of the third quarter. Warren Wells got the scoring started when he caught a nine-yard pass from Lamonica. Later, Wells sprinted 41 yards to paydirt on an end around.

The Raiders went into an uncharacteristic slump after beating the Patriots. They lost to San Diego, 23-14, and Kansas City, 24-10. It was their first two-game losing streak since early in the 1966 season.

Coach Rauch got his troops back on track the next week with a 31-10 win over the Cincinnati Bengals. The victory started another eight-game winning streak. Included in that string was a 38-21 triumph over Kansas City in which Daryle Lamonica and George Blanda combined for 469 passing yards to set an AFL one-game record. Even more dramatic was an Oakland win over the New York Jets in a nationally televised game.

The Jets' Jim Turner kicked a 26-yard field goal with 1:05 left in the game to give New York a 32-29 lead over the Raiders. At that point NBC executives had their own decision to make. They could either broadcast a special production of "Heidi" at its scheduled time, or they could continue coverage of the football game. NBC decided to broadcast "Heidi." Football fans across the country flooded the network with complaints. They also missed one of the great comebacks in Raider history.

After the ensuing kickoff Oakland moved the ball to the Jets 43-yard line. With 40 seconds to go, Daryle Lamonica hit rookie Charlie Smith at the New York 20. Smith turned on the afterburners and sprinted into the end zone to give Oakland the lead, 36-32. But that wasn't all.

Oakland kicked off and New York's Dick Christy fumbled the ball. The Raiders' Preston Ridlehuber recovered in the end zone. Oakland had scored 14 points in 28 seconds to defeat the Jets, 43-32.

The Raiders went into the final game of the season with an 11-2 record. The Kansas City Chiefs were also 11-2 and tied with Oakland for first place in the western division. Oakland was matched with the San Diego Chargers. Kansas City faced the Denver Broncos. If both teams won they would meet in a playoff.

Kansas City did its part, defeating Denver, 30-7. Oakland needed a win to remain in the playoff picture.

San Diego made it tough on Oakland, taking a 13-10 lead in the first half. Oakland's only touchdown came on Lamonica's 13-yard pass to Biletnikoff. Then the Raiders got a break in the second half when Rodger Bird picked off a John Hadl pass and returned it 23 yards for a touchdown. It gave Oakland its first lead of the day, 17-13.

Bird set up the Raiders' next score when he returned a punt 13 yards to give Oakland good field position at its 45-yard line. Two plays later Lamonica hit Wells on a 55-yard pass to give Oakland a 24-13 lead.

Oakland added 10 more points and seemed to be in control in the fourth quarter when disaster struck. The Chargers cut the score to 34-19, then Raider defensive back Nemiah Wilson fumbled a punt. The ball was batted into the San Diego end zone where Charger Ken Dyer recovered. San Diego added a two-point conversion and Oakland held a precarious 34-27 lead with nine minutes to play.

The Chargers had two more opportunities to score in the final period, but the Oakland defense turned back the challenge. The Raiders won, 34-27, and would face the Kansas City Chiefs in a playoff.

Oakland had the home field advantage, but

Jim Otto 1960-74

Oakland joined the AFL early in 1960 as the new league's eighth and possibly sorriest franchise. First called the Dons, then the Senors, the team actually was an afterthought—a last-ditch replacement for a Minnesota entry that had defected to the NFL.

At first, the Raiders—they finally settled on a name—had no players. Those drafted by Minnesota the previous November had been dispersed across the league. Running back Abner Haynes, for one, went to Lamar Hunt's Dallas Texans. A 217-pound center from the University of Miami, for another, signed with Houston.

Scrambling to stock the Raider roster, the AFL reassigned certain contracts. One belonged to the 217-pound center. He reported to training camp that summer in Santa Cruz along with 100 other scraggly hopefuls. He was small for a lineman, but he stood out in the drills. The coaches could see right away he was a player. His name, of course, was Jim Otto.

Not only did Otto make the lineup that year, he became an enduring star. He was the Raiders only starting center for their first 15 years and the AFL's only All-Star center in its 10 years of existence.

From 1960 to 1974, Jim Otto played with ironman consistency. During his 15 years with the Raiders, he appeared in 210 consecutive regular season games and 13 AFL all-star or NFL Pro Bowl games.

All of it came at a crippling price—11 knee operations, five of them since retiring, two artificial knee joints, several back and shoulder surgeries. Otto played a long career through infirmity and pain he was too stubborn to recognize. He admits as much.

But he claims he would do it again the same way. Pro football was his passion, being All-Pro center for the Oakland Raiders was his identity.

"I was a football player," he said firmly, "and I wanted to play."

If not for the AFL, he might never have gotten the chance. Otto was a two-way performer at the University of Miami, center and middle linebacker. What notoriety he earned in college came from his defense. NFL scouting systems were primitive then, surviving through word of mouth, newspaper reports, magazine ratings and occasional phone tips. Otto had a couple big games his senior year, against Tulane and Navy. He intercepted a few passes, made something like 14 unassisted tackles.

Word was circulating in 1959. Miami U. had this senior middle linebacker who was hitting people.

Otto stood 6'2" at the time, but he weighed only 205 pounds. The 49ers and the Packers put out some feelers. But Otto's size plus some shoulder injuries cooled their interest. He not only wasn't drafted by the NFL, he didn't even attract a free agent contract.

The AFL was a different story. Otto was picked by Minnesota, signed by Houston, and sent to Oakland, a sequence that didn't faze him. He wanted to play football and he says he was fiercely loyal to his new team, "from the day I first pulled on the helmet."

Otto had something to prove. The fact he was playing for the worst team in an inferior league only tested his confidence and loyalty.

"I kept my barometer high," Otto said. "We were just fledglings, team and league. I looked at the best at my position in the National Football League. Jim Ringo, supposedly, and Chuch Bednarik. I thought to myself, 'I'm as good or better than they are. I'm in a league that's going to be better than theirs.'"

Otto himself progressed faster than either the AFL or the Raiders, at least if measured by NFL standards.

"After I finished my first year," Otto said, "the NFL was knocking at my door, wanting me to jump leagues. They knocked every year until the merger, but I wouldn't do it. I had faith in the Raiders."

Otto bulked up starting his rookie year.

He lifted weights religiously and supplemented his diet with high-protein drinks, including his favorite, and a Raider staple, beer. He played that first year at 243 pounds. He started out as number 50.

He was number 50, through the first game of his second year, 1961. His nickname on the field and in the clubhouse was "Ott," which sounded like "Ought", zero. The equipment man, Frank Hinek, had an idea. He called the commissioner, Joe Foss, and received permission to give Otto the double-0 number.

"Frank thought it would be a good gimmick," Otto said, "Jim Otto, Double-0, and I didn't mind."

Double-0 became his trademark in Oakland. Around the league it became a symbol for fiery and active play, for unstoppable energy. Rosters were small in those days ("one year we only had 32 players," Otto said), and he was on every special team, making a deliberate nuisance of himself.

"First one down on punts," he recalled, "I made the majority of tackles on punts. I went down on kickoffs. I received kickoffs. I was in on some punt returns, because we'd be on offense right afterwards. I'd go in and replace a defender. I foiled a fake punt one time in New York. Lined up as a linebacker, flew in and hit the center. They snapped to the up back. They thought they

could block me. I dropped the guy for a loss."

Otto loved it, all the play on special teams, in addition to every down on offense.

"I loved to hit the center on punts," he said. "I knew when he was about to snap the ball. I could see his knuckles whitening on his hands. I used to time it just right, flying in. I had a lot of fun."

Al Davis told Otto that when he was an assistant coach in San Diego he used to yell at the Chargers, "Get Otto out of the game, get him out. He goes down, and they don't have anyone else."

Otto cherishes the memory.

"They had guys trying to clip me all the time," he said. "But I outlasted them. I played on the punt team for 12 years. It was only after Dave Dalby was drafted in 1972 that they had another long snapper and could give me a rest. So my last three years I only did field goals and extra points."

As the Raiders grew in stature, Otto grew as well. He started as an All-Pro on a laughingstock in a suspect league. He became an All-Pro on a first-rate team in a league that established parity—if not superiority—by winning Super Bowls III and IV. Otto had believed from the outset it would happen.

He worked too hard not to. John Madden used to marvel at Otto's diligent film study, the way Otto would ask to see his mistakes backed up and rerun time after

time, the way he would ignore what he did well.

"He was a model, that guy," said Madden.

"I wanted to be perfect," Otto said. "I strived for perfection. When I had a problem, I wanted to see it over and over again until I figured how I was going to correct it. I didn't need to see the good ones."

Otto played at All-Pro levels for a decade before the injuries began to hit with cruel regularity.

"My first ten years," he says, "I didn't have a single serious injury. Oh, I broke my nose a lot of times, broke a few ribs, my jaw, a few fingers, but no knees. Then the luck ran out. From my eleventh season on, it was knee surgery every year."

Otto played through 1974, the year the Raiders beat Miami in the playoffs, 28-26, on Kenny Stabler's desperation pass to Clarence Davis in the end zone. Oakland was eliminated by Pittsburgh the following week, 33-14, and, though he didn't know it at the time, Jim Otto had played in his last game.

He had offseason knee surgery once more, but this time the knee couldn't respond. He had pushed it to the wall. The previous year, his fifteenth as a Raider, he was voted second team All-Pro. But now it was over.

"I was stubborn," he said, "I played hurt, but I went out at the right time, the way I wanted to. When I still rated higher than 27 other guys in the league."

The Raiders cover a Pittsburgh Steeler fumble. Gus Otto (34) recovered for Oakland.

Kansas City was a five-point favorite. Despite bitter cold and a driving rain, 53,605 fans were on hand. It was the largest attendance of the season at the Oakland Coliseum.

Lamonica went to the air in the first quarter and tossed three touchdown passes. He connected with Biletnikoff on scoring passes of 24 and 44 yards, and added a 23-yarder to Warren Wells. The early scores forced Kansas City to abandon its ball-control offense and rely on quarterback Len Dawson's arm. The Raider defense ate him alive.

Dawson had completed 58 percent of his passes during the regular season, but against the Raiders he could complete just 49 percent. He faced defensive pressure throughout the second half and had four of his passes intercepted.

Lamonica threw two more touchdown passes before the day was over—a 54-yard pass to Biletnikoff and a 35-yard toss to Wells—as Oakland destroyed Kansas City, 41-6. The win gave Oakland its second straight western division title and a shot at the New York Jets in the AFL Championship Game.

Lamonica ended the day completing 19 of 39 passes for 347 yards and five touchdowns. Biletnikoff caught seven of those passes for 180 yards.

Wells caught four for 94 yards. Charlie Smith was the leading rusher with 74 yards on 13 carries.

An AFL record crowd of 62,627 packed into Shea Stadium to watch the Raiders take on Joe Namath and the New York Jets. Namath got the Jets on the scoreboard first by hitting Don Maynard on a 14-yard pass.

On the Raiders' next possession they drove to the 35-yard line where George Blanda attempted a field goal. The kick hit the cross bar and bounced away.

New York kicker Jim Turner booted a 33-yard field goal at the end of the first quarter to give the Jets a 10-0 advantage. It turned out to be the largest margin in the game.

Early in the second quarter, Lamonica took the Raiders on an impressive 80-yard drive. He mixed plays beautifully, picking up yardage on short passes to Biletnikoff and quick openers to fullback Hewritt Dixon. Lamonica capped the drive with a 29-yard pass to Biletnikoff. Blanda added a field goal just before the half ended and

New York took a 13-10 lead into the locker room.

The Raiders went right at the Jets to start the second half. They drove nearly the length of the field, but the drive stalled at the New York two-yard line. Blanda kicked a nine-yard field goal to tie the game, 13-13.

Oakland took the lead for the first time midway through the fourth period. George Atkinson made a spectacular interception and returned it to the New York five-yard line before Namath ran him out of bounds. One play later Pete Banaszak bulled his way through the Jets' line to score. The touchdown put Oakland in front, 23-20.

The lead lasted just 31 seconds. New York took over on its own 20 after the ensuing kickoff and Namath went to work. He completed a 22-yard sideline pass to George Sauer, then hit Don Maynard on a 50-yard toss over the middle. On the next play he hit Maynard again for the touchdown. In just three plays Namath moved the Jets 80 yards to regain the lead, 27-23.

The Raiders still had plenty of time left. Lamonica had the ball at his own 15-yard line with 3:09 to play. On first down he drilled a 25-yard pass to Biletnikoff. After throwing incomplete, Lamonica went to the air again and floated a pass in the direction of Warren Wells. Wells outjumped Jet safety Randy Beverly to make the catch and pick up another 34 yards. New York was also hit with a 15-yard penalty on the play for unsportsmanlike conduct. The Raiders were now just 22 yards away from the end zone with two minutes to play.

On first down from the 22, Lamonica attempted to pass but could not find an open receiver downfield. He spotted halfback Charlie Smith still in the backfield and tried to hit him with a pass as Smith ran parallel to Lamonica. The pass went behind Smith, where it bounced around before New York's Ralph Baker picked it up. The referees then ruled the toss was a backward pass, similar to a lateral, and therefore a free ball. New York took over and ran down the clock to win, 27-23. The Jets advanced to the Super Bowl and became the first AFL team to beat an NFL club by downing the Baltimore Colts, 16-7.

Quarterback Daryle Lamonica continued to confound defenses with the long ball in 1968. Although he completed just 49.5 percent of his 416 passes, he threw for 25 touchdowns and 3,245 yards. Hewritt Dixon was the club's leading ground gainer with 865 yards. Kicker George

Blanda set a team scoring mark with 117 points.

Jim Otto was picked to the all-league team for the ninth straight year. He was joined by teammates Hewritt Dixon, Gene Upshaw, Dan Birdwell, Dan Conners, Willie Brown and Dave Grayson. Grayson had 10 interceptions to lead the league.

1969 Prior to the 1969 season, Raider linebackers coach John Madden was named head coach, replacing John Rauch. Rauch left the Raiders to take over the head coaching job at Buffalo. In his three years with Oakland, Rauch compiled a 33-8-1 record. He also led the club to two division championships and one Super Bowl.

At 33, Madden became the youngest head coach in professional football. He had been an assistant coach at San Diego State for three years before taking a job with the Raider staff.

Oakland finished the preseason with a 2-3 record then started the regular season with wins over Houston, Miami, Boston, San Diego, Buffalo and Denver. The club also played Miami to a 20-20 tie. Against Buffalo, Daryle Lamonica tied a club record by throwing six touchdown passes in the first half. It was also the first of 137 consecutive sellouts at the Oakland Coliseum.

The Raiders were upset by the Cincinnati Bengals midway through the season, 31-17, then went on to win their next five games. On the final day of the season they were matched with the Kansas City Chiefs. Oakland had an 11-1-1 record. Kansas City was 12-1. The winner would be crowned western division champ.

The Raider defense played errorless football against the Chiefs. Kansas City was limited to 170 yards of total offense. Just 29 of those yards were gained on the ground.

Kansas City's defense was just as stingy. In the first half, Oakland threatened only once. Lamonica connected on a 72-yard bomb to Warren Wells putting the ball on the Kansas City 12. But Buck Buchanan stormed through the Raider line

Rod Sherman celebrates after scoring an 87-yard touchdown on a pass from Daryle Lamonica.

on the next play to sack Lamonica and move the ball back to the 25. Oakland had to settle for a field goal.

The score stayed at 3-0 until midway through the fourth period when Lamonica marched the Raiders to the eight-yard line. From there he connected with running back Charlie Smith in the end zone.

Kansas City retaliated with its own 62-yard drive. Wendell Hayes scored on a one-yard run and Oakland had just a 10-7 lead. With 5:30 left, the Chiefs were confident they could regain the ball and score again. Lamonica had other plans. Oakland picked up three consecutive first downs to run out the clock and preserve the win.

Under a new AFL playoff system the Raiders were slated to meet the eastern division runner-up. The eastern division champ played the western division's second-place club. Oakland was matched with the Houston Oilers. Houston, led by quarterback Pete Beathard, had a 6-6-2 record.

Oakland humiliated the Oilers, 56-7, on a muddy field at the Oakland Coliseum. Lamonica completed 13 of 17 passes for six touchdowns as the Raiders built a 49-0 lead before Houston could score midway through the fourth period. Starting wide receiver Warren Wells was sidelined with a separated shoulder, but backup Rod Sherman was sensational in his absence. Sherman and Biletnikoff each hauled in two touchdown passes.

The victory meant that Oakland would face the Kansas City Chiefs for the AFL Championship at the Oakland Coliseum. Kansas City made its way to the league final by knocking off the New York Jets in the playoffs, 13-6.

The championship game was nearly a replica of the final regular season contest between the two clubs. Defense was the dominating factor.

The Raiders scored first on Charlie Smith's three-yard run late in the first quarter. Oakland's slim 7-0 lead held until late in the second quarter when Kansas City quarterback Len Dawson hit receiver Frank Pitts on a 41-yard pass to the Oakland one-yard line. Wendell Hayes punched the ball over to tie the game, 7-7.

Midway through the third quarter, Tom Keating recovered a Kansas City fumble and the game seemed to turn in the Raiders' favor. From there, Lamonica threw two incomplete passes.

On the second one he hit his hand on an opposing lineman's helmet and had to be removed from the game. George Blanda relieved Lamonica. He threw incomplete, then missed a 40-yard field goal. Kansas City took over and marched 95 yards in 10 plays to post a 14-7 lead.

Lamonica returned to action late in the third quarter, but the fingers on his throwing hand were badly bruised and swollen. He moved the club downfield to the Kansas City 39, then had a pass intercepted by safety Jim Kearney.

Two plays later, Oakland recovered a fumble. On the first play from scrimmage, Lamonica had a pass intercepted by defensive back Jim Marsalis. He threw his third interception on the club's next possession. Kansas City converted the turnover into a field goal and held on to win, 17-7.

The Chiefs went on to Super Bowl IV, where they faced the Minnesota Vikings. The Vikings were 13-point favorites but the Chiefs upset Minnesota, 23-7.

The Raider loss ended another promising season. Daryle Lamonica finished the year with a club record, 34 touchdown passes. He was selected all-league along with nine other Raiders. Making the all-star team for the tenth straight time was Jim Otto. Gene Upshaw, Harry Schuh, Fred Biletnikoff, Warren Wells, Willie Brown, Dave Grayson, Dan Conners and Tom Keating also made the squad.

Page 64: Tony Cline (84) and Otis Sistrunk (60) stack up Atlanta's Dave Hampton (43) in a 37-34 Raiders overtime win.

1970–1979

CHAPTER TWO

JOINING THE NFL

In 1970, the National and American Football Leagues completed their merger. Several minor points needed to be worked out before the start of the season. Among the issues that were settled was whether to use the two-point conversion, as prefered by the AFL, or stick to the NFL's rule of a single point after touchdown. The NFL's rule was adopted for all of football. The two leagues also agreed to use the NFL-style game ball.

Both leagues were then reorganized with the Baltimore Colts, Pittsburgh Steelers and Cleveland Browns of the NFL being placed in the newly named American Football Conference. The NFL became known as the National Football Conference. The two conferences were arranged into three divisions. The Raiders found themselves in the western division with the San Diego Chargers, Kansas City Chiefs and Denver Broncos.

Tragedy struck the Raiders just prior to training camp when running back Roger Hagberg was killed in an auto accident. Hagberg started his career with the Raiders in 1965 after starring at the University of Minnesota. In five seasons with the club, he carried the ball 194 times for 766 yards. He also caught 58 passes and scored eight touchdowns for Oakland.

Among the rookies in camp in 1970 were Raymond Chester, a 220-pound tight end from Morgan State, and linebacker Carl Weathers of San Diego State. Weathers later gained fame as Apollo Creed in the movie "Rocky."

The Raiders looked uninspired during the exhibition season dropping all three home games and finishing with a 2-4 record. In the team's final pre-season game, all-league linebacker Dan Conners was injured and lost for five weeks.

The regular season started just as poorly. Oakland lost its opener to the lowly Cincinnati Bengals, 31-21, then tied San Diego and lost to the Miami Dolphins. The loss to Cincinnati was particularly aggravating for Coach John Madden. The Bengals, in only their third season of professional football, were never behind. They blocked a punt by Raider kicker Mike Eischeid just one minute into the game and recovered at the Oakland seven-yard line. Two plays later, Bengal quarterback Sam Wyche ran five yards for the score.

Cincinnati completely dominated line play. The Bengals gained 247 yards on the ground and averaged 6.2 yards per carry. Cincinnati running back Jesse Phillips picked up 130 yards in 15 tries to lead all rushers. The Raiders managed just 48 yards on the ground.

Oakland turned the season around in the fourth week when the Denver Broncos visited the Oakland Coliseum. Denver led, 23-21, at the start of the fourth period when Lamonica struck on a 50-yard pass to Warren Wells. The play moved Oakland into field goal position at the 20-yard line. On the next play from scrimmage, Lamonica went for the end zone. He threw to

Jack Tatum (32) and Monte Johnson tip a pass intended for San Diego's Gary Garrison (27).

Wells, who was closely guarded. The ball was tipped into the air by Denver defensive back Bill Thompson, but Wells made a magnificent catch for the touchdown.

Raider halfback Charlie Smith added a five-yard scoring run late in the game as Oakland beat Denver, 35-23. Daryle Lamonica completed 20 of 37 passes for 364 yards and four touchdowns. Warren Wells had seven receptions for 198 yards and three scores.

It was a bittersweet win for the Raiders, however. They lost all-league defensive back Willie Brown for at least five weeks with a separated shoulder.

A week later, Oakland ran its record to 2-2-1 with a 34-20 win over the Washington Redskins. The Pittsburgh Steelers were next on the schedule.

Oakland was clinging to a 17-14 lead against Pittsburgh when Lamonica was injured late in the first half. Backup quarterback George Blanda

was summoned from the bench. He threw two touchdown passes to pace the Raiders to a 31-14 win.

The 43-year-old Blanda was in his 21st season of professional football. With the Raiders he performed mostly as a kicker and emergency backup to Lamonica. But for five consecutive games in 1970 he proved more valuable off the bench than anyone could have imagined.

A week after beating Pittsburgh, Blanda kicked a 48-yard field goal with three seconds left to tie Kansas City, 17-17. The following week he kicked a 52-yarder with three seconds on the clock to beat Cleveland, 23-20. In the next game at Denver, Lamonica was ineffective. Blanda came off the bench in the fourth quarter and marched the Raiders to the winning touchdown in a 24-19 victory. Blanda topped it off by kicking a field goal against San Diego with seven seconds remaining in a 20-17 win.

Oakland won two of its final three games to finish with an 8-4-2 record, best in the western division. The Raiders were matched with the Miami Dolphins in the playoffs. Under Coach Don Shula, Miami finished with a 10-4 mark.

A capacity crowd of 54,401 gathered at the Oakland Coliseum to watch John Madden's men

take on Miami. The Dolphins scored first on a 16-yard pass from Bob Griese to Paul Warfield, but Oakland tied the game in the second quarter when Lamonica hit Biletnikoff on a 22-yard pass. The first half ended in a 7-7 tie.

The Raiders seemed determined to give the game away in the second half. They fumbled four times, but Miami was unable to capitalize on the turnovers.

In the third period Oakland got its first break. Willie Brown intercepted a Bob Griese pass and sprinted 50 yards down the sideline to score. Early in the fourth quarter Oakland extended its lead when Lamonica caught Miami in man-to-man coverage. Oakland receiver Rod Sherman beat rookie defensive back Curtis Johnson and Lamonica laid the ball right in his hands. Sherman took the pass in stride at the Miami 45 and outran everyone to the end zone, completing the 82-yard pass play. Griese drove the Dolphins 63 yards to score one last time, but Oakland held on to win, 21-14.

Meanwhile, the Baltimore Colts beat the Cincinnati Bengals to set up an AFC Championship Game between the Colts and Oakland. Baltimore, led by veteran quarterback Johnny Unitas, had the home field advantage.

Clarence Davis looks for running room behind the blocks of tight end Bob Moore (88) and tackle John Vella (75).

The Raiders were behind most of the game. Then with about 12 minutes remaining the momentum seemed to switch. Daryle Lamonica left the game with a pulled groin and was replaced by the ageless George Blanda. Blanda responded by throwing a 15-yard touchdown pass to Warren Wells and Oakland was within three points, 20-17.

The game was now in the hands of the Raider defense. Willie Brown knocked away a Johnny Unitas pass on first down, then Ben Davidson sacked Unitas for a one-yard loss on second down. On third-and-11, Unitas found receiver Ray Perkins behind the Oakland secondary and unloaded a 68-yard touchdown pass. Oakland never recovered. Baltimore went on to win, 27-17. It was the third straight year Oakland lost in league championship play.

Two weeks later, the Colts defeated the Dallas Cowboys in Super Bowl V, 16-13. Rookie kicker Jim O'Brien was the hero of the day for Balti-

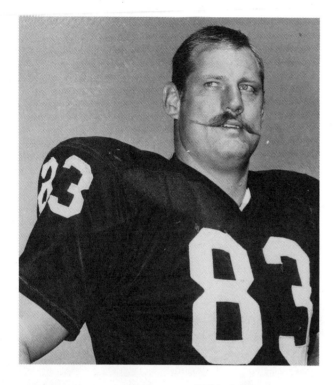

more. He booted a 32-yard field goal as the clock ran down to win it for the Colts.

Once again, the Raiders dominated the all-league team. Receivers Warren Wells and Fred Biletnikoff both made the club as did Daryle Lamonica, fullback Hewritt Dixon, center Jim Otto, tackle Harry Schuh and guard Gene Upshaw. Tom Keating and Willie Brown were the only defensive players to make the squad.

George Blanda's late game heroics were not lost on the country's sports writers. He was voted AFC Player of the Year. Tight end Raymond Chester was named AFC Rookie of the Year.

Hewritt Dixon retired after the 1970 season, along with defensive back Kent McCloughan and guard Wayne Hawkins, one of the original Raiders. Dixon ended his eight-year career with 3,090 total yards and a 4-yard rushing average. He was also a reliable receiver, nabbing 263 passes for 2,819 yards.

1971 The Raiders made several lineup changes in 1971. During the preseason, Ken Stabler competed with Daryle Lamonica at quarterback. Despite several impressive performances by Stabler, Lamonica won back the starting job.

Lamonica found himself at a disadvantage, however. Warren Wells, his favorite deep threat and an all-league performer in 1970, ran into trouble with the law and was declared ineligible to play pro football. Receivers Fred Biletnikoff and Ray Chester picked up the slack. Biletnikoff responded by catching 61 passes in 1971 to lead the AFC.

There were changes in the backfield as well. Marv Hubbard and Pete Banaszak won the starting jobs, while Clarence Davis, a rookie from USC, also saw considerable playing time.

On the defensive side, two rookies made their presence known. Jack Tatum, a safety from Ohio

Top: Defensive end Ben Davidson. **Bottom:** In his first game as a professional in 1968, George Atkinson set an AFC record by returning five punts for 205 yards. **Page 69:** Ken Stabler (12) leaves the game in pain after injuring his ribs. Concerned teammates and trainers come to his aid.

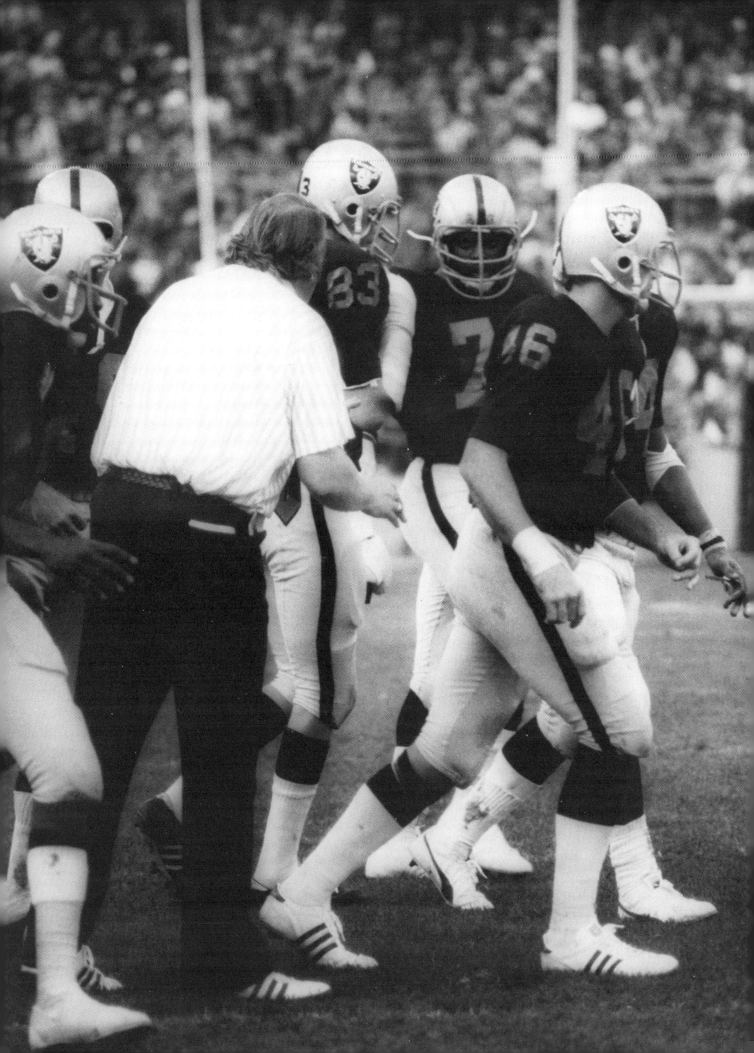

State, moved into the starting lineup and intercepted four passes. Bowling Green linebacker Phil Villapiano teamed with Gerald Irons, Dan Conners and Gus Otto to give the Raiders a solid linebacking crew.

The Raiders had an excellent preseason, stringing together wins over the New York Jets, Los Angeles Rams, Green Bay Packers, San Francisco 49ers and Baltimore Colts.

They dropped their opening game of the year against New England at Schaefer Stadium, 20-6, but came back the following week to wallop San Diego, 34-0. It was the first shutout by a Raider team in nearly four years.

Oakland had just a 6-0 lead over San Diego at halftime. But the Raiders added a touchdown on their first possession of the second half, driving 74 yards in eight plays. Lamonica hit Biletnikoff on a 36-yard pass for the touchdown.

The defense took over from there, limiting the Chargers to 73 yards rushing and only 13 first downs in the game. Charger quarterback John Hadl had five of his passes intercepted.

Lamonica completed 11 of 17 passes for 174 yards and two touchdowns. Clarence Davis was the leading rusher with 75 yards in nine carries.

Oakland went 6-0-2 during its next eight games to post a 7-1-2 record and gain first place in the western division. Kansas City was right behind them with a 7-2-1 mark.

The Raiders picked a bad time to go into a slump. They lost two straight games and went into the 13th week of the season 1/2 game behind the Chiefs. They traveled to Kansas City that week. The winner would become the western division champion.

Kansas City jumped out to a 10-0 lead behind Len Dawson's 29-yard pass to Otis Taylor and Jan Stenerud's 33-yard field goal. Oakland got its offense moving in the second quarter after Nemiah Wilson intercepted a Dawson pass and returned it to the Kansas City 32. Coach Madden sent Blanda into the game to replace the ineffective

Top: Pete Banaszak (40) turns the corner against Atlanta and heads for the end zone. **Bottom:** Punter Ray Guy (8) is greeted by Neal Colzie after getting off a booming punt. **Page 70:** Coach John Madden fires up his kickoff team as the Raiders take the field against Atlanta in 1975.

Lamonica and he responded by hitting Biletnikoff on two consecutive passes to move the ball to the eight. Three plays later Marv Hubbard scored.

The Raiders took a 14-13 lead at the start of the fourth quarter after Hubbard scored again on a one-yard run. Late in the fourth period Blanda lined up to try a 37-yard field goal that would put the Raiders in front, 17-13. The kick was blocked. Kansas City recovered and Chief quarterback Len Dawson steadily moved his club downfield. Jan Stenerud came on with 1:44 left in the game to kick a 10-yard field goal and beat Oakland, 16-14. The loss knocked Oakland out of the western division title race. It was the first time in five years the Raiders failed to make the playoffs.

Fred Biletnikoff ended the season with 61 receptions for 929 yards and nine touchdowns. His 61 catches topped the AFL. Hubbard ground out 867 yards on 181 carries and averaged 4.8 yards per carry. Banaszak had 563 yards on 137 carries.

Four members of the Raider offensive line were selected all-league. Center Jim Otto made the team once again as did tackle Bob Brown, guard Gene Upshaw and tight end Ray Chester. Cornerback Willie Brown was the sole member of the defensive unit to make the team.

1972 In 1972 the Raiders began to revamp their defensive line. Defensive end Ben Davidson retired after suffering a heel injury, and veterans Tom Keating and Carleton Oats were replaced by youngsters Art Thoms, Tony Cline and Otis Sistrunk.

The offense began to show signs of change, too. Backup quarterback Ken Stabler looked impressive in the preseason opener against New England. He rallied the Raiders to 17 points in the third quarter, connecting with rookie receiver Cliff Branch on a 26-yard pass and later directing the club on a 72-yard scoring drive for another touchdown. Oakland defeated the Patriots, 31-

Running back Harold Hart (34) grinds out tough yardage against the Kansas City Chiefs.

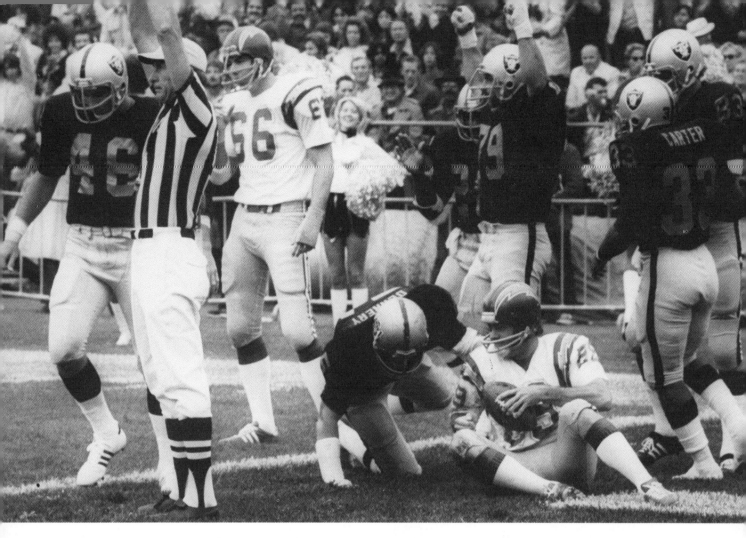

Oakland draws first blood when Mike Dennery (54) and Louis Carter (33) drop San Diego punter Dennis Partee for a safety.

24, then completed the exhibition schedule with a 4-2 record.

Among the other rookies to stick with the club were center Dave Dalby of UCLA, receiver Mike Siani of Villanova, offensive lineman John Vella of USC and defensive back Skip Thomas of USC.

The Raiders opened the season against the Pittsburgh Steelers. Pittsburgh had not won a championship in 40 years, but under the guidance of quarterback Terry Bradshaw, the Steelers finally had a contender. They dominated Oakland for three quarters, intercepting three Stabler passes enroute to a 27-7 lead.

Daryle Lamonica replaced Stabler at the start of the fourth quarter. He directed the Raiders 70 yards and capped it with a a 24-yard pass to Mike Siani. Pittsburgh scored on its next possession and seemed to put the game out of reach. With just nine minutes to play the Steelers led, 34-14.

After the kickoff, Lamonica marched the Raiders 77 yards, closing the score to 34-21. Then

Oakland's defense held Pittsburgh on four downs and the Raiders regained the ball. On their second play from scrimmage Lamonica unloaded a 70-yard scoring pass to Mike Siani. Less than two minutes remained and Pittsburgh was now clinging to a 34-28 lead. But the Steelers had time in their favor. They were able to run out the clock and end Lamonica's heroics.

Lamonica regained the starting quarterback job and led Oakland to nine wins in its next 12 games. Nevertheless, the Raiders needed a win on the last day of the season to ensure a playoff spot.

The Chicago Bears did not make things easy for Oakland. Despite a 4-8-1 record, the Bears refused to roll over. In a freezing rain at Oakland, the Bears jumped out to a quick 7-0 lead when Ron Smith returned the opening kickoff 94 yards. The Raiders tied the game just before the half when Lamonica hit Charlie Smith with a 14-yard touchdown pass.

Stabler replaced Lamonica in the third quarter and got the sluggish offense in gear. He directed the club 66 yards and connected with Smith on a 19-yard pass to give the Raiders the lead, 14-7.

The Raiders put together their most impressive drive in the fourth quarter when they needed it

Marv Hubbard 1969-75

Until Marcus Allen came along in 1982 to give it a touch of glitter, the Raider running game always had been as blue collar as a day at the foundry.

Always. The prevailing Raider method was domination, man-on-man football. Beat your man at the point of attack, and all else follows. Show by the run you're bigger, stronger, tougher, and more durable. Prove it in the pits. Bowl over a defense with the run, and the pass becomes much more effective.

In the old days in Oakland, the Raider running game went tackle to tackle. There were no attempts at deception, no tosses, traps, or pitches. They relied instead on such elemental plays as the ''68 and 69 Boom Man,'' weak side slants to either side, the fullback carrying.

The halfback would hit the hole first, clearing it of any filling linebacker. The fullback came behind, taking the snap, plunging through, cutting past bodies into whatever open space the line had ripped free.

It was not a glamorous way to gain yards, but it was brutally effective. It required halfbacks unafraid of riding point. It required a fullback the size of a middle linebacker who hit like a sledge hammer and backed up not an inch, someone like Marv Hubbard, the Raiders' starting fullback from 1971 to 1975.

Hubbard played his part to the hilt. He had such little regard for the subtleties of the running back position he selected his equipment only for one reason— how effectively it withstood collision.

''I wore lineman's pads,'' Hubbard said. ''They covered me down to my belly. I wore lineman's knee and thigh pads. I wore cardboard liners inside my socks to protect my shins and heavy leather shoes with round safety heels. I didn't take many chances.

''I had a helmet that the manufacturer guaranteed would withstand 200 g's of force before it would pop. It takes nine g's on your body to make your lungs collapse. I busted about 12 of those helmets, but I never had any headaches with them.''

Hubbard was an 11th-round draft choice from Colgate in 1968. He was a little on the eccentric side, a true Raider in that respect. One year in training camp he asked John Madden to assign him a new roommate. The one he had, a kicker from Syracuse, wore pajamas and liked to go to bed early. Hubbard despised him for the sheer regularity of his habits.

It took longer for his playing personality to rise to Raider standards. Hubbard was tough, fearless and determined. He had excellent balance. He had been skiing since he was four years old, giant slalom and downhill, and he loved contact. If a stone wall were put up before him he would try running through it.

"You want to ride this train, you better buy a ticket," Hubbard said of his earlier style.

But the earlier style had drawbacks. Hubbard lacked abundant speed. And nowhere else had he ever been asked to block. In college at Colgate he ran from an offense that had him "sweep left, sweep right, and run up the middle." In Santa Rosa that first camp, Al Davis liked him, but only as a project, a future.

That was 1968, when the Raiders already had Hewritt Dixon and Roger Hagberg as fullbacks. Hubbard predictably fell victim to the numbers. But 24 hours after Oakland cut him, he was claimed by Denver.

He did well enough in the Denver camp the week he was there, ringing up runs in full-scale scrimmages of 90, 46 and 44 yards. But once again he was cut, this time after a dispute with a defensive assistant.

"I should have made the Denver club that year," Hubbard maintained, "but I got into a small argument with a linebacker who tried to clothesline me in a no-contact drill. The linebacker coach jumped in and chewed me out. Then the head coach, Lou Saban, jumped in and said things. The next morning I was gone."

From there—what Hubbard calls "stopping in Denver and saying hello to Lou Saban"— he went to the football minors, Hartford in the Continental League. He had a good enough year in Connecticut to attract the interest of Green Bay, Dallas, New England and the New York Jets. He envisioned a bidding war.

He found out that wouldn't happen and why. The Raiders still owned his rights. Al Davis had signed him to two one-year contracts in 1968, one for that year, which was dissolved when the Raiders released him, and one for 1969. Hubbard appealed. He didn't want to return to Oakland and risk being waived again. But the commissioner's office backed up the Raiders' claim, so Hubbard went once more to Santa Rosa.

By then John Madden was head coach. Madden had moved Hagberg to backup tight end, opening a spot behind Hewritt Dixon. In Hartford, Hubbard had lost none of his running skill, plus he had acquired an aptitude for taking on 280-pound defensive linemen, a skill he was only too happy to demonstrate in camp.

"I was knocking people down," Hubbard recalled. "I just said,

there's nobody who's going to keep me off this team, and if I have to drive my helmet through somebody to prove it, that's what I'm going to do."

He had only one crisis of doubt, that on the anniversary of the day he was cut in 1968. He figured it down to the calendar page. When the anniversary hit he started packing. They couldn't fire him if he quit first. Someone saw him preparing to leave and told John Madden. It took some reassurance before Madden could convince Hubbard he was making the team.

Once a Raider, his whole personality emerged, on field and off. Hubbard had been raised amid poverty. He came from a small upper Appalachian town in western New York called Red House, where "some people still live in dirt floor shacks." He attended a one-room school until the seventh grade. He was bright. He skipped a grade in high school, then went to Colgate on an academic scholarship, but he still was country in many ways.

He'd spend nights at training camp drinking beer in the card rooms around Santa Rosa, or he'd stay in his room plunking out country and western ballads on his guitar.

He once told Madden, "I don't understand California. Where I come from, you go out drinking on Saturday night. The night goes on. You start a fight and cold cock some guy. You pick him up, dust him

off, buy him a drink, and the night goes on some more.

"But in California, you go into a bar, you start a fight and cold cock some guy . . . and he turns around and sues you. I don't like California very much."

But he liked football, and he was born for the Raiders' straight ahead running game. Without speed and slick moves, he still led the team in rushing all four years he started, 1971 through 1974, averaging 4.8 yards a carry and close to 1,000 yards a year.

He was entrenched as the starting fullback in 1975 when he was hit by a series of shoulder separations beginning in a preseason game with Atlanta. The shoulder injuries never quite healed, and his playing career was cut short before he was 30.

Hubbard once had this idea. Someday he'd be sitting in a rocking chair holding a grandchild on his lap, showing him a studded diamond ring on his finger, telling him, "Once upon a time, son, your grampa was full-back for the best team in all of football."

He missed by a year. He went out in 1975, a season before the Raiders won Super Bowl XI with Mark van Eeghen, another Colgate grad, as their starting fullback. But for the time he was there— Super Bowl ring or no— he made his impact, gaining more than 4,000 yards, all of them coming the hard way— through the space between the tackles.

Dave Dalby (50) dives to block Atlanta's Don Hansen (58) as Mark van Eeghen (30) slashes for yardage.

most. Oakland held a slim 21-14 advantage when running back Clarence Davis burst off-tackle and followed a Gene Upshaw block to score on a 45-yard run. The touchdown enabled Oakland to win, 28-21, and clinch the western division crown.

Stabler had one of his best days as a Raider. He connected on 10 of 11 passes for 124 yards and one touchdown despite playing less than a half.

Oakland was slated to meet the Pittsburgh Steelers in the first round of the playoffs. Pittsburgh beat the Raiders earlier in the year, 34-28. The Steelers ended the season with an 11-3 record. Oakland finished 10-3-1. The game proved to be one of the most memorable playoff contests in NFL history.

The first half was a defensive struggle and ended in a scoreless tie. Pittsburgh got on the board with two Roy Gerela field goals in the second half. Midway through the fourth quarter the Steelers led, 6-0.

Daryle Lamonica had been ineffective most of the game, hitting on just six of 18 passes in three quarters of play. Ken Stabler replaced Lamonica in the fourth quarter and went to work. He threw to tight end Ray Chester for 10 yards, then unloaded a 12-yard pass to Pete Banaszak. He

connected on another 12-yarder to Biletnikoff, moving the ball to the Pittsburgh 42-yard line. It was the Raiders' deepest penetration of the day.

Stabler then hit Mike Siani with a 12-yard pass to the 30-yard line. With barely 1:30 left to play Stabler dropped back to pass and was almost sacked. He broke free and outran the Pittsburgh defenders 30 yards into the end zone. Blanda added the extra point to give Oakland its first lead of the game, 7-6.

After the ensuing kickoff, Pittsburgh had less than a minute to get on the scoreboard. Steeler quarterback Terry Bradshaw took over at his own 20 and completed two passes to the Pittsburgh 40. The Steelers needed a miracle to win it. Instead, they got the "Immaculate Reception."

With 22 seconds on the clock, Bradshaw looked for wide receiver Barry Pearson on a down-and-in pattern. Pearson was covered so Bradshaw lofted a pass to John Fuqua, who was running a pattern toward the middle of the field. Safety Jack Tatum had the play well covered and hit Fuqua just as the pass arrived. But the ball bounced into the air and rookie running back Franco Harris grabbed it just inches off the turf. Harris shook off safety Jimmy Warren's diving tackle attempt, then sprinted down the sideline to score.

The stunned Raiders protested that the pass had bounced off Fuqua not Tatum and therefore could not be caught by another Steeler. The referees disagreed. They awarded Pittsburgh a touchdown on the controversial play, eliminating the Raiders from further playoff competition.

1973 Daryle Lamonica opened the 1973 exhibition season as the Raiders' starting quarterback. Before the year was over, Ken Stabler had replaced him and become the AFC's leading passer.

Kicker Ray Guy, drafted out of Southern Mississippi, was a welcome addition to the club, as were linebacker Monte Johnson and veteran defensive end Bubba Smith. Smith, a former All-Pro, was acquired from the Baltimore Colts.

Oakland closed out the preseason schedule with a 4-1-1 record, but the offense was less than explosive. In the opening game of the regular season at Minnesota the trend continued. Lamonica was unable to put a touchdown on the scoreboard as the Raiders lost, 24-16. Three field goals by George Blanda and a 63-yard punt return by George Atkinson accounted for all of Oakland's points. Lamonica completed just 13 of 29 passes and had two intercepted.

The following week, Oakland met the Miami Dolphins at the University of California's Memorial Stadium. Miami finished the 1972 season with a 17-0 record, including a win over the Washington Redskins in Super Bowl VII. A curious crowd of 74,121 was on hand to see Oakland upset the defending world champions, 12-7. Despite the victory, Lamonica was unable to generate much

George Blanda (16) uncorks while Pittsburgh's Steve Furness strains to no avail.

offense. All of Oakland's scoring came on field goals.

The Raiders' inability to score touchdowns became increasingly evident in the third week of the season when they were defeated by the Kansas City Chiefs, 16-3. Coach Madden was faced with a difficult decision. Sporting a 1-2 record, he benched Lamonica after the Kansas City game and replaced him with Ken Stabler.

Stabler's style of play was completely different from Lamonica's. Whereas Lamonica liked to score quickly with the long bomb, Stabler preferred a controlled offense that featured high percentage passes. Stabler's style worked well for the Raiders because they were blessed with three sturdy running backs—Marv Hubbard, Clarence Davis and Charlie Smith—who made the ball-control offense work. In addition, wide receiver Fred Biletnikoff was one of the game's great possession receivers.

In his first start, Stabler led the Raiders to a 17-10 victory over the St. Louis Cardinals. Under Stabler's guidance Oakland went on to beat San Diego, tie Denver, then defeat Baltimore and the New York Giants.

Against the Giants, Stabler completed 16 of 21 passes for 212 yards and two touchdowns enroute to a 42-0 victory. The win moved the Raiders a game ahead of the Kansas City Chiefs in the western division. Mike Siani and Fred Biletnikoff each nabbed four passes for Oakland.

In his first five games as the starting quarterback Stabler put on a remarkable display. He completed 69.9 percent of his passes and had only three balls intercepted.

Oakland's winning streak came to an end a week later at the hands of the Pittsburgh Steelers, 17-9. It was the first meeting between the two clubs since the dramatic 1972 playoff game when Franco Harris' "Immaculate Reception" gave Pittsburgh a victory with 22 seconds to play.

The Raiders got back on track with a win over San Diego, 31-3, and finished the season with four straight victories to clinch the western divi-

John Vella (75) leads the blocking downfield for running back Mark van Eeghen (30).

sion title. In their final game Oakland beat the second-place Denver Broncos, 21-17.

Several members of the club won individual honors at the conclusion of the season. Stabler topped the AFC with a 62.7 passing percentage. It also bettered the old club mark of 54 percent set by Tom Flores in 1960. Punter Ray Guy just missed winning the league's punting title. His 45.3 yard average was topped only by Kansas City's Jerrel Wilson, who had a 45.5 yard average. Running back Marv Hubbard had an outstanding season. He rushed for 903 yards and averaged 4.7 yards per carry.

For the second straight year Oakland's opponent in the playoffs was the Pittsburgh Steelers. This time the Raiders had the home field advantage. Ticket prices at the Oakland Coliseum were $11, $10, $9 and $6.50. A capacity crowd of 53,662 was on hand.

The revenge-minded Raiders got things started midway through the first period. They posted a 7-0 lead after marching 82 yards in 16 plays. Marv Hubbard scored on a one-yard run.

The Raiders added a field goal in the second quarter after a Pittsburgh turnover. Defensive tackle Otis Sistrunk tipped a Terry Bradshaw pass and linebacker Phil Villapiano snared it. The interception gave Oakland good field position at its own 40. Later, George Blanda connected on a 25-yard field goal.

Oakland put the game away in the third quarter. Blanda added two more field goals and defensive back Willie Brown returned an intercepted pass 54 yards to score. The Raiders went on to win, 33-14.

Ken Stabler made the most of his first playoff start, completing 14 of 17 passes for 142 yards. Marv Hubbard chalked up 91 yards on the ground to lead all running backs.

Top: Skip Thomas (26) knocks Pittsburgh fullback Reggie Harrison (46) out of bounds. **Bottom:** Dave Casper hauls in a fourth quarter touchdown pass that helpted Oakland beat the Pittsburgh Steelers, 31-28, in 1976. **Page 82:** A fight breaks out between Oakland and San Diego on the sideline during a game in 1975. Raider running back Clarence Davis is on the bottom of the pile as San Diego's Dan Goode (50) and Glen Booner (21) work him over.

Marv Hubbard, Fred Biletnikoff, George Blanda, and Ken Stabler watch from the sideline.

Meanwhile, the Miami Dolphins defeated the Cincinnati Bengals, 34-16, to set up an AFC title match between the Raiders and the Dolphins. Both clubs relied on ball-control offenses. Miami was led by quarterback Bob Griese and a running attack that featured fullback Larry Csonka and speedster Mercury Morris. The Dolphins bruising running game proved to be the difference.

On the first series of the game, Oakland seemed to have the Dolphins stopped at midfield. Facing third-and-11, Griese dropped back to pass. He ducked under a hard pass rush, then headed upfield to pick up 27 yards and a first down. Four plays later Csonka put Miami in front on an 11-yard run. He scored again early in the second quarter on a one-yard run and Miami took a 14-0 lead into the locker room at halftime.

The Raiders got on the scoreboard in the third quarter on a George Blanda field goal. They closed the gap to 17-10 when Stabler connected on a 25-yard pass to Mike Siani. But that was as

close as Oakland would get. The Raiders had one final chance to turn the game around with six minutes to play. Miami led, 20-10, but Oakland was driving at its own 46. Stabler was faced with a fourth-and-one situation. He called on fullback Marv Hubbard, who was met at the line of scrimmage by Miami safety Dick Anderson. Hubbard fumbled the football and it bounced back into Stabler's arms. Stabler sprinted toward the first down marker at the sideline, but was stopped short. Miami took over and added one final touchdown to win, 27-10.

Csonka dominated the game, gaining 117 yards on 29 carries. Mercury Morris added 86 yards on 14 carries. Quarterback Bob Griese threw just six passes and connected on three of them.

Stabler had a good day, completing 15 of 23 passes for 129 yards. Charlie Smith grabbed five passes for 43 yards.

Miami advanced to the Super Bowl and demolished the Minnesota Vikings, 24-7. It was their second straight Super Bowl win.

Among the Raiders selected to play in the Pro Bowl at the conclusion of the season were quarterback Ken Stabler, tackle Art Shell, wide receiver Fred Biletnikoff, defensive back Willie

John Madden 1967-78

His first year out of coaching, when he had just started with CBS, John Madden was doing a Denver Bronco-New Orleans Saints game from Mile-High Stadium. He looked over at his broadcast partner, Lindsey Nelson, and said, ''You're going to see something when the Saints come out. These Denver fans go crazy.

''The Saints came out,'' Madden went on. ''I'm waiting . . . I'm waiting.'' He told Nelson, ''Well, wait till they start playing and do something like score or make a first down.'' He waited some more. Same thing.

''It was then,'' Madden said, ''that I realized I only knew Mile-High Stadium as coach of the Oakland Raiders. And that was different from anything else.

''We'd come in there to play, and people would throw snowballs at us. I got death threats so often in Denver, I regularly had police protection.''

The Oakland Raiders under John Madden. They blend together into one huge entity of game day wildness and winning. The silver and black horde that inspired rage in opposing fans and snatched victories in the final two minutes. The Raiders and their huge coach, with his tolerance for weirdness, his shrewd mind for strategy, erupting together on autumn Sundays.

Madden was never hard to find on the sidelines of Oakland Raider games. His outbursts were legendary if seldom printable—6'4'', 260-pounds of molten redhead, gesticulating lava. But the image belies what really made Madden distinct as a coach. What set him apart were his intelligence, and the ways his intelligence manifested in victories.

''He's double smart,'' Paul Brown, the legendary coach of the Cleveland Browns and Cincinnati Bengals, once

said. ''He always comes in with more than one way to beat you.''

On an afternoon in Oakland in 1974, Madden's Raiders found themselves behind Paul Brown's Bengals, 27-23, with little more than three minutes left in the game. Oakland had the ball, fourth-and-eight from the Bengal 31. As 51,281 fans were screaming, ''Go for it!'' Madden motioned in Ray Guy and the punting team.

To him, it was automatic. He figured Ray Guy would back up the Bengals inside their own 20. Guy did, punting out of bounds at the seven.

Madden figured Paul Brown would take no chances nursing his four-point lead. He wouldn't pass, not wanting to risk stopping the clock nor having the ball intercepted. Madden saw the Raider defense stopping the Bengals on three runs. He had saved his timeouts. He knew he could stop the clock

after each down and have the ball back in something like 20 seconds.

All of which happened. The Bengals punted. Kenny Stabler and the offense took over in good field position. Stabler had a fresh start. He had had time on the sidelines to plan. He moved the Raiders down the field to the four. With the clock ticking, and the Bengals set up to stop a pass, Madden called a sweep. Charlie Smith carried it in with eight seconds showing.

John Madden was a giant on game days, literally and figuratively. He blew off steam and berated officials, but never in a way that clouded his brain. It was part of his makeup as a winning coach.

Another was the touch he had with the unusual people he seemed to attract. Madden took over as head coach of the Raiders in February of 1969, still in the era before big money and high technology had automated pro football and made it more corporate.

In 1969, NFL players were more characters than clones, meaning NFL coaches had to be zookeepers more than they had to be chief executive officers.

The character profile in Oakland was high when Madden was coaching. The job of zookeeper was one he took on with relish. He was raised on the streets in Daly City, and spent more time in pool halls than he did in libraries. He worked one summer in a steel foundry in South San Francisco. He had a job in junior college one semester as a shill in a card room. He knew life and appreciated its outlandish forms.

One incident stands typical of so many. It involved eccentric cornerback, Alonzo "Skip" Thomas, who liked to emulate what he saw on television.

"Skip had a motorcycle one year," Madden recalled, "a big Harley. It was the day of a preseason game, a Saturday. We were in Santa Rosa. We were going to play in Oakland that night. Skip had seen Evel Kneival jump some cars on television. In the back of the motel where we stayed there was a fence and an empty lot.

"Skip had gotten a board and leaned it against the top of this six-foot high wooden fence. He was going to run his bike up this homemade ramp, go over the fence and onto the empty lot. A crowd

of players was gathered around and were cheering him on.

"Skip was astride his bike, vroom, vroom, vroom, making passes, getting ready for his big jump. I heard it from my room and went out and put a stop to it. No telling what would have happened otherwise."

Oakland had so many renegades and flakes that when Ted Hendricks was acquired in 1975 he made the statement, "Everywhere else I've played I've been known as colorful. But around here I'm quite boring."

Madden tolerated the oddness, maybe encouraged it with his tolerance, not only for amusement but because it squared with his thinking. He believed great players have distinct personalities. That is part of their greatness. He believed if you tried toning them down, that would be tampering. He thought you might lose the weirdness all right, but you might also tamper with the part that makes them excel on the field.

The Raiders under Madden weren't presentable, not like, say, the Dallas Cowboys or the Seattle Seahawks. But in the only ways that meant anything to him, John Madden's teams were highly disciplined.

"I admit we weren't too well groomed," he said. "But you never saw us jumping offsides when it was fourth-and-inches. We didn't go into motion before the ball was snapped. That was us. We didn't do

stupid things on the field. We performed too many times under pressure, boom, boom, boom. Going right down the field and scoring in the last few minutes of so many games to be anything but disciplined.

"My guys were different," he said, stating the obvious, "but they rarely broke the only three rules I ever laid down: be on time, pay attention, and play like hell when I tell you to."

Through Madden's ten years as head coach of the Raiders, he rang up 103 victories and posted a .763 winning percentage, the all-time high among NFL coaches, higher than Shula, Lombardi, Landry, or Halas.

Madden's most satisfying game, of course, was Super Bowl XI, the 32-14 victory over Minnesota in 1976. But his proudest win— one that stands testimony to his coaching—came one month earlier, in the 13th week, a Monday night against the Cincinnati Bengals.

The Raiders had already clinched the western division. Cincinnati was still fighting Pittsburgh for the lead in the central. In fact, if Oakland lost to Cincinnati, the hated Steelers would be eliminated. Some in the media took note and suggested the Raiders would go into the tank. Madden was incensed.

"There's only one way to play," he said at the time, "and that is hard, all the way. To suggest we'd do anything else, that's just stupid."

Madden made sure. He conducted fierce practices all week, priming the Raiders for war. They launched on Cincinnati, beating the Bengals, 35-20, with such suddenness and force that Bengal defensive tackle Coy Bacon said afterward, "Man, if them guys was laying down, I'd hate to see them when they decided to play."

When he first started coaching the Raiders, Madden had set some career goals. Winning the Super Bowl was one. He did that in 1976. He wanted to win more games than Vince Lombardi, and he wanted to win 100 games in 10 years, something achieved only by Don Shula before him. He accomplished both of the latter in 1978, the season he decided to retire.

The job had taken its toll by then. Madden had done what he set out to do, and he had bleeding ulcers to show for it. It was time, and he knew it.

He retired from coaching football at the young age of 42. But with all the craziness from his players, all the big games, the victories and adulation, the police escorts and the hostile crowds on the road, all the years of single-minded focus on football. With all that, he knew he had experienced a whole lifetime in his ten years as head coach of the Oakland Raiders.

He figured he had more lifetimes to live, and it was damn well time to get on with them.

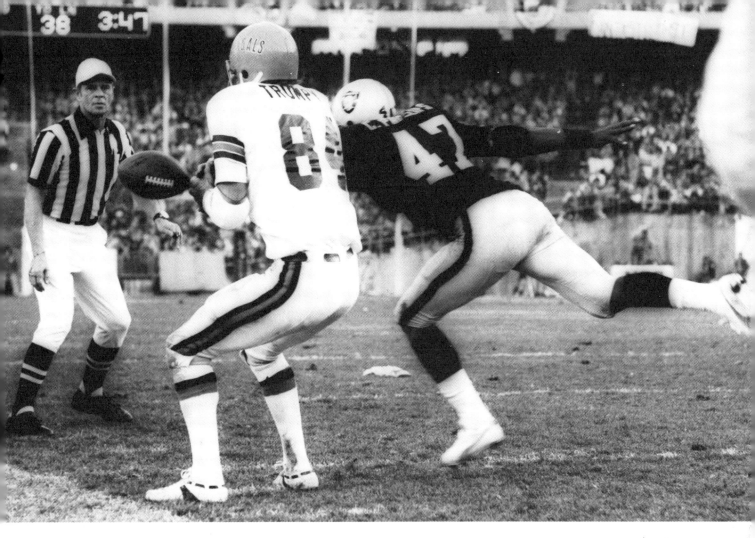

Brown and punter Ray Guy.

Defensive back Charles Phillips (47) breaks up a pass intended for Cincinnati Bengal receiver Bob Trumpy.

1974 The World Football League began operation in 1974. Among the established NFL stars coveted by the new league were Raider quarterbacks Ken Stabler and Daryle Lamonica. Lamonica signed with the league's Southern California franchise. Stabler signed a contract that would allow him to play with the Birmingham Americans when his Raider contract ran out in 1976. The league folded before Stabler's contract was to take effect.

Meanwhile, the NFL Players Association called a strike just as training camp was about to open in an effort to create a new free agent system. Many veteran players spent the early part of camp walking picket lines. The exhibition games consisted mainly of rookies and free agents while the veterans worked out by themselves. Among the rookies in the Raider camp were fullback Mark van Eeghen from Colgate and tight end Dave Casper from Notre Dame.

The NFL also adopted some new rules in 1974. Management decided to move the goal posts from the front to the back of the end zone, adopt the sudden-death overtime to eliminate tie games and move kickoffs from the 40 to the 35-yard line. The passing game was also given a shot in the arm. It became illegal to cut down wide receivers or to make contact more than once with a potential receiver coming off the line.

Despite the absence of many veterans, Oakland posted a 5-1 record in the exhibition season. By opening day most of the club's established stars were back in camp.

Stabler started the new season right where he left off in 1973. After losing the opener to the Buffalo Bills, 21-20, Oakland strung together nine straight victories.

Wide receiver Cliff Branch broke into the starting lineup during that stretch after Mike Siani was sidelined with an injury. Branch quickly developed into one of the club's most reliable receivers. He ended the year with 60 receptions for 1,092 yards and 13 touchdowns. He topped the league in reception yardage and touchdowns.

Oakland breezed to a 12-2 record and its seventh western division championship in eight years. The second-place Denver Broncos finished 4½ games behind the Raiders.

Oakland closed out the regular season with a tough game against the Dallas Cowboys at Oakland. It took the efforts of 47-year-old George Blanda to finally subdue the hard-charging Cowboys.

Blanda saw action at quarterback for the first time in over two years and responded by throwing a 28-yard touchdown pass to Cliff Branch the first time he handled the ball. He also kicked two field goals and three extra points as Oakland dumped the Cowboys, 27-23.

The Raiders found themselves matched with the Miami Dolphins in the first round of the playoffs. A capacity crowd of 54,020 was on hand at the Oakland Coliseum to watch one of the most exciting games in Raider history.

The game started on a bad note for Oakland. Miami's Nat Moore returned the opening kickoff 89 yards to give the Dolphins a quick lead, 7-0. It wasn't until the second quarter that Oakland began to move the football. Stabler hit Charlie Smith on a 31-yard scoring pass and at the end of the half Miami had a 10-7 edge.

The two clubs matched touchdowns in the third period. Oakland scored on Stabler's second touchdown pass of the day, a 13-yard toss to Fred Biletnikoff. Miami scored on a 16-yard pass from Griese to Warfield. Then, in the fourth quarter, the real action started.

Garo Yepremian gave Miami a 19-14 edge after he booted a 46-yard field goal early in the final period. The score stayed that way until the Raiders took over with just under five minutes to play in the game. On second down Stabler unloaded a 72-yard scoring pass to Cliff Branch and Oakland took the lead, 21-19.

Miami quarterback Bob Griese was not to be outdone. He methodically marched his club downfield after the kickoff. Csonka picked up yardage through the middle, while Griese hit Warfield and Nat Moore on quick passes. The Dolphins moved the ball to Oakland's 23-yard line with 2:12 to play. On second down, running back Ben Malone burst through tackle to score and give Miami a 26-21 lead.

Ron Smith handled the ensuing kickoff for Oakland and returned it to the 32. With less than two minutes to play, the Raiders had to travel 68 yards to score and advance to the AFC Championship Game.

Guard Gene Upshaw recalled the scene as Oakland took the field, "Ken (Stabler) gave us confidence. He was so cool, so calm. He said, 'Just give me a little time and we'll get the job done.'"

Stabler was good on his word. He moved the club downfield on sideline passes to Biletnikoff, while Marv Hubbard added tough inside yardage. In five plays, Stabler guided the Raiders 60 yards to the Miami eight. Only 31 seconds remained on the clock. Oakland needed a touchdown to win it.

On third down, the Raiders lined up with three receivers to the right side. Stabler dropped back and found his receivers covered. He rolled to his left to avoid defensive end Vern Den Herder and spotted running back Clarence Davis in the end zone. Davis was surrounded by three Dolphin defenders. Den Herder grabbed Stabler and was in the process of hurling him to the turf when Stabler unloaded the ball. Davis made a spectacular grab in the end zone between a horde of Miami defenders. Oakland won, 28-26.

The Pittsburgh Steelers were next on the Raiders' schedule. The Steelers made their way to the AFC Championship Game by defeating O.J. Simpson and the Buffalo Bills, 32-14. They hoped to counter Oakland's quick striking offense with one of the toughest defensive units in the league.

The game was fought in the trenches. Pittsburgh's defensive line, consisting of L.C. Greenwood, Joe Greene, Ernie Holmes and Dwight White, was matched against Oakland's Jim Otto, Gene Upshaw, Art Shell, John Vella and Henry Lawrence.

The Steelers dominated line play and nullified Oakland's ground game. The Raiders gained just 29 yards rushing. Nevertheless, early in the game, the breaks went Oakland's way. In the first quarter, Pittsburgh's Lynn Swann fumbled a punt. Oakland recovered and six plays later George Blanda kicked a field goal to give the Raiders a 3-0 edge. The first half ended in a 3-3 tie.

With the running game at a standstill, Stabler went to the air in the second half. Midway through the third quarter he moved the Raiders

Left, top: The Raider defense prepares to do battle with the Washington Redskins in Super Bowl XVIII. From left to right are Rod Martin (53), Lyle Alzado (77), Reggie Kinlaw (62), Howie Long (75) and Mike Davis (36). **Left, bottom:** Line coach Oliver Spencer reviews blocking schemes with the offense. Looking on are Clarence Davis (28), Dave Dalby (50), John Vella, Henry Lawrence (70) and Art Shell (78). **Right, top:** Defensive linemen Otis Sistrunk (60) and John Matuszak (72) humor one another before taking the field in a crucial game against the Minnesota Vikings in 1977. **Right, middle, left:** A Raider fan cheers on his heroes at the Oakland Coliseum. **Right, middle, right:** Linebacker Monte Johnson (58) teamed with Phil Villapiano and Ted Hendricks during the 1970s to give Oakland one of the most respected linebacking crews in the NFL. **Right, bottom:** Members of the Raiders' defensive unit take a break. From left to right are defensive tackle Art Thoms, linebacker Gerald Irons and defensive end Bubba Smith. **Below:** Coach John Madden signals instructions to his offensive unit during a hotly contested game in 1974. During his ten years as the Raider head coach, Madden led his club to eight playoff appearances.

Below, top: Wide receiver Dokie Williams (85) has averaged nearly 23 yards per catch since joining the Raiders as a fifth-round draft choice in 1983. **Below, bottom:** Cliff Branch (21) makes a catch over a Pittsburgh Steeler defender. Branch is the NFL's all-time pass receiver in post-season play. **Right:** Pete Banaszak (40) turns upfield and battles for extra yards. He set a club record in 1975 by rushing for three touchdowns in two different games. **Page 96:** Jim Plunkett releases a pass against the Washington Redskins in Super Bowl XVIII. Plunkett completed 16 of 25 passes, including one for a touchdown as the Raiders defeated Washington, 38-9.

80 yards in eight plays and capped it with a 38-yard pass to Cliff Branch. Branch made an excellent catch over cornerback Mel Blount, putting Oakland in front, 10-3. Meanwhile, the Raider defense shut out the Steelers in the third period. Oakland seemed to be on the way to another Super Bowl.

The momentum changed in the final period. Franco Harris tied the game early in the fourth quarter on an eight-yard touchdown run and the Steelers dominated the rest of the way. Pittsburgh's defense held the Raiders to just three points in the final quarter, while Terry Bradshaw directed the Steelers to two more touchdowns. Pittsburgh scored 21 points in the fourth period to beat Oakland, 24-13.

The game's most revealing statistic was the rushing yardage. Pittsburgh pounded out 224 yards on the ground, while Oakland managed just 29. The leading ball carrier was Franco Harris, who picked up 111 yards for Pittsburgh. Rocky Bleir added 98 yards.

Most of Oakland's offense was supplied by Ken Stabler and Cliff Branch. Branch set a playoff record by catching nine passes for 186 yards. Stabler completed 19 of 36 passes for 271 yards, but had three passes picked off.

The win gave Pittsburgh its first conference championship. The Raiders failed to advance past the AFC title game for the sixth time in seven years.

Center Jim Otto played in his last game against the Steelers. He retired prior to the 1975 season marking the end of an era in Oakland. Otto started in the club's first game in 1960 and was in the starting lineup for 210 consecutive games, a Raider record. Otto was an all-pro each year from 1960 to 1972. He was inducted into Pro Football's Hall of Fame in 1980.

1975 The Raiders assembled one of the deepest rosters in the NFL in 1975. Ted Hendricks was acquired from the Green Bay Packers and joined Gerald Irons, Monte Johnson and All-Pro Phil Villapiano at linebacker. The defensive line already featured Tony Cline and All-Pros Otis Sistrunk and Art Thoms. In the secondary were George Atkinson, Skip Thomas, and All-Pros Jack Tatum and Willie Brown.

The offense consisted of five strong running backs—Pete Banaszak, Mark van Eeghen, Clarence Davis, Jess Phillips and Marv Hubbard. All-Pro quarterback Ken Stabler kept opponents honest with his accurate passing. Snake's main receivers were Fred Biletnikoff, Cliff Branch, Mike Siani and Bob Moore.

Oakland opened the regular season at the Orange Bowl, where the Miami Dolphins had not lost a game in nearly four years. The Dolphins were playing without star running backs Larry Csonka and Jim Kiick. Both men jumped to the new World Football League.

The Raiders took control of the game in the first period. Stabler directed a 73-yard drive on his second possession with Banaszak scoring on a two-yard run. In the second quarter, Oakland took advantage of a Miami turnover to tally again and run up a 17-0 advantage.

Oakland's offense moved at will against Miami. The Raiders picked up 159 yards rushing while Stabler threw for another 108. But it was the defense that was the difference in the game. Oakland forced five Miami turnovers, intercepting four passes and recovering one fumble, enroute to a 31-21 victory.

Madden's troops put together a 3-0 record before suffering two straight losses at the hands of the Kansas City Chiefs and Cincinnati Bengals. Going into the sixth week of the season, Oakland was tied with Denver and Kansas City for the western division lead.

The San Diego Chargers were unfortunate to be the next team on the Raider schedule. Earlier in the season Oakland blanked the Chargers, 6-0. The Chargers wouldn't get that close this time.

The game was as good as decided after the first series of plays. On its first possession, San Diego was forced to punt from its own 17-yard line. Punter Dennis Partee fumbled the snap and Oakland linebacker Mike Dennary tackled him in the end zone. Oakland had a 2-0 lead.

The Charger offense was stymied the rest of the afternoon. Oakland held San Diego to 157 yards of offense including just 17 passing yards. Meanwhile, the Raiders piled up points. They scored at least once in every quarter enroute to a 25-0 win. Pete Banaszak had a pair of one-yard scoring runs in the first half, and Stabler hit Cliff Branch with a 45-yard touchdown pass in the third quarter. Late in the final period, Oakland linebacker Ted Hendricks downed Charger

quarterback Jesse Freitas in the end zone for a safety. The play allowed Oakland to tie an NFL record with two safeties in a single game.

The victory marked the beginning of a seven-game winning streak for the Raiders that allowed them to clinch the AFC Western Division crown. In the final game of the season, Oakland defeated the Kansas City Chiefs, 28-20. But more importantly George Blanda reached a personal milestone. He became the first man in NFL history to score 2,000 points during his career.

Pete Banaszak scored three touchdowns against the Chiefs to give him 16 for the season. He tied the club single-season touchdown record set by Art Powell in 1963. Banaszak was also the team's leading rusher with 672 yards in 187 carries.

Oakland was guaranteed the home field advantage throughout the playoffs by virtue of their 11-3 record. Their first opponent was the Cincinnati Bengals. The Bengals also finished the year with an 11-3 mark.

From the start, the Raiders looked like they would rout the Bengals. They had a 10-0 first quarter lead and were about to pad that margin with a 14-yard field goal. But George Blanda's kick was blocked. Cincinnati recovered and drove the length of the field, closing the gap to 10-7.

Oakland went to work again and built a 31-14 lead early in the fourth quarter. Most of the offense was generated by quarterback Ken Stabler who ended the day completing 17 of 23 passes for 199 yards. He threw touchdown passes to Mike Siani, Bob Moore and Dave Casper.

In the final 10 minutes of play, the Raiders tried to give the game away. Bengal defensive back Ken Riley picked off a Stabler pass and returned it to the Oakland 34-yard line. Two plays later quarterback Ken Anderson had Cincinnati in the

Top: Otis Sistrunk played eight seasons with Oakland between 1972-79. He was selected to the Pro Bowl team in 1974.
Bottom: George Atkinson (43) and Ted Hendricks (83) watch the Oakland offense from the sideline. **Page 99:** Defensive back Skip Thomas picks off a pass against the Cincinnati Bengals in 1976. He led the club in interceptions with six in both 1974 and 1975.

end zone. The Bengals made the score 31-28 on their next possession after Anderson hit receiver Issac Curtis on a 14-yard pass.

With nearly six minutes left to play the once formidable Oakland lead had dwindled to three points. When Pete Banaszak fumbled the ball away on Oakland's next series of plays, it seemed like only a matter of time before Cincinnati would take the lead. But the Raider defense had seen enough. They shut down the Bengals the rest of the way to preserve the 31-28 victory. Oakland had another date in the AFC Championship Game.

For the fourth consecutive season Oakland met the Pittsburgh Steelers in post-season play. Pittsburgh finished the year with a 12-2 record and clobbered the Baltimore Colts in the first round of the playoffs, 28-10. The Steelers were six-point favorites to beat Oakland at Three Rivers Stadium.

A howling wind and snowstorm greeted the Raiders when they arrived at Pittsburgh. Several hours before the two teams were to meet, the tarp protecting the stadium's artificial turf was ripped loose by the wind. On Sunday afternoon the field was caked with ice and snow. Workmen needed picks to chip away the ice prior to game time. On the field the temperature was about three degrees with the wind-chill factor.

The miserable playing conditions contributed to a boring game for three quarters. Both clubs combined to fumble nine times and drop numerous passes. As the two clubs retreated to the warmth of their locker rooms at halftime, Pittsburgh held a 3-0 lead.

After a scoreless third quarter the two offenses came to life in the final period. The Steelers struck first as quarterback Terry Bradshaw moved his club 70 yards. Franco Harris capped the drive with a 25-yard dash to the end zone.

Quarterback Ken Stabler (12) eludes the Pittsburgh Steeler rush. **Pages 102-103:** Running back Pete Banaszak (40) is hemmed in by a swarm of Atlanta defenders. **Page 104:** Clarence Davis (28) charges forward against the Vikings during Super Bowl XI. **Page 105:** Jack Tatum grabs the face mask in an attempt to bring down Seattle Seahawk receiver Sherman Smith (47). Smith broke the tackle and scored anyway.

Bob Moore, Gene Upshaw (63), Fred Biletnikoff (25), Dave Casper (87), and Neil Colzie (45) load up on Stick'em prior to a game against the Atlanta Falcons in in 1975.

The Raiders countered with their own drive. With the wind at his back, Ken Stabler completed three straight passes to tight end Dave Casper covering 46 yards. He then found Mike Siani alone in the end zone and hit him with a 14-yard pass.

Pittsburgh scored again on its next possession. This time Bradshaw marched his club 48 yards before hitting John Stallworth on a 20-yard touchdown pass.

With 1:31 to play the Steelers had a 16-7 lead. It looked like it would be enough, but Stabler had other plans. The Raiders retained the ball and marched 40 yards to the Pittsburgh 24. The drive stalled there, but George Blanda came in to kick a 41-yard field goal and cut the Steeler lead to six points. There were only 20 seconds left on the clock.

The Raiders needed a miracle to pull the game out. Kicker Ray Guy tried an onside kick and it

was recovered by Marv Hubbard at the Oakland 45. The Raiders were still alive, but with just seven seconds to go.

Oakland had enough time for one play. Stabler dropped back and completed a pass to Cliff Branch at the Pittsburgh 15. Branch tried to find running room, but was hemmed in by several Steelers. He was knocked out of bounds as time ran out. Final score: Pittsburgh 16, Oakland 10.

Although there was no Super Bowl for Oakland, five Raiders were selected All-Pro in 1975. End Cliff Branch and tackle Art Shell were picked from the offensive team, while linebacker Phil Villapiano and safety Jack Tatum were selected off the defensive squad. Punter Ray Guy was also named All-Pro.

The amazing George Blanda decided to retire at the end of the season. Blanda's longevity will probably never be matched. He played pro football a record 26 seasons beginning in 1949 with the Chicago Bears. After 10 years as a quarterback and kicker with the Bears, Blanda joined the Houston Oilers. He led the Oilers to two AFL titles, then joined the Raiders in 1967. He scored an NFL record 2,002 points in his career, and threw 236 touchdown passes. The second leading scorer in NFL history, Lou Groza, is nearly

200 points behind Blanda. Groza retired with 1,608 points. Blanda was selected to Pro Football's Hall of Fame in 1981.

Halfback Carl Garrett (31) sidesteps Pittsburgh Steeler linebacker Jack Lambert. **Page 108:** John Madden holds the game ball high after a playoff victory against Miami.

1976

The Raiders came to camp in 1976 determined to win a world championship. They signed veteran running back Carl Garrett and rookies Charles Philyaw, a defensive end from Texas Southern, and Mike Rae, a quarterback from USC. After the first game of the season, the Raiders added free agent defensive end John Matuszak to the roster.

The Raiders swept through the exhibition schedule with a 5-1 record then opened the regular season against their bitter rival—the Pittsburgh Steelers. Pittsburgh dominated the game early and held a 28-14 lead with just over five minutes to play.

The Raiders began to click in the waning minutes of the game. Pittsburgh knew the Raiders had to pass so Steeler coach Chuck Noll set loose his ferocious pass rush. The Raiders were ready for it. The offensive line, consisting of Art Shell, Gene Upshaw, Dave Dalby, John Vella and George Buehler held off the Steelers. Stabler had time to throw and he completed consecutive

passes of 22, 25 and 10 yards to Dave Casper. Casper caught the final pass in the end zone, making the score, 28-21. But there was just 2:55 to play.

Oakland's defense took the field and held the Steelers to no gain on three plays. Pittsburgh was forced to punt. The kick was partially blocked by Warren Bankston, giving the Raiders excellent field postion at the Pittsburgh 29 with 1:47 left.

On his first three plays from scrimmage, Stabler went to the air and failed to complete a pass. Facing fourth-and-10, Stabler dropped back and was rushed hard by Pittsburgh's Joe Greene. Stabler ducked under the big defensive end's reach, then rolled out and found Cliff Branch open at the 15-yard line. Branch made the catch then sprinted down the sideline to the two. Stabler ran the ball in on the next play. Kicker Fred Steinfort added the extra point to tie the game.

The Raiders got another break on Pittsburgh's

Ken Stabler 1970-79

The Oakland Raiders of the 1970's were as disciplined on the field as they were reputed misfits and brigands elsewhere. For such a team, one so widely split in personality, John Madden may have been the perfect coach. If so, Kenny Stabler was the perfect quarterback. He was a Raider in every sense.

Stabler was a Bobby Layne kind of performer, maybe the last of the breed, a swaggering field general who called his own plays and ran his own huddle. Like Layne, Stabler completed more passes and won more games—many in the last few minutes—than creaky knees and limited arm strength suggested he should.

Above all, he was a winner. In his years as a starter, the Raiders' won

their division five times. They made it to the AFC Championship Game five times. They won the Super Bowl once, number XI against the Minnesota Vikings, a 32-14 triumph, another Stabler masterpiece of play-calling and execution.

Off the field, Stabler was something of a legend as well—a swinger from the ''Redneck Riviera'' on the gulf coast of Alabama. He loved speedboats, girls and beer. When he was a college senior, Stabler persuaded a Chevrolet dealer in Tuscaloosa to ''sell'' him a new Corvette. He put nothing down and told the dealer payment would come when he signed a pro contract. He wrecked the car before ever paying a dime.

Stabler says he was a man of ''big pickup trucks, fat belt buckles and a few laughs.'' He admits to dancing all night to jukebox lights with his share of blondes, to drinking his share of distilled spirits and to closing his share of roadhouses.

But Madden says that the fiesty part of Stabler emerged mostly in the off season. ''Kenny liked to live wild for a few months. He would let loose now and then, but not so often as was portrayed, and never when winning and losing football games was on the line. He was too much of a competitor to let anything else affect his game.''

Kenny ''Snake'' Stabler came of age rather late for an NFL star. Unwillingly, he rode the Raider bench for

parts of his first six seasons. The Raiders had drafted him in the second round in 1968. He was still available because a knee injury suffered in the Sugar Bowl made him a question mark as a first-round talent.

Oakland already had Daryle Lamonica, then in his second year with the team. Lamonica had led the Raiders to Super Bowl II in 1967. He had thrown 30 touchdown passes and was named AFL Player of the Year. Backing up Lamonica was George Blanda, who, at age 41, after 19 years in the NFL and the original AFL, still had some spectacular football ahead.

Stabler spent all of 1968 convalescing. In 1969, he walked out of camp in Santa Rosa, announcing, ''there wasn't any sense of staying if I wasn't enjoying myself. I got some things to sort out."

The real reason was more specific if unmentioned at the time. Stabler was having trouble with his first wife back in Alabama. John Madden, in his rookie season as head coach, watched him go, as only a coach would do who already had a Lamonica backed by a Blanda.

"I've got 65 players who want to play," Madden said then, "I can't worry about one who doesn't."

That was then. Now Madden says, "If I knew at the time what I found out later about Stabler, I'd have been on the next train to Selma with a butterfly net."

Stabler returned in 1970 fully committed and began a period of serious apprenticeship. On the sidelines during games, he kneeled beside George Blanda, and the two of them drew up ways to beat the defense. In idle hours during the practice week, he discovered weightlifting through his buddy, defensive end Tony Cline. Stabler lifted until his arm grew strong, and he could throw deep like a Raider quarterback should.

"I wouldn't have a starting quarterback who couldn't throw upfield better than he could then," Davis had said of the early Stabler.

Stabler established himself the fourth week of the 1973 season, when defenses had caught up with Lamonica's "Mad

Bomber" style of play, and the Raider offense had collapsed. After a loss to Kansas City, with the Raiders' record 1-2, and the offense having been held without a touchdown in 12 quarters, Stabler went to Madden and said he could no longer stand moping-up behind Lamonica, playing only in situations he didn't create. Madden said he was sorry to hear it, but he would do nothing about it.

Stabler nodded and asked if he could throw the St. Louis offense that week on defense day. Madden said go ahead. Simulating Cardinal quarterback Jim Hart the next Wednesday, Stabler completed nearly every pass he threw against the Raider defense. Madden made a move that day he'd been thinking about for some time. He replaced Lamonica as the starter, naming Stabler.

"Not because he came in and bitched about not playing," Madden clarified. "But because he didn't give up and pout. He went out on the field and backed his claim for the position."

With Stabler at quarterback, the Raiders beat the Cardinals that week. The next week against the Colts, the Raiders won again. Stabler threw for more than 300 yards and three touchdowns. He completed 25 of 29 passes, breaking a record for completion percentage previously held by Washington Redskin quarterback Sammy Baugh. Stabler

finished the year as the second leading passer in the AFC.

His numbers from then on were glittering, but they never overshadowed what he did best, which was to lead. In areas of motivation, execution and composure, Stabler may have been the best of his time.

"When Snake called a play," said tackle Art Shell, "we knew it was the right play. Because if it wasn't the right play, he wouldn't have called it.

"He had a great mind for football," Madden agreed. "He always saw the big picture."

The playoff game against New England in 1976, the year of Super Bowl XI, was vintage Stabler. The Raiders came back from a 21-10 deficit to win, 24-21. Neither Stabler nor the offense could fire up for the first three quarters. But Gene Upshaw remembers the fourth quarter.

"Snake came into the huddle with ice water in his veins," Upshaw said. "I thought to myself, 'this is why we do it all the time, because he's like that.'"

The Raiders won after Stabler drove for touchdowns twice in the last 16 minutes—two scoring drives, eight pass completions in nine attempts, no yards lost, no crossed signals, no penalties, false starts, or turnovers. The winning points came with Stabler rolling left behind Upshaw's block, diving into the end zone with ten seconds showing.

Madden added another memory— between the fifth and sixth periods of the double overtime playoff game against Baltimore in 1977. "Snake came over to where I was," Madden said. "It was a tense situation. The score had seesawed for 75 minutes. The loser would go home, the winner on to the American Conference championship. I thought he had some play on his mind."

He didn't. Stabler raised his facebar up to his forehead and took a swig of Gatorade, sloshed it around, swallowed and told Madden, "The fans are really getting their money's worth today. Think so, John?"

"He was unflappable," Madden said.

Stabler said later that 37-31 Raider victory over the Colts was the most exciting game he ever played in. But it was downhill from there. The Raiders lost the following week in Denver in the AFC Championship Game. They went 9-7 each of the next two seasons. Madden had retired by then. The years were catching up. Stabler had lost something off his fastball. He threw 30 interceptions in 1979. He was 34, and his relationship with Al Davis had soured.

Davis traded him to Houston for Dan Pastorini before the 1980 season, and an era ended in Oakland. The last of a breed had been sent on his way.

first play after the kick off. Bradshaw's pass was tipped by defensive lineman Dave Rowe and linebacker Willie Hall intercepted. He returned the ball to the Steeler 12-yard line. With 21 seconds left, Steinfort kicked a 21-yard field goal to win the game for Oakland.

Oakland took a 3-0 record to Foxboro, Massachusetts and was stunned by the New England Patriots, 48-17. Not since 1963 had a Raider team given up so many points. The Patriots gained 296 yards on the ground, the most ever allowed by Oakland. The club's lone bright spot was tight end Dave Casper. He caught 12 passes for 136 yards.

Oakland rebounded to win its next 10 games and finish the season at 13-1, the best record in the NFL. The Raiders closed the regular season with a 24-0 win over the San Diego Chargers. Mark van Eeghen gained 95 yards on 22 carries to give him 1,012 for the season. Only Marv Hubbard with 1,100 yards and Clem Daniels with 1,099 ever gained more for the Raiders.

Coach John Madden gave Ken Stabler the day off against San Diego. He was replaced by David Rae, who completed 13 of 22 passes for 143 yards and three touchdowns.

Stabler ended the regular season as the NFL's highest rated passer. He completed 194 of 291 passes for 2,737 yards and 27 touchdowns. His phenomenal 67 percent completion rate, was second best in NFL history. Dave Casper caught 53 passes for 10 touchdowns, Cliff Branch had 46 receptions for 12 touchdowns and Fred Biletnikoff caught 43 passes for seven touchdowns.

The New England Patriots visited Oakland for the first round of the playoffs. New England finished the season with an 11-3 record. More importantly, the Patriots handed Oakland its only loss of the season, a 48-17 thumping. The Raiders were determined to avenge themselves.

The game didn't go quite as planned for Oakland. After three quarters of play they were behind, 21-10. The Raiders only scoring came on a 40-yard field goal by Errol Mann and a 31-yard pass from Stabler to Biletnikoff. Meanwhile, New England controlled the ball with a potent rushing attack that featured Sam Cunningham and Don Calhoun.

In the fourth quarter the Raiders began to battle back. Midway through the period Banaszak scored on a one-yard run to cut the Patriots' margin to 21-17.

Oakland retained the ball with 4:12 to play and Stabler began to work his magic. Starting from his own 32-yard line, Stabler connected on passes of 12 yards to Fred Biletnikoff and 21 yards to Dave Casper. Clarence Davis kept the defense honest, picking up eight yards on two running plays.

With a first down at the Patriot 35, Stabler missed on three straight passes. On fourth down, Patriot tackle Ray Hamilton was called for roughing the passer. The controversial call gave Oakland a first down at the New England 13 with 57 seconds to play.

On first down, Pete Banaszak gained eight yards. In addition, Patriot defensive back Prentice McCray was penalized for unsportsmanlike conduct. With 30 seconds left, Oakland had the ball at the two-yard line.

Banaszak got the call again on first down and was stopped short of the goal line. Stabler took a time out with 13 seconds on the clock. In the huddle he called a run-pass option play. Stabler faked a handoff to Banaszak then took off around left end behind guard Gene Upshaw. Upshaw leveled a Patriot defender and Stabler dove into the end zone to score the winning touchdown.

Oakland had another date with the Pittsburgh Steelers in the AFC Championship Game. The Steelers were looking for their third consecutive win over Oakland in post-season play.

Pittsburgh coach Chuck Noll had assembled one of the most feared defensive units in NFL history. "The Steel Curtain" had allowed only 14 touchdowns all season and won five games by shutout. The Steelers finished the 1976 season with nine straight wins. During that stretch they allowed just 28 points, an average of three points per game.

The Steelers were without their starting running backs—Franco Harris and Rocky Bleir. Both

Dave Casper, though upended, holds on for the reception.
Pages 114-115: The Falcon's Dave Hampton (43) heads into heavy traffic in Oakland.

men gained over 1,000 yards during the regular season. They were injured during Pittsburgh's 40-14 playoff win over Baltimore. Without Harris and Bleir the offensive burden fell on quarterback Terry Bradshaw.

Steeler turnovers set up the Raiders' initial scores. Early in the game Oakland's Hubie Ginn blocked a punt by Bobby Walden and the Raiders took over at the Pittsburgh 38. Seven plays later, Errol Mann put Oakland in front with a 39-yard field goal.

In the second quarter, linebacker Willie Hall intercepted a Bradshaw pass and returned it to the one-yard line. Clarence Davis scored from there and Oakland had a 10-0 lead.

Terry Bradshaw put together an impressive second quarter drive with clutch third down passing to get Pittsburgh back in the game. Fullback Reggie Harrison scored from the three, cutting Oakland's lead to 10-7.

Stabler completely demoralized the Steelers by coming back with his own 72-yard drive. He capped it by completing a four-yard pass to Warren Bankston just 19 seconds before the half ended.

Oakland ran right at Pittsburgh's feared defense in the second half, eating up valuable time and yardage. Late in the third period, Stabler was knocked out of the game after being blitzed by linebacker Jack Ham. Ham knocked a cap off Stabler's tooth and left a large welt on his back. Before he was hit, Stabler was able to get off a five-yard touchdown pass to Pete Banaszak. That was all the scoring Oakland needed. The defense shut down Pittsburgh the rest of the way to capture a 24-7 victory. It propelled Oakland to the Super Bowl for the first time since 1967. That year the Raiders were beaten by the Green Bay Packers, 33-14.

Minnesota defeated the Los Angeles Rams, 24-13, in the NFC Championship Game and would

Top: John Matuszak catches his breath after a long battle. **Bottom:** Defensive back Charles Phillips (47) breaks up a pass intended for Cincinnati Bengal receiver Bob Trumpy. **Page 116:** Mark van Eeghen (30) struggles for yardage against the Minnesota Vikings in 1977. Van Eeghen led the team in rushing that season with 818 yards on 223 carries.

face Oakland in Super Bowl XI at Pasadena, Ca. The Vikings, led by quarterback Fran Tarkenton, had lost in three previous Super Bowl appearances.

A record crowd of 100,421 was on hand at the Rose Bowl. Minnesota had a chance to score first after blocking a Ray Guy punt and recovering at the Oakland three-yard line. The Vikings failed to score on three straight plays and decided to go for the end zone on fourth down. The Raiders held and the first quarter went scoreless.

Oakland's offense began to click in the second quarter. Errol Mann kicked a 24-yard field goal and Stabler guided the Raiders on two long drives to build a 16-0 halftime lead. Pete Banaszak scored on a one-yard run and Stabler completed a one-yard pass to Dave Casper for the other score.

Minnesota finally put some points on the board late in the third quarter on an eight-yard pass from Tarkenton to Sammy White. But it just wasn't the Vikings' day. Oakland scored twice in the fourth quarter to put the game out of reach. The Raiders' final touchdown came on a 75-yard interception return by defensive back Willie Brown.

Tarkenton was removed from the game after Brown's interception and replaced by quarterback Bob Lee. Lee directed the Vikings to a touchdown, but it wasn't enough. Oakland handed Minnesota its fourth Super Bowl loss, 32-14.

Oakland completely dominated the line of scrimmage. The Raiders picked up 266 yards on the ground while Minnesota gained just 71. Clarence Davis gained 137 yards rushing, his best game as a professional and Mark van Eeghen added 73 yards. Stabler completed 12 of 19 passes for 180 yards and one touchdown. Fred Biletnikoff was the game's Most Valuable Player. He caught four passes for 79 yards and set up scores with each reception.

At the conclusion of the season, John Madden was named Coach of the Year by the Washington Touchdown Club. Al Davis was named NFL Executive of the Year.

1977

The world champions started the 1977 season by humiliating the Houston Oilers, 40-0, in their opening preseason game. Coach John Madden sent four quarterbacks into action—Ken Stabler, Mike Rae, Dave Humm and Jeb Blount—and each produced at least one touchdown.

Several new faces appeared on the defensive unit, including veteran linemen Pat Toomay and Mike McCoy, rookie linebackers Rod Martin and Jeff Barnes, and rookie defensive back Lester Hayes. The only notable addition to the offensive squad was guard Mickey Marvin, a 270-pound rookie from Tennessee.

The Raiders started the regular season with Stabler at quarterback. He was joined in the backfield by Mark van Eeghen and Clarence Davis. In the club's first league game, however, it was the defense that deserved the praise. They shut out the dangerous San Diego Chargers, 24-0, before 51,022 fans at Oakland. It was the third consecutive time the Raiders shut out San Diego at the Coliseum.

Oakland's defense did not allow the Chargers to penetrate any farther than the 30-yard line and that was due to a 15-yard penalty. The defense and special teams also set up Oakland's scores. Lester Hayes blocked a punt in the first quarter, which was recovered by Randy McClanahan on the 13. Five plays later Oakland was in the end zone.

The punting team also came through in the second quarter. Ray Guy's booming kick was fumbled and rookie Jeff Barnes recovered on the 10. Three plays later the Raiders had another touchdown.

Oakland strung together eight wins in its first nine games. The club's sole loss during that stretch was a 30-7 defeat at the hands of the Denver Broncos. In the tenth week of the season, the Raiders traveled south to take on the San Diego Chargers again. The Chargers got revenge for their earlier shelling with a 12-7 win.

Entering the final week of the season Oakland had a 10-3 record, but was in second place in the AFC Western Division. The surprising Denver Broncos had already clinched the division title. Nevertheless, the Raiders needed a win on the last day of the season to ensure the club of a wild card spot in the playoffs.

Oakland was matched with the Kansas City Chiefs in the final league contest. The Raiders were nine-point favorites over the Chiefs, who ended the season with a 2-11 record. Oakland won, but it wasn't easy. The Raiders weren't as-

Jack Tatum 1971-79

When all else about him is forgotten, Jack Tatum will be remembered for two infamous moments in Oakland Raider history. The so-called "Immaculate Reception" occurred at the beginning of his career in 1972, and the Darryl Stingley episode near the end in 1978.

The first took place in Pittsburgh, round one of the AFC playoffs. The Raiders had gone ahead, 7-6, on a Kenny Stabler run late in the fourth quarter.

Now Pittsburgh had the ball, third down and ten from its own 40. Less than a minute remained in the game. Steeler quarterback Terry Bradshaw took the snap and dropped to pass. Halfback

"Frenchy" Fuqua broke into a curl pattern over the middle. Bradshaw saw him. He threw as he was hit by four Raider linemen.

Upfield, Jack Tatum came flying into view. Tatum said later he was trying to time it so he would smash Fuqua just as the ball arrived and the gun went off. He hit Fuqua as planned, jarring him senseless, the ball caroming off the collision and floating 20 yards back toward the line of scrimmage.

Franco Harris, running an outlet pattern, saw the football floating toward him. He picked it off at shoetop level and ran 60 yards for a winning touchdown. One that couldn't have taken place if Jack

Tatum hadn't hit Fuqua as hard as he did.

The Stingley episode came on a dreary August night nearly six years later. The Raiders were facing New England in an otherwise forgettable preseason game. They were on defense deployed in a three-deep zone. On one play, Stingley—New England's sixth-year wide receiver from Purdue—slanted across the middle into the no-man's land where Jack Tatum always lurked.

Tatum saw an intimidating hit in his sights and went straight to it, running hard. He smashed Stingley as the ball had passed through his hands. It was a clean play under the rules, but one that left Stingley

crumpled on the ground, looking lifeless. He was paralyzed, as it turned out, with a broken neck.

Tatum would have escaped such a moment only by the sheerest of luck. The Stingley collision was by no means the hardest of his career, only the worst in terms of effect. But it or something similar was almost inevitable. Because Jack Tatum was perhaps the hardest hitting defensive back in NFL history.

Tatum surfaced as a gridiron entity when he was 15 years old. He was one of two sophomores on his high school varsity in Passaic, New Jersey. At first a nonstarter, he was sent in at linebacker early in the season opening game. A few plays later, he bore in on the opposing quarterback and knocked him cold.

Later, the second-string quarterback tried running for a first down and Tatum knocked him out too. Passaic won the game, and the other team finished with its tight end under center. Tatum was elevated to first-string, and a hitting legend was born.

Oakland drafted him in 1971, the 19th pick of the first round. The year before, 1970, the Raiders had finished 8-4-2. They won the western division, but their record amounted to a decline from the peak year of 1969 when they had gone 12-1-1. Al Davis and John Madden agreed, the team needed restocking. They sensed in particular the defense was losing its Raider trademark, intimidating toughness.

They went into the draft looking for a hammer, someone who could be an enforcer in the secondary. Tatum was a two-time All-America monster back from Ohio State. He was still on the board when the Raiders' turn came around, so their choice was made for them.

"Jack Tatum could hit a man so hard that it would lift both his feet off the ground," said Woody Hayes, his coach at Ohio State. "We always played him to the open side of the field, and in the 1969 Rose Bowl game, Southern California chose to run away from Tatum into the sideline . . . as many other teams had tried."

At his peak, Tatum

blended with one of the best and fiercest defensive backfields of all time. Future Hall of Famer Willie Brown played one corner. Alonzo "Skip" Thomas (who John Madden said was the most talented defensive player he ever coached) was the other. Tatum's running buddy, George Atkinson, played strong safety. Tatum himself was the free safety. It was a solid marriage of ability and instinct.

"In our system," Tatum explained, "the cornerbacks covered the wide receivers on most formations. Our strong safety almost always took the tight end. I didn't have anyone specifically to cover. My job was to help out, just clean up, maybe like a sheriff. I'd position myself so that when they go after the ball, I'd go for the receiver."

Going after receivers, intimidating them into submission, that was Jack Tatum's special mission in the Raider secondary. He was a warrior at heart, one who played within the rules but with such aggressiveness that critics often called him dirty.

Chuck Noll, coach of the Pittsburgh Steelers, for instance, said in 1976 that Tatum and Atkinson were part of the NFL's "criminal element." He said that because Pittsburgh receiver Lynn Swann left so many Raider-Steeler games with disabling injuries.

"I guarantee you one thing," John Madden said in rebuttal. "Jack Tatum never hit anybody

from behind."

He was just unbelievably tough, so much so it formed his destiny as a Raider, his reputation as a player. It was visible even before he reported to Oakland. In the 1971 College All-Star Game, Baltimore Colt tight end John Mackey had eluded a Tatum tackle.

"Hard hitting rookie, what a joke," Mackey said.

Tatum caught him later reaching back for an Earl Morrall pass. He bore in full speed and blasted him in the rib cage. Mackey lay on the ground twitching his legs, trying to suck in air, while Tatum stood over him asking, "How funny was that joke, sucker?"

Before Tatum learned to harness his energy, he was knocking out friend and enemy alike. In one game his rookie year, the Raiders were holding off New Orleans, 21-14, late in the fourth quarter. The Saints threw into the middle looking for receiver Danny Abramowicz, who was well covered by George Atkinson.

Tatum blasted in from the weak side to assist. In the collision, he knocked out Abramowicz . . . and Atkinson. He knocked out Atkinson again later in the year, knocked out Willie Brown and Nemiah Wilson as well.

"I was pretty bad as a rookie," Tatum admitted.

Tatum learned technique without relinquishing power. He became a first-rate defensive back, but his

steady play as a free safety always was overshadowed by the big hits. The one against Riley Odoms in Mile-High Stadium that caused Odoms to say later, "Damn Tate, you almost killed me." The two knockouts of Frank Pitts in the same game against Cleveland. The knockout of Miami's Paul Warfield in the 1973 playoffs. The hit on Minnesota's Sammy White in Super Bowl XI, the one that slammed White backwards and sent his helmet flying one direction, his chinstrap another.

The irony is, Jack Tatum is a docile gentleman off the field, polite and intelligent. But when he laced on his football shoes, it tapped some well of rage. Put him in pads and a helmet, and he was a warhead.

In their Super Bowl year of 1976, the Raiders were in Philadelphia in November playing the Eagles. Early in the first quarter, Eagle wide receiver Harold Carmichael ran a listless decoy pattern over the middle, the area Tatum patrolled so fiercely.

Passing by him, Carmichael said, "Hey man, I won't try blocking you today, you promise not to hit me."

"Okay by me," Tatum said as Carmichael loped by. Then under his breath to himself: "My job's done."

Throughout his career, one way or another, Jack Tatum could enforce that kind of submission.

Gene Upshaw (63) and John Madden prepare to celebrate as the clock winds down at Super Bowl XI. Oakland beat Minnesota 32-14 to win its first world championship.

sured of a victory until Kansas City kicker Jan Stenerud shanked a 35-yard field goal attempt with 10 seconds to play. Final score: Oakland 21, Kansas City 20.

The Raiders flew into Baltimore to meet the Colts in the first round of the AFC playoffs. Baltimore put together an outstanding year. They finished with a 10-4 record to edge the Miami Dolphins in the AFC's Eastern Division. The game turned out to be one of the most exciting in playoff history.

Baltimore capitalized on four Raider turnovers to build a 31-28 lead late in the fourth quarter. The Colts scored lightning quick. Their first touchdown came on a 61-yard interception return by Bruce Laird, the second was an 87-yard kickoff return by Marshall Johnson. Oakland put points on the board through long, sustained drives.

The real action started with two minutes to play and Baltimore leading, 31-28. Working from his own 44-yard line, Stabler sent Casper streaking down the sideline. Stabler hit his tight end in full stride and Casper was dragged down at the Colts' 14. From there, Errol Mann kicked a field goal to send the game into overtime.

After 15 minutes of overtime the game was still tied, 31-31. The Raiders were driving, however. With 43 seconds gone in the second overtime period the Raiders lined up in a three tight end formation at the Baltimore 10-yard line. The Colts were looking for a running play. Instead, Stabler sent Casper to the corner of the end zone, where he was wide open. Casper's reception ended the game after 75 minutes and 43 seconds. The win gave Oakland a shot at the Denver Broncos for the AFC championship.

Denver's tough defensive unit, nicknamed "Orange Crush," was the team's driving force. On offense the Broncos were led by veteran quarterback Craig Morton and receivers Haven Moses and Riley Odoms.

Oakland had more experience and as the defending Super Bowl champion, they were slight favorites to beat Denver at Mile High Stadium.

The game's first big blow was struck by Denver. Oakland took a 3-0 lead on Mann's 20-yard field goal. But the Broncos came right back two plays later and scored on a 74-yard pass from

Morton to Haven Moses. The rest of the half was a defensive struggle and Denver went into the locker room with a 7-3 advantage.

The most controversial call of the season occured in the third quarter and it went against the Raiders. Denver marched downfield and faced a first-and-goal at the Raider two. Denver's Rob Lytle took a handoff from Morton and tried to vault into the end zone. He was met head on by safety Jack Tatum. The ball popped loose and Oakland's Mike McCoy scooped it up. However, the officials, who were apparently screened out on the play, ruled that it wasn't a fumble and awarded the ball to Denver. The Broncos scored on the next play to take a 14-3 lead.

The Raiders played catch-up in the fourth quarter. Stabler teamed with Dave Casper on scoring passes of seven and 17 yards, but it wasn't enough. Denver also added a touchdown on a 12-yard pass from Craig Morton to Haven Moses and Denver had a 20-17 victory.

Mark van Eeghen had his most productive year as a Raider gaining 1,273 yards and scoring seven touchdowns. Clarence Davis added 787 yards. Ken Stabler proved again he was one of the most accurate quarterbacks in the league. He completed 58 percent of his 294 passes for 2,176 yards and 20 touchdowns. Dave Casper was the club's leading receiver with 48 catches.

Casper was selected for the Pro Bowl along with Cliff Branch, Art Shell, Gene Upshaw, Jack Tatum, Ray Guy and Errol Mann.

1978 The Raiders were a team in transition in 1978. The offensive line, led by 31-year-old Art Shell and 33-year-old Gene Upshaw, was gradually growing old. Furthermore, tackle John Vella was sidelined for the season with a chest injury.

Several other veterans were gradually phased out. Rookie Arthur Whittington replaced Clarence Davis in the backfield, and receiver Morris Bradshaw began to take playing time away from

Mark van Eeghen bolts off tackle for one of three Raider touchdowns during the second quarter against San Diego.

Fred Biletnikoff. Second-year guard Mickey Marvin also worked his way into the starting lineup.

Among the club's acquisitions in the offseason were quarterback Jim Plunkett and tight end Raymond Chester. Rookie tight end Derrick Ramsey, defensive end Dave Browning and tackle Lindsey Mason were also signed.

The Raiders opened the new season against the Denver Broncos at Mile High Stadium. Denver's Orange Crush defense was still a force to be reckoned with, but the Raiders also had one of the best defensive units in football. After 55 minutes of football at Denver, the Broncos were clinging to a 7-6 lead.

Oakland took over with 4:24 remaining. Methodically, Stabler moved the Raiders downfield and into scoring position. He tried a quick pass over the middle to Fred Biletnikoff, but the ball went through the hands of the usually sure-fingered receiver and was intercepted by Denver defensive back Bernard Jackson. Jackson returned the ball 27 yards to Oakland's 37-yard line. It was Oakland's last chance. The Broncos ran down the clock and scored again with 30 seconds to play to clinch a 14-6 win.

Oakland got back on track the following week at San Diego in another controversial game. The Chargers held a 20-14 lead with 1:07 to play when the Raiders regained the football at their own 20-yard line. Stabler moved the Raiders downfield to the Charger 23 with key passes to Biletnikoff, Ray Chester and Morris Bradshaw. There was five seconds remaining on the clock when Stabler dropped back to pass on the last play of the game. Charger linebacker Woodrow Lowe smothered Stabler as time ran out, but the Raider quarterback was able to heave the ball forward before he hit the ground. The ball

Top: Mark van Eeghen on his way to gaining 143 yards against the Buffalo Bills in 1977. **Bottom:** Running back Carl Garrett (31) bursts through the Minnesota Vikings' line on the way to a big gain. Garrett joined the Raiders in 1976 and helped the club during its drive toward the Super Bowl. **Page 124:** Seattle's Steve Largent plays David to Oakland's Goliath. **Page 126:** O.J. Simpson and Ken Stabler greet one another coming off the field at halftime. **Page 129:** Ken Stabler displays the form that made him one of the most accurate passers in the history of football.

Phil Villapiano 1971-79

The Oakland Raiders began a drastic retooling of their defense in 1971, the only year between 1967 and 1978 they failed to make the playoffs.

By then, the nucleus from the teams of 1967 through 1970, winners of four straight western division championships, was gone. Defensive linemen Ben Davidson, Dan Birdwell and Ike Lassiter had departed, as well as linebackers Gus Otto and Bill Laskey. Defensive backs Rodger Bird and Dave Grayson were also gone.

In their place would come the nucleus of the championship teams of the early and mid-1970's. Among the newcomers were linemen Tony Cline, Otis Sistrunk and Art Thoms, linebackers Gerald Irons and Phil Villapiano, and defensive backs Jack Tatum, Nemiah Wilson and Alonzo ''Skip'' Thomas.

Villapiano, a starting outside linebacker from 1971 to 1978, arrived from Bowling Green in the second round of the 1971 draft. He was an undersized defensive end in college (6'1'', 222), but was so aggressive—he averaged ten tackles a game and was conference player of the year his senior season—he was almost destined to become an Oakland Raider.

''College prepared me pretty well,'' agrees Villapiano. ''It was physical in the MAC, not much finesse, just hit, hit, hit. That carried over into the pros. In fact, it's probably not right to say, but at Oakland I remember pursuing plays and hoping my own guy would miss a tackle so I'd get my shot.''

Villapiano started as a rookie, one of two first-year players to join the Raiders' defense in 1971. The other was Jack Tatum. Villapiano's position, strong side linebacker, had opened up somewhat unexpectedly. His predecessor was Ralph ''Chip'' Oliver from U.S.C. who in 1968 also had been a rookie starter.

The Raiders liked Oliver, but the 1960's had turned him slowly into a hippie, souring him on an establishment indulgence like professional football.

After the 1968 season, Oliver—who had resided for a time in his Volkswagen van parked in the Oakland Coliseum—took his macrobiotic diet, put his van into gear, and drove off to a north woods commune, leaving football and the Raiders forever behind.

Oliver had been an instinctive football player with the kind of quickness, agility and hostility the Raiders relished in an outside linebacker. They drafted Phil Villapiano in 1971 in part because he reminded them of Chip Oliver.

Villapiano was rougher in his pass defense instincts than Oliver, but he compensated with a love for contact he seemed to have been born with.

''I never had a problem with that part,''

127

Villapiano remembers. "When I was a kid in New Jersey, we moved from a tough city environment to the suburbs. They didn't have Pop Warner in the city where I was from. But they did in this suburb, Asbury Park.

"I tried out," he adds with a smile, "but the people in charge wouldn't let me on a team because of the way I played. I guess I was a little too rough."

The Raiders knew they were taking a short-run chance putting Tatum and Villapiano in the lineup in 1971, knew they'd have to live with rookie mistakes. But a defensive future was being formed, and while it did, one fact was fast becoming clear. Tatum and Villapiano were the team's two best tacklers.

"They liked my aggressiveness," Villapiano recalled. "Al Davis told me not to worry about my mistakes. Those would be corrected over time. He told me to keep on playing aggressively, and the rest would take care of itself."

It did. In 1971, the Raiders finished second in the western division behind Kansas City, but Villapiano was named to the rookie all-pro team. He was in the Pro Bowl his third season, and the Raiders were back to winning their division more or less automatically.

From the beginning Villapiano had something that made him Raider material, what John Madden always called

"linebacker's eyes"—a spark that gleamed at the prospect of savage contact and that made the personality behind them run on rather a lean mixture.

"All good linebackers are the same," confirmed Villapiano. In Oakland he knew what was expected, and he was eager to deliver in great abundance.

"When you played for Oakland," he said, "you played to win and you played tough. It's not something the coaches teach or talk about. It's just there, like in the air. It's an attitude. You're going to hit people and smash them if you're an Oakland Raider."

Madden tells the story of Super Bowl XI, when for a brief moment in the first quarter he had dire dread of losing. A reporter had asked Madden during the week if he were worried about the Viking's special teams, specificaly about their success in blocking punts.

Madden answered, "No, because we have Ray Guy, and Ray Guy's never had a punt blocked in his life."

Now with ten minutes gone in the first quarter, the Raiders were punting from their own 34. Ray Guy took the snap, spun the laces, and stepped into his kick—just as Minnesota's Fred McNeill smothered the ball for the block. The ball rolled backward to the three, where the Vikings recovered.

"All I could think about," said Madden, "was that statistic I kept hearing where the

team that scores first in the Super Bowl almost always wins it."

In the defensive huddle, Villapiano yelled out, "Okay, now we got them where we want them."

Two plays later, Brent McClanahan took a handoff from Fran Tarkenton and blasted into the hole off-tackle. He hit a pileup led by Villapiano, who stuck his helmet into the crook of McClanahan's arm and knocked the ball loose for Willie Hall to recover.

Madden later explained Villapiano's reasoning.

"He figured down that close they weren't going to pass or run any special plays. He liked that. It was pure football, hitting and smashing. He said he knew all he had to do was hit the quarterback, the ball carrier and the ball all at the same time.

"I guess that makes sense because it sure worked."

The Super Bowl was really the high point of Villapiano's career. The next year, he and the Raiders traveled to Pittsburgh in the second week to settle a score, and a lot of things began to change.

The Steelers claimed the reason they lost the 1976 AFC Championship Game to Oakland was because Franco Harris and Rocky Bleier had been hurt. Madden and the Raiders believed the victory they had earned at Super Bowl XI would be tarnished until that stain from the conference championship win over Pittsburgh could be wiped clean.

They deplaned from Oakland International as though part of a crusade. Departure time for a road trip is usually loose and informal, players' wives taking group polaroids or showing each other whose kids had new teeth. But this was more like waving good-bye to soldiers headed off to the Pacific in 1943.

It had such a grim aura about it, John Madden remembers telling Al Davis, "Jesus, Al, it feels like we're going off to war." And in a way they were. Madden still believes it was the "most meaningful second game of the season in the history of professional football."

The Raiders validated their claim as world champions that day, beating the Steelers 16-7, but at a fearful price. The game was so fierce Villapiano and offensive tackle John Vella went out for the year, Vella with a shoulder, Villapiano with a knee. Cliff Branch and Jack Tatum were lost for most of the season, and Clarence Davis was out for several games.

Villapiano, who loved to hit, had come in with the nucleus of that 1977 team six years earlier. But the Pittsburgh game marked the beginning of the end.

He went into decline and was traded to Buffalo two years later. Once again, it was time for the Raiders to retool their defense.

Wide receiver Bob Chandler (85) takes a pass from Jim Plunkett and heads up field. Chandler played just three seasons with the Raiders from 1980-82.

bounded toward Pete Banaszak at the 11-yard line and Banaszak, who was surrounded by Chargers, batted the ball in the direction of the goal line. The ball reached Dave Casper at about the five. Casper kicked the football into the end zone then pounced on it to score the winning touchdown.

The Chargers protested that the play was either an incomplete forward pass or intentional grounding. The referees claimed it was a fumble and a Raider touchdown.

Afterward Stabler said, "It certainly wasn't a pass. We had no time outs left. I tried to fumble. If he sacks me its over. I just threw it out there to get rid of it."

Banaszak had the next shot at the football, but he was surrounded by Chargers and would have been tackled if he picked it up. "You bet I batted it toward the goal line," he said. "If I'd picked it up, I'd never have scored. It was the logical thing to do."

"At first I tried to pick it up," added Casper, "but I kept missing it. So I just tried to kick it into the end zone. When I saw that goal line go by, I knew I could fall on it."

The Raiders then won five of their next six games. Three of those games were decided in the final minute of play, including a 25-19 overtime win at Chicago.

Their most impressive victory during that stretch was a 28-6 thrashing of the Kansas City Chiefs. Stabler had one of his best days of the season against Kansas City. He completed 15 of 20 passes for 222 yards and one touchdown. Dave Casper was Stabler's favorite receiver. He caught five passes for 51 yards, including a four-yard touchdown pass.

Oakland hit a cold spell and dropped two straight games to division rivals Seattle and San Diego. The two losses gave the Raiders a 5-4 record. Denver was on top of the division at 6-3.

After winning three straight games, Oakland was in excellent position to win at least a wild card spot in the playoffs. Instead, the club went into a tailspin and lost to Seattle, Denver and Miami. Although the Raiders had one game left on their schedule, the season came to an end in Miami. They were statistically eliminated from

playoff competition.

The Miami game was a comedy of errors for the Raiders. Stabler had five passes intercepted, was sacked three times and fumbled once. Nevertheless, Oakland and Miami were tied at the end of three quarters, 6-6. In the fourth period, the turnovers caught up with Oakland. Linebacker Larry Gordon intercepted his third pass of the day to set up a Garo Yepremian field goal. Shortly thereafter, a Stabler pass bounced off the hands of Cliff Branch and into the arms of Miami defensive back Gerald Small. Small returned the interception 46 yards for a touchdown.

Oakland finished the season with a 9-7 record, but was only 3-5 within its division. Denver clinched the AFC Western Division crown with a 10-6 mark. Oakland tied for second place in the division with the surprising Seattle Seahawks and the San Diego Chargers.

The game marked the end of John Madden's coaching career. He retired and was replaced by former Raider quarterback Tom Flores. Madden served the Raiders for 10 seasons as head coach and another two years as linebacker coach. He compiled a record of 103-32-7 in league play, and guided the Raiders to seven AFC Western Division titles and one Super Bowl victory.

Throughout the season running back Mark van Eeghen was the cornerstone of the Raider offense. He gained 1,080 yards and averaged four yards per carry. Stabler had one of his toughest seasons with Oakland. Although he completed 58 percent of his 406 passes, he also led the league in interceptions with 30.

Several players retired after the 1978 season including Pete Banaszak, All-Pro cornerback Willie Brown, Skip "Dr. Death" Thomas, Clarence Davis and Stabler's favorite target for nine seasons, Fred Biletnikoff.

Biletnikoff joined the Raiders in 1965 out of Florida State. At the time of his retirement he was ranked fourth on pro football's all-time reception list with 589 catches. He gained 8,974 yards receiving and scored 76 touchdowns. He holds the Raiders' record in all three categories. Biletnikoff was selected to play in the Pro Bowl four times.

Oakland obtained Willie Brown in a trade with

131

the Denver Broncos in 1967. The seven-time All-Pro was the Raiders' defensive captain for 10 years. During his career he intercepted 54 passes. One of his most memorable interceptions came against the Minnesota Vikings in Super Bowl XI. He set a Super Bowl record by returning it 75 yards for a touchdown. Brown was selected to the Hall of Fame in 1984.

Banaszak played 13 seasons with the Raiders beginning in 1966. During that time he became one of the club's most reliable running backs. Although he led the team in rushing just once, when he gained 672 yards in 1975, he pounded out 47 touchdowns on the ground and is the club's all-time leader in that category. In 1975 he scored 16 touchdowns to lead the team in scoring.

1979 Tom Flores had a tough act to follow after the departure of John Madden. It was even tougher with the retirement of key players like Banaszak, Biletnikoff, Davis, Thomas and Brown. He still had a solid offensive line and veteran Ken Stabler at quarterback. But the position that really stood out was tight end, where Flores had two of the best in the business—Ray Chester and Dave Casper.

Flores took advantage of the abilities of Chester and Casper by installing a double tight end formation. Nevertheless, the offense didn't function properly. The Raiders had a hard time putting points on the board.

Oakland opened the season with four consecutive road games. Their first opponent was the eventual NFC champion Los Angeles Rams. The Rams jumped out to a 14-0 lead, but Oakland's special team play got the Raiders on the scoreboard. In the second period, Reggie Kinlaw and Derrick Jensen broke through the Ram line to

Top: Dave Dalby became only the second starting center in Raider history when he replaced Jim Otto in 1975. **Bottom:** Cliff Branch during the closing moments of another Raider victory. **Page 133:** Running back Clarence Davis (28) winds his way through the San Francisco 49ers defense during a game in 1977.

block a punt and set up the first Raider touchdown. Kinlaw recovered the ball for Oakland at the one-yard line. Derrick Ramsey scored from there.

Late in the third quarter with the game tied, 17-17, Oakland got a break. Ram quarterback Pat Haden's pass bounced off the hands of tight end Terry Nelson. It was intercepted by Monte Jackson and returned to the Ram 26-yard line. Five plays later, Stabler connected with Raymond Chester on a four-yard touchdown pass. It proved to be the winning score.

The Raiders then lost three straight games to division rivals San Diego, Seattle and Kansas City. With Denver coming to town in week five of the season, Oakland desperately needed a win to keep the club's playoff hopes alive. Fortunately they got it, beating a strong Denver team, 27-3.

Atlanta visited Oakland a week later and was crushed by the Raiders, 50-19. It was the most points scored by a Raider team in 10 years. Running back Mark van Eeghen scored three touchdowns. Stabler was hot, completing 16 of 22 passes for 186 yards. Rich Martini was on the receiving end of six passes.

Oakland finished up the season by winning five of its last eight games. The San Diego Chargers clinched the western division championship, but on the last day of the season the Raiders still had a shot at a wild card spot. All they needed was a victory over the Seattle Seahawks.

Seattle started the game at a disadvantage. The club's star receiver, Steve Largent, was sidelined with a broken wrist. Despite missing the game, Largent was eventually the league's leader in reception yardage with 1,237.

Lester Hayes got things started for the Raiders by intercepting Jim Zorn's first pass and returning it 30 yards for a touchdown. Late in the

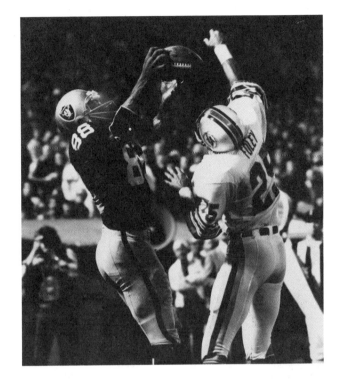

Top: Tight end Raymond Chester grabs a touchdown pass over Miami's Tim Foley. **Bottom:** Running back Mark van Eeghen holds the Raiders' career rushing mark with 5,907 yards on 1,475 attempts. Van Eeghen was the club's workhorse from 1974-81. **Page 134:** Running back Arthur Whittington (22) tries to elude Seattle linebacker Keith Butler. He had his best year with the Raiders in 1978, gaining 661 yards on 172 carries.

second period, Stabler put together an impressive drive that started from his own 10-yard line. He moved the ball 90 yards in 18 plays. Whittington capped the drive with a two-yard touchdown run. Seattle battled back and at halftime the score was tied, 17-17.

In the third quarter the momentum began to swing in favor of the Seahawks. A touchdown pass from Stabler to Ray Chester was nullified because of a holding penalty. Later, Stabler was sacked and he fumbled the ball away. Seattle recovered and marched 76 yards to take the lead, 24-17.

The mistakes continued late in the third quarter. Center Steve Sylvester snapped the ball over punter Ray Guy's head and out of the end zone for a safety.

Behind 29-17, Stabler was forced to throw in the fourth quarter. He did an admirable job, but the Raiders didn't score again until 1:27 was left in the game. Oakland still needed another touchdown. They tried an onside kick but it was unsuccessful. Seattle held on to win, 29-24.

Stabler completed 31 of 47 passes for 342 yards against Seattle. He finished the season with 3,615 yards passing, nearly 700 yards more than he accumulated in 1978. With Biletnikoff gone, Stabler no longer looked for just one receiver. Cliff Branch ended the year with 59 receptions, Ray Chester had 58, Dave Casper had 57 and Mark van Eeghen had 51. Van Eeghen also led the club in rushing with 818 yards in 223 carries.

Nevertheless, the Raiders failed to make the playoffs for the second straight year. The last time Oakland missed the playoffs in successive seasons was in 1965-66. The following year the Raiders played in the Super Bowl. That statistic proved to be an omen for Oakland in 1980.

Top: Defensive back Monte Jackson played five seasons with the Raiders between 1978-82. **Bottom:** Cliff Branch races toward the end zone after taking a pass from Ken Stabler. **Page 138:** NFL commissioner Pete Rozelle awards the Vince Lombardi trophy to Raider owner Al Davis and coach Tom Flores after Oakland beat the Philadelphia Eagles, 27-10, in Super Bowl XV.

1980–1986

CHAPTER THREE

THE SUPER BOWL YEARS

The Raiders opened the 1980 season with a completely re-vamped roster. Gone were such familiar names as Ken Stabler, Jack Tatum, Otis Sistrunk, Phil Villapiano, Charles Philyaw and John Vella. Among the new faces in camp were quarterback Dan Pastorini—acquired from Houston in a trade for Stabler—rookie quarterback Marc Wilson, veteran running back Kenny King, receiver Bob Chandler, defensive end Cedrick Hardman and rookie linebacker Matt Millen.

Pastorini, Wilson and Jim Plunkett competed for the starting quarterback spot. Pastorini won the job after a sterling performance in the preseason. In the league opener against the Kanasas City Chiefs, he demonstrated his passing skill. Pastorini teamed up with veteran receiver Bob Chandler on two touchdown passes and led the Raiders on a 70-yard scoring drive to give Oakland a 21-7 halftime lead.

The Raider defense took over from there. Kansas City was able to score just one more touchdown in the closing minutes of the game as Oakland defeated the Chiefs, 27-14.

In his first game in an Oakland uniform, Pastorini completed 19 of 37 passes for 317 yards. Chandler led the Raider receivers with five receptions for 85 yards.

Oakland then hit the skids, losing three of its next four games. In the fourth game, a rematch with the Chiefs at Oakland, Pastorini suffered a broken leg and was lost for the year. The starting job was handed to Plunkett. His only backup was rookie Marc Wilson and emergency quarterback Ray Guy.

Plunkett responded valiantly. He directed the Raiders to six straight wins and nine victories in their last 11 games. During that stretch, Plunkett was the soul of the offense. He completed 52 percent of his 320 passes for 2,299 yards and 18 touchdowns. Mark van Eeghen was the club's workhorse, gaining 838 yards and averaging 3.8 yards per carry. Kenny King added 761 yards rushing.

But the heart of the Raider club was its defense. Ted Hendricks and Lester Hayes consistently came up with clutch plays to turn ball games around. Hayes led the league in interceptions with 13, the most ever by a Raider, while the 32-year-old Hendricks had three interceptions and numerous fumble recoveries. Oakland intercepted 35 passes to top the league and was second in sacks with 54.

The Raiders went into the final game of the season with a 10-5 record. The San Diego Chargers were also 10-5. If the Chargers won their final game they would clinch the AFC Western Division crown according to the league tie-breaker rules. Oakland needed a victory over the New York Giants to ensure a wild card playoff spot.

Oakland whipped the Giants, 33-17, but the Chargers also came up with a victory. The Raiders had to settle for a wild card match with the Houston Oilers.

Houston quarterback Ken Stabler returned to the Oakland Coliseum to face his ex-teammates for the first time since being traded. The Raiders gave their former leader a rude homecoming.

Oakland's defense put on a superb performance, sacking Stabler seven times and intercepting two of his passes. Lester Hayes was outstanding. He had two sacks and both interceptions. Hayes returned one interception 20 yards for a touchdown.

The game was in doubt until the fourth quarter. At the start of the final period, Oakland led, 10-7. Plunkett then moved the club 80 yards on just four plays capping the drive with a 45-yard pass to Arthur Whittington. Oakland added another fourth quarter touchdown on Hayes' interception return as the Raiders defeated Houston, 27-7.

The Raiders traveled to Cleveland to meet the Browns in the second round of the playoffs. It was Cleveland's first post-season appearance since 1972.

Cleveland was led by quarterback Brian Sipe. During the season, he completed 61 percent of his 554 passes for 4,132 yards. Running back Mike Pruitt gave the Browns a strong inside running attack. He gained 1,034 yards during the season.

The game was played in arctic conditions with the wind-chill factor at 30 degrees below zero. Even so, it attracted 77,655 diehard Cleveland fans.

The field was almost completely frozen, limiting the rushing game on both sides. Cleveland could generate just 85 yards on 27 carries. The Raiders managed to gain 76 yards on 38 carries. In reality, it was a game that was decided in the final two minutes.

Cleveland took a 12-7 lead into the fourth quarter on two Don Cockroft field goals and an intercepted pass returned by Ron Boulton for a

Quarterback Jim Plunkett (16) prepares to hit wide receiver Bob Chandler. Plunkett was obtained by the Raiders in 1978 after being waived by the San Francisco 49ers.

touchdown. Oakland's only score came on a two-yard run by Mark van Eeghen.

Midway through the fourth quarter, the Raiders began to move the ball against Cleveland. Plunkett directed the club 80 yards with van Eeghen scoring on a one-yard plunge. It gave Oakland the lead for the first time in the game, 14-12.

Cleveland took the ensuing kickoff and drove steadily downfield into the bitter wind that howled off Lake Erie. Sipe moved the Browns into field goal position at the 14-yard line with 56 seconds to play. Kicker Don Cockroft was successful on two earlier attempts. His third field goal would give Cleveland the game.

Instead of running down the clock and attempting a cinch field goal, Coach Sam Rutigliano decided to go for the end zone. On second down, Sipe dropped back and looked for tight end Ozzie Newsome over the middle. Raider safety Mike Davis read the play perfectly and stepped in front of Newsome to intercept the pass. Oakland won it, 14-12.

The Raiders next venture was to San Diego to meet the explosive Chargers in the AFC title game. San Diego was a solid favorite. Coach Don Coryell had assembled one of the most dangerous passing attacks in the NFL. It featured All-Pro quarterback Dan Fouts and spectacular receivers John Jefferson, Kellen Winslow and Charlie Joiner. Chuck Muncie led the ground game.

Oakland put together the perfect defense to counter the Charger attack. The Raiders planned to use a ball control offense that would eat up time and keep Fouts off the field.

The Raiders scored quickly on their first possession. Plunkett tried to hit Kenny King with a short pass over the middle, but it bounced off his hands and into the arms of Ray Chester. Chester outran the Charger secondary 65 yards to the end zone.

San Diego tied the game on Fouts' 48-yard pass to Charlie Joiner, then the Raiders utilized their game plan. On their next possession they marched 76 yards and scored on a five-yard run. Later in the quarter Plunkett directed a 50-yard drive as Oakland built a 21-7 lead.

Oakland's defense went to work after that. In the second quarter, Ted Hendricks recovered a fumble on the San Diego 29. The Raiders quickly added their fourth touchdown of the day on van Eeghen's three-yard run.

The complexion of the game began to change in the third quarter. San Diego scored on its first two possessions of the half and suddenly the Raiders' lead was cut to 28-24 with over 15 minutes to play.

The Raiders returned to their ball control offense to eat up the clock. On their next two possessions they used 19 plays to consume nearly eight minutes of playing time and score six points. It was all they needed. San Diego could muster just three points the rest of the way and Oakland had a convincing 34-27 victory.

The win was particularly satisfying for Plunkett. He completed 14 of 18 passes for 261 yards. Ray Chester was the club's leading receiver, nabbing five passes for 105 yards. Van Eeghen pounded out 85 yards on the ground, while Kenny King added 36 yards. More importantly, the Raiders advanced to the Super Bowl.

Most NFL observers were surprised to see Oakland playing for the world championship against the Philadelphia Eagles. The Raiders were stocked with several veterans who had been released by other clubs. Included in that group were key starters like quarterback Jim Plunkett, running back Kenny King and defensive end John Matuszak.

Philadelphia beat Oakland earlier in the season, 10-7. Plunkett was sacked eight times in that game and completed just 10 of 36 passes. Oddsmakers liked the Eagles' tough defense and their quick striking offense, led by quarterback Ron Jaworski. The Eagles were three-point favorites.

Once again, it was the defense that got the Raiders moving. Linebacker Rod Martin intercepted Jaworski's first pass of the day and returned it 17 yards to the Philadelphia 30. It was the first of Martin's three interceptions. Plunkett took just seven plays to get the ball into the end zone, hitting Cliff Branch for the touchdown.

Late in the quarter Oakland took possession at its own 20-yard line. Plunkett dropped back to pass and hit Kenny King at the 38. King sidestepped a tackler then outran the Eagle secondary to score the Raiders' second touchdown. In the process he set a Super Bowl record for the longest touchdown reception.

The Raiders took the field in the second half with a 14-3 lead. They returned the kickoff to the 24-yard line and Plunkett went to work again. He connected on a 13-yard pass to King and a 32-yard pass to Chandler to move into Eagle territory. On second down from the Philadelphia 29, Plunkett hit Cliff Branch for the touchdown. Oakland led, 21-3.

The game was just about over at that point. Oakland added two Chris Bahr field goals to post a decisive 27-10 win. Plunkett was the game's Most Valuable Player. He completed 13 of 21 passes for 261 yards and three touchdowns. Van Eeghen was the game's leading rusher with 80 yards in 19 carries.

1981 The world champion Raiders started the 1981 season full of optimism. Jim Plunkett had come back from adversity to establish himself as one of the game's clutch performers in Super Bowl XV. He was backed by Marc Wilson, who replaced Dan Pastorini as the second-team quarterback.

The passing game was bolstered by the acquisition of wide receiver Cle Montgomery from Cleveland and rookie receiver Malcolm Barnwell. Guard Curt Marsh and fullback Frank Hawkins were expected to improve the running attack.

The defense, led by linebackers Rod Martin, Matt Millen and Ted Hendricks, countinued to be one of the toughest units in the league. Cornerback Lester Hayes, who ended the 1980 season with 13 interceptions in the regular season and four in post-season play, dared quarterbacks to throw in his direction. Defensive end Howie Long, a second-round draft pick, was expected to strengthen the pass rush.

The Raiders started the season in federal court in Los Angeles engulfed in a $213 million antitrust suit against the NFL. The suit originated a year earlier when the NFL owners voted against a Raider move to Los Angeles. The 13-week trial ended in a hung jury in August after an 8-2 vote in favor of the Raiders moving to Los Angeles. A second trial was set for April of 1982.

The season started badly for the Super Bowl champions. Despite a superb defensive perfor-

Page 145: During the 1981 AFC Championship, Mark van Eeghen carries to sustain a time-consuming fourth-quarter drive.

Marcus Allen 1982-

When talk turns to great all-around running backs, names like Lenny Moore, Hugh McElhenny and Lydell Mitchell are sure to be mentioned. All of them were dangerous receivers as well as outstanding running backs. In Marcus Allen, the Raiders may have the most versatile back of all-time.

Allen came out of the University of Southern California with all the right credentials. As a college senior he became the first man in NCAA history to rush for over 2,000 yards in a single season. He set an NCAA record by gaining 2,343 yards. Eight times in his senior year he rushed for over 200 yards in a game, another NCAA record. Allen convincingly beat Georgia's Herschel Walker for the 1981 Heisman Trophy. He also received the Walter Camp and Maxwell Club awards as college football's Player of the Year. The Raiders made him their first-round draft choice.

But the road to the top was not an easy one for Allen. Although he was always a gifted athlete, his early football coaches steered him away from the backfield. At San

143

Diego's Lincoln High School, Allen started out as a free safety and once made 30 tackles in a game. He loved the contact and envisioned himself as a secondary man in college and possibly the pros.

That desire hit a snag in his junior year at high school when his coach asked him to give the quarterback position a shot. Allen resisted at first because he didn't expect to play quarterback in college. Eventually he took over as the starting signal caller and as a senior guided his team to the San Diego County football championship. Allen scored five touchdowns in the title contest.

Allen caught the attention of college football scouts across the country. Oklahoma wanted him as a quarterback, while USC envisioned Allen as a defensive back. Allen chose USC where he could be the hard-hitting safety he always wanted to be. But he also harbored a secret desire—to someday play tailback at USC like his idol, O.J. Simpson.

John Robinson, Allen's coach at USC and now the head coach of the Los Angeles Rams, turned Allen into a running back in his sophomore year. There was one problem, however. Robinson wanted Allen to be the USC fullback, not the tailback. Allen's main function would be to block for tailback Charles White. Although he balked at the idea initially, Allen took over the fullback spot. His

blocking ability helped White capture the Heisman Trophy in 1979.

Allen got his chance at tailback the following season. He would follow in the footsteps of such USC greats as Mike Garrett, Anthony Davis, Ricky Bell, Clarence Davis, Charles White and his boyhood idol, O.J. Simpson. In 1980, Allen gained 1,563 yards and was the nation's second leading rusher, yet critics said he didn't have the right stuff to be a USC tailback.

In his senior year, Allen erased the belief that he was an inferior back with his 2,342 yards. He figured his Heisman Trophy would make him a cinch to be the first or second player chosen in the draft. The pro scouts thought differently.

The Raiders made Allen their first-round pick in 1982, but he was the 10th player chosen overall and the third running back selected. Stanford's Darrin Nelson and Arizona State's Gerald Riggs were the backs picked ahead of him. Allen was both surprised and upset at not going higher.

Scouts pointed to Allen's 4.65 speed in the 40, or his tendency to fumble as reasons he wasn't the league's top pick. Even USC coach John Robinson was critical. He was quoted as saying Allen would not be a dominant player in the NFL.

In reality, Allen's speed is deceptive. He is quicker than most people give him credit

for and has the ability to put on the jets once he breaks in the open. Although he's listed at 6-2, and just 205 pounds, Allen still likes contact and can hit like a fullback.

Raider coach Tom Flores got his first look at Allen at the Gold Bowl in San Diego after Allen's senior year. Flores ran him through some receiving drills and Allen proved to be an excellent pass catcher. He was just the type of player Flores was looking for, a sure-handed receiver coming out of the backfield. But Flores saw something else in that game, Allen's insatiable desire to excel.

"Having the proper mental attitude is an important part of this game," Allen said. "I've always wanted to be rated among the best at my position. If you seek to be the best, there is a good chance you'll reach it."

Allen proved the critics wrong once again in the pro ranks. In the strike shortened 1982 season, Allen rushed for 697 yards and a 4.4-yard average. He was named NFL Rookie of the Year. The next year he gained 1,014 yards and led the Raiders to a 38-9 Super Bowl win over the Washington Redskins. He picked up 191 yards rushing in that game, a Super Bowl record, and was the game's MVP. More importantly, he flashed the speed he supposedly lacked, outracing the Redskin secondary on a 74-yard touchdown run. It was the longest run in Super Bowl history.

Allen has gradually improved his yearly statistics and in 1985 he reached a pinnacle when he led the NFL with 1,759 yards. The awards continue to come as well. He has been selected to three straight Pro Bowls and was the NFL's MVP in 1985.

But what really sets Allen apart from most NFL running backs is his pass-catching skill. He has caught 60 passes in each of the last three seasons and has averaged nearly 11 yards per reception. Lydell Mitchell formerly of the Baltimore Colts, is the only other running back in NFL history to catch at least 60 passes and rush for over 1,000 yards for three straight years.

An untiring work ethic is also responsible for Allen's success. He routinely carried the ball 35 times a game as the USC tailback. With the Raiders he averages 23 carries and four receptions.

Allen has always wanted to be more than a running back, however. He constantly badgers Flores to use him on special teams and has even volunteered to play defensive back in a pinch.

"Sometimes you have to keep an eye on Marcus because once he's in a game he won't come out, even if he is seriously hurt," Flores said. "But that's the kind of pride he has. He really wants to be the best, to be a winner. I'm just glad he's on our side."

mance by the Raiders in their opening league game, they were defeated by the Denver Broncos, 9-7.

Plunkett spent most of the day running away from Denver pass rushers. He was sacked five times. Three times the Raiders advanced within 35 yards of the goal line and were held scoreless.

Oakland regrouped and got a pair of wins over Minnesota and Seattle, then the Raiders went into the worst slump in club history. Oakland was shut out in three consecutive games. No professional football team since the hapless 1942-43 Brooklyn Dodgers had been shut out in three straight games. The Raiders lost to Detroit, 16-0, Denver, 17-0, and Kansas City, 27-0.

Against the Chiefs, Coach Tom Flores tried to spark the offense by starting Marc Wilson at quarterback instead of Plunkett. In addition, Curt Marsh replaced Gene Upshaw at guard and Derrick Ramsey started at tight end for Raymond Chester. The lineup changes did nothing to influence the scoreboard. Oakland crossed the 50-yard line just four times and only once in the second half.

Wilson was ineffective at quarterback. He completed just two of 11 passes in relief of Plunkett. Kenny King was the club's leading rusher with only 46 yards.

The Raiders broke the shutout jinx a week later by squeaking past the Tampa Bay Bucs, 18-16. They played .500 ball the rest of the year, winning five of their last 10 games. Wilson got most of the playing time at quarterback. He ended the season with 173 completions in 366 attempts for 2,311 yards and 14 touchdowns. Derrick Ramsey was his favorite receiver. Ramsey snared 52 passes for 674 yards. Kenny King led the Oakland ground game all season with 828 yards in 170 carries.

Oakland finished the year with a 7-9 record. The San Diego Chargers won the western division title with a 10-6 record. It was Oakland's first losing season since 1964 when they were 5-7-2 under Coach Al Davis.

Bob Chandler is dropped after a long reception against the Chargers.

1982 During the offseason, a second trial began in federal court in Los Angeles. This time the jury decided in favor of the Raiders' proposed move to Southern California. The club then signed a 10-year lease to play at the Los Angeles Coliseum.

On August 29, 1982, the Raiders played their first game before a home crowd at Los Angeles. The preseason contest against the Green Bay Packers attracted 54,268 spectators. The Raiders beat Green Bay handily, 24-3.

After posting a 2-2 preseason record, the Raiders opened the regular season at San Francisco against the 49ers, winners of Super Bowl XVI. Los Angeles had a new backfield that featured Heisman Trophy winner Marcus Allen and veteran halfback Greg Pruitt. Pruitt was obtained from Cleveland in a trade. Jim Plunkett won the starting quarterback position.

Allen was the difference in the opener. He gained 116 yards on 23 carries and caught two passes for 30 yards. He scored on a three-yard run in the second period, bringing the Raiders to within a point, 14-13.

The second half belonged to the Raiders. They added a touchdown on a three-yard pass from Plunkett to Todd Christensen and Bahr kicked a 43-yard field goal as Los Angeles posted a 23-17 win.

The Raiders won their second game of the season at Atlanta, 38-14, then the NFL Players Association went on strike. Two months later the strike was settled and play resumed under a reduced scheduled.

Los Angeles restarted the season at the Coliseum and beat San Diego, 28-24, before 55,060 fans. The club went on to win four of its next five games, including victories over division rivals Seattle, Denver and Kansas City. On the final day of the season Los Angeles had a 7-1 record and was matched with the second place San Diego Chargers. San Diego had a 6-2 record and could clinch the division title under league tie-breaker rules by beating the Raiders.

Los Angeles jumped out to a 20-3 lead in the third quarter and seemed well in control of the game until San Diego quarterback Dan Fouts came to life. He guided the Chargers to 24 unanswered points and San Diego took a 27-20 lead. Fouts was accurate on a 25-yard touchdown pass to Wes Chandler and set up two other scores with

passes to tight end Kellen Winslow.

In the final eight minutes of the game the Raiders demonstrated their character. Plunkett directed the club 88 yards on eight plays to tie the game, 27-27. Marcus Allen scored the touchdown when he swept two yards around left end with 5:20 to play.

Three minutes later Los Angeles took the lead when defensive back James Davis intercepted a Fouts pass and returned it 52 yards to score. Allen added an insurance touchdown with 1:37 to play as the Raiders stormed to a 41-34 victory.

Allen finished the day with 126 yards in 20 carries. He gained 697 yards on 160 carries during the season, an average of 4.4 yards per attempt. Jim Plunkett returned to the form he showed during Super Bowl XV. He completed 58 percent of 261 passes for 2,035 yards.

The victory over San Diego gave Los Angeles an 8-1 record, best in the AFC, and the home field advantage for the playoffs. The Raiders were matched with the Cleveland Browns in the first round. Cleveland sneaked into the playoffs with a 4-5 record.

The game attracted only 56,555 spectators to the Coliseum. Midway through the third period the score was tied, 10-10, but the Browns were driving. They had a first-and-10 at the Raider 14-yard line. Cleveland running back Charles White got the call on first down, but he was met at the line of scrimmage by defensive end Lyle Alzado. White fumbled and the Raiders recovered. Los Angeles marched the length of the field and posted 17 unanswered points enroute to a 27-10 win.

The Raiders dominated the game offensively. They rolled up 510 total yards to set a new playoff record.

The New York Jets were the next AFC team to face the Raiders. New York defeated the Cincinnati Bengals in the first round of the playoffs.

Los Angeles spotted the Jets a 10-0 halftime lead, then came back to score twice in the third quarter. Marcus Allen got the Raiders on the board with a four-yard run, capping a 77-yard drive. Four minutes later Plunkett unloaded a 57-yard pass to Malcolm Barnwell and the Raiders were in front, 14-10.

New York responded with a fourth quarter touchdown to resume the lead, 17-14. But with 3:50 to play, Los Angeles took over at its own 20. Plunkett missed on his first pass, then was sacked

Al Davis 1963-

In 1963, at the age of 33, Al Davis took over as head coach and general manager of a Raider team that had lost 25 of its last 28 games. It was a team that had hired and fired three coaches in as many years. One that played its games in a high school stadium, Frank Youell Field. The stadium held only 23,000 people and was named after an undertaker.

Davis inherited linemen Jim Otto and Wayne Hawkins, running back Clemon Daniels, quarterbacks Tom Flores and Cotton Davidson, and precious little else. He went searching and signed free agent end Art Powell. He traded three rejects to Buffalo for a middle linebacker, Archie Matsos. A week before the opening game, Davis cut two ineffective offensive tackle candidates and signed Frank Youso, just waived by Minnesota. That one move strengthened the line and simultaneously sent a message—produce or leave.

The Raiders started slowly in 1963, 2-4 in the first six games. But they won their last eight, with wild finishes in the final three. They ended the season 10-4, in second place by a game behind the champion San Diego Chargers. To the surprise of no one, Al Davis was named NFL Coach of the Year.

It went from there, Davis building the Raider organization in his own image. He rented headquarters without windows and barred the use of clocks (he himself never wears a watch). He wanted the Raiders to run like a Las Vegas casino— open 24 hours and riveted to the single cause, in this case, winning. He didn't want anyone looking out the window at the traffic or watching the clock thinking it was time to go.

"It's easy working for Al," former special teams assistant coach Joe Scannella once said. "You just can't like sleep too much."

Davis sent his ideas out like tentacles. He is color blind, and there are those who say he picked silver and black as the team colors because that's how he sees the world anyway. The truth is, he wanted colors that themselves chilled the air.

"We wanted to be the most feared team in the game," Davis said, "We wanted other teams to come into dark, gray Oakland, see those black shirts on the other side and feel something frightening."

Of course, it went deeper than costumes and cosmetics. Davis wanted his Raiders to chill the opponents on the field as well. He always loved the passing game, cradled as he was in Sid Gillman's wide open attacks with the Los Angeles and San Diego Chargers. He took a Gillman idea, five

149

receivers in the pattern to stretch the defense horizontally, and customized it for use in Oakland.

He wanted five receivers, all right, but not just for the horizontal stretch. He wanted to extend the defense vertically as well. That meant a strong-arm quarterback eager to trade a high percentage of completions for a profusion of bombs.

That's why he traded for Daryle Lamonica in 1967. It's one reason Kenny Stabler didn't play until he had lifted weights and strengthened his upper body. It's why Davis in turn acquired Jim Plunkett, Dan Pastorini, and Marc Wilson. They all could throw deep.

It also meant high speed receivers on the weak side (Art Powell, Warren Wells and Cliff Branch) and halfbacks who could split the deep zones up the middle and catch like a receiver. Charlie Smith, a Raider back from 1968-74, was the prototype. And Marcus Allen may be even better at it than Charlie Smith was.

Davis' offensive ideas meant two other things. First, the team needed tight ends who could catch, which is why Davis acquired running back Billy Cannon in 1964 and, over Cannon's strenuous objections, converted him to tight end. And it is why the Raiders signed free agent Todd Christensen in 1979 after Dallas had cut him as a running back.

Secondly, Davis needed blockers who could protect the passer, not for the duration of a timing pattern, or a dumpoff to a back, but as long as it took Tom Flores, Cotton Davidson, Daryle Lamonica, Kenny Stabler, Jim Plunkett, or Marc Wilson to spot the open man and cut loose. To that end he acquired big men with first-round talent and paid them star wages. Gene Upshaw, Art Shell, Jim Otto, George Beuhler, Bob Brown and John Vella are just a few of the linemen on that list.

On defense, he tinkered. Davis was fascinated by the success John Wooden was having with UCLA basketball beginning in 1963. Particularly, he liked the idea of Wooden's 1-3-1 zone press, the way it started with the inbound pass and tied up the other team's offense before it could get up the floor.

Davis adapted the press to football and came up with the bump-and-run. The idea was starkly effective. He had the corners confront and attack the wide receivers at the line of scrimmage, making them spend energy evading contact at the line rather than using it downfield running their routes.

In Davis's system, the cornerbacks—Kent McCloughan was the pioneer followed by Willie Brown—stifled receivers long enough for the pass rush to reach the quarterbacks. It was a defensive scheme that differed dramatically from others in professional football.

Of course, none of this laboratory work would succeed without talented players. Al Davis was never particular about what the Raiders did as long as they were talented. Middle linebacker Dan Conners remembers one year going in to see Davis about a raise in salary. Conners said he hadn't had that great a year, so he stressed his citizenship. He listed all the ways he was more stable and civic-minded than the renegades and outlaws across the Raider roster.

Davis looked at him with an expression that resembled scorn. "I don't care anything about that," Davis said. "It's what you do on Sunday."

In the process, the Raiders developed into a halfway house where off-center players found refuge and developed, in turn, the allegiance a pit bull might have for his keeper. The pay was good, their talent was respected, the rewards were victories and playoff money. And the best part—no one was suggesting they had to sing in the church choir to be accepted.

The renegades prized the freedom from personal judgement that went with being a Raider. Few would jeopardize it with action that went across the irregular grain their peers had established.

"We don't prejudge players," said Davis. "A guy has to prove he can't get along with us."

Not all of Al Davis' early football ideas have been retained by subsequent coaches John Rauch, John Madden and Tom Flores. But the bases have. An offensive pressure, a defensive force, a Raider kind of player—those are remarkably intact.

In the years since Davis took over, man coverage has given way to zone defenses in the NFL, the zones to the wolfpack assaults of the 46. But look up, and there are Mike Haynes and Lester Hayes, jamming receivers at the line and covering them tight, just like Kent McCloughan and Willie Brown did when Davis put in the bump-and-run in the 1960's.

In that same time, NFL passing games have gone the way of ball control, short routes to the backs for modest gains. But look up, and there is the Raider quarterback—Plunkett, Wilson, or someone new—staying in the pocket waiting until the last second for a Jesse Hester or a Dokie Williams to break free on a "flag," a "post," or an "up."

As a coach, general manager, administrator, even adversary, Davis has shown a restless and inventive mind. Not since Vince Lombardi and George Halas has one individual wielded such a significant impact on a franchise. Even his detractors, including Pete Rozelle and the fans he left behind in Oakland, would have to admit as much. The man has made his imprint on the Raiders. And the Raiders, the way they play football, continue to make their imprint on the entire NFL.

on second down to force a third-and-18 situation. Plunkett dropped back and threw over the middle to Cliff Branch. The pass was picked off by Jet linebacker Lance Mehl.

The Raider defense desperately tried to get the ball back. On third down Raider safety Burgess Owens popped running back Freeman McNeil causing a fumble. Ted Hendricks recovered for the Raiders at the Los Angeles 32.

Plunkett brought his offense back onto the field with 2:26 to play. There was plenty of time to get within field goal range and tie the score. Plunkett directed the Raiders 26 yards to the New York 42-yard line. With 1:50 to play Plunkett threw to Cliff Branch. Mehl made another interception, ending the season for Los Angeles.

Tackle Art Shell retired at the end of the year after an outstanding 15-year career with the Raiders. Shell appeared in 207 games for the silver and black. Only Gene Upshaw (217) and Jim Otto (210) played in more games for the Raiders. Shell also appeared in eight Pro Bowls.

1983 Los Angeles opened the 1983 season against the Cincinnati Bengals. Among the new faces in Raider uniforms were defensive lineman Bill Pickel, defensive end Greg Townsend, linebacker Tony Caldwell, center Don Mosebar, wide receiver Dokie Williams and veteran linemen Shelby Jordan and Charley Hannah. Midway through the season All-Pro defensive back Mike Haynes was acquired from New England.

The Raiders took advantage of three Bengal turnovers in the opener to post a 17-0 halftime lead. Marcus Allen scored both Los Angeles touchdowns and Chris Bahr added a 38-yard field goal. The Raider defense did the rest of the work. Cincinnati quarterback Ken Anderson was pressured all afternoon and was sacked four times during the game. The Bengals were held to just one field goal until the final minute of the

Top: Cornerback Lester Hayes (37) prepares to play bump-and-run on San Diego's John Jefferson. Hayes intercepted 13 passes in 1980 to set a team record. **Bottom:** John Matuszak fires up the crowd prior to Super Bowl XV.

game when quarterback Ken Anderson tossed a nine-yard touchdown pass to make the final score 20-10.

After beating the Bengals, the Raiders won four of their next six games before facing the undefeated Dallas Cowboys at Irving, Texas. Quarterback Jim Plunkett, who threw 10 interceptions in three games, was benched. Marc Wilson got the starting assignment. Wilson had been wooed by the New Jersey Generals of the United States Football League, but signed a new contract with the Raiders just two days before the game.

Both clubs put on an offensive show. Midway through the second period, Dallas led, 24-17, on the strength of Danny White's passing arm. With six minutes to go in the half Wilson connected with Frank Hawkins on a 17-yard strike to tie the score.

Late in the half, Los Angeles took over again and drove to the 28-yard line where Bahr came in to attempt a field goal. Instead, Wilson took the snap and passed to tight end Todd Christensen in the end zone. Cowboy linebacker Anthony Dickerson was called for pass interference and the Raiders took over at the one. On the next play, Wilson hit Christensen for the touchdown as time ran out.

Dallas came back to take a 38-37 lead late in the fourth period, but again Wilson rallied the Raiders. He started at his own 25-yard line with 3:09 to play and completed five straight passes, including two 18-yard tosses to receiver Dokie Williams. With 23 seconds left Bahr kicked a 26-yard field goal. The Raiders won, 40-38.

Los Angeles finished with six wins in its last seven games to post a 12-4 record and clinch the western division championship. Tight end Todd Christensen ended the season with 92 catches to lead the NFL. He also set a club single-season reception record. Marcus Allen was the team's leading rusher. He totaled 1,014 yards on 266 carries.

Los Angeles had the home field advantage for

Safety Odis McKinney (23) goes high in the air to take a pass away from San Diego tight end Kellen Winslow. McKinney joined the Raiders in 1980 after playing two seasons with the New York Giants.

the playoffs and nearly 91,000 fans crowded into the Coliseum to watch the Raiders play the Pittsburgh Steelers in the opening round. It was never a contest. Los Angeles defeated the Steelers, 38-10.

The Raiders dominated line play, paving the way for Allen to gain 121 yards on 13 carries. Allen also scored two touchdowns. Plunkett completed 21 of 34 passes for 232 yards.

On defense, the Raiders sacked Pittsburgh quarterback Cliff Stoudt five times. Defensive end Lyle Alzado led the charge with three sacks. Stoudt had one pass picked off by Lester Hayes. Hayes returned the interception 18 yards for a touchdown.

The surprising Seattle Seahawks were the Raiders' next hurdle. It was Seattle's first appearance in the playoffs. The Seahawk offense featured AFC rushing champion Curt Warner and one of the league's most dangerous receivers in Steve Largent. Los Angeles defeated the Seahawks in their two regular season meetings, 38-36 and 34-21.

Los Angeles did not take the Seahawks lightly. The Raider defense limited Warner to just 18 yards on nine carries in the first half while the offense posted 17 second quarter points enroute to a 20-0 halftime lead. The Raiders outgained Seattle 226 yards to 16 in the half and sacked quarterback Dave Krieg three times for 21 yards in losses. Los Angeles coasted the rest of the way.

Plunkett lit up the Raider offense, completing 17 of 24 passes for 214 yards and one touchdown. Barnwell caught five passes for 115 yards. Marcus Allen paced the ground game with a season high of 154 yards on 25 carries. He also had seven catches for 63 yards.

Seattle backup quarterback Jim Zorn replaced Krieg in the second half and managed to put two touchdowns on the scoreboard. Zorn completed 14 of 27 passes. Curt Warner ended the game with just 26 yards on 11 carries, his lowest total of the season.

The Raiders' convincing 30-14 win over Seattle gave them another date in the Super Bowl. This time their opponent would be the Washington Redskins. Washington finished the regular season with a 14-2 record including an early season win over the Raiders, 37-35. In the playoffs the Redskins destroyed the Los Angeles Rams, 51-7, then squeaked by the San Francisco 49ers,

24-21. Nevada bookmakers tabbed Washington as a three-point favorite. It turned out to be one of the most lopsided games in Super Bowl history.

Los Angeles scored early and often. The Raider special teams got into the act first when Derrick Jensen blocked a Redskin punt and recovered it in the end zone. Los Angeles had a quick 7-0 lead.

Next, it was the offense's turn. On first down early in the second quarter, Plunkett hit Cliff Branch on a 50-yard pass to the Washington 15. Two plays later he hit Branch in the end zone and Los Angeles led, 14-0.

After the Redskins got on the scoreboard with a Mark Mosley field goal, the Raider defense got a chance to score. With just 10 seconds left in the half, the Redskins were deep in their own territory. Quarterback Joe Theismann tried an ill-advised screen pass to Joe Washington at the five-yard line. The pass went directly to Raider linebacker Jack Squirek. Squirek could have walked the five yards to the end zone.

Sporting a 21-3 halftime lead, the Raider defense teed off in the second half. The heralded Redskin offense, led by Theismann, and running backs Joe Washington and John Riggins, never got untracked. Riggins gained just 64 yards in the game, while Washington had eight.

Theismann was forced to throw in the second half and had little success. Cornerbacks Mike Haynes and Lester Hayes shut down Redskin wide receivers Charlie Brown and Art Monk, and Theismann completed just 16 of 35 passes. Two of his tosses were picked off as the Raiders stormed to a 38-9 win. It was the Raiders' third Super Bowl victory in eight years.

Marcus Allen had his finest day as a pro. He gained 191 yards to set a Super Bowl rushing mark. And his 74-yard touchdown burst in the third quarter was the longest run from scrimmage in Super Bowl history. He was unanimously selected MVP of the game.

1984

The Raiders began their 25th year of football in 1984. During that span they were the most successful team in the game with a record of 215-115-11. The Dallas Cowboys were next with a 214-119-6 mark.

The Raiders also started a new tradition in 1984, moving from their former training camp at Santa Rosa to their new facility at El Segundo. Several outstanding draft picks were in camp including defensive end Sean Jones, a second-round pick from Northeastern, tight end Andy Parker, a fifth-round pick from Utah, safety Stacey Toran, a sixth-round choice from Notre Dame and wide receiver Sam Seale, an eighth-round choice from Western State.

Tight end Dave Casper returned to the Raiders after a brief stint in Houston. Casper played well in preseason, but could not take the starting job from Todd Christiansen.

The competition at quarterback heated up with Plunkett battling Marc Wilson for the number-one spot. Plunkett opened the season at quarterback against the Houston Oilers at the Astrodome. After teasing Houston for 30 minutes, the Raiders beat the Oilers, 24-14.

Los Angeles' defense set up much of the scoring. The Raiders started all three of their touchdown drives from within the 50. Plunkett completed 15 of 36 passes, but had several dropped. Allen was the leading receiver, catching five passes for 40 yards. He also gained 83 yards on 22 carries.

The Raiders continued to play strong defense and surged to seven wins in their first eight games. The club's sole loss came at the hands of the Denver Broncos. During that streak, Plunkett was sidelined with a torn abdominal muscle and was replaced by Marc Wilson.

In the club's rematch with Denver at the Coliseum, Los Angeles lost in overtime, 22-19, before 92,469 spectators. It kicked off a three-game losing streak for the Raiders. Wilson played with a bruised thumb on his throwing hand during that stretch and failed to produce.

The Raiders also lost to the Seattle Seahawks, another division rival. In that game, Seahawk quarterback Dave Krieg guided his club to 17 points in the third period and a 17-14 lead. But the Raiders still had a chance to win the game late in the final quarter.

With five minutes to play, Krieg was sacked by defensive end Greg Townsend and fumbled the ball. Raider tackle Bill Pickel recovered at the Seahawk 25 and Los Angeles was in business. Instead, the Raiders gained just three yards on two running plays, then Wilson was sacked for a seven-yard loss. Chris Bahr's 45-yard field goal attempt to tie the game was blocked. Seattle held

Jim Plunkett 1978-

It's doubtful any professional athlete has had more ups and downs than Jim Plunkett.

As a senior at Stanford in 1970, Plunkett lived a fairy tale existence. He was a collegiate hero, finishing his three-year varsity career with an NCAA record 7,544 passing yards and 52 touchdowns. He was presented the Heisman Trophy and Maxwell Club Award as college football's Player of the Year.

More importantly, Plunkett proved he was a winner. He led Stanford to its first Rose Bowl victory in 30 years, defeating a powerful Ohio State team. He was named the game's Most Valuable Player.

Predictably, the New England Patriots made Plunkett the first player chosen in the NFL draft. His future seemed unlimited.

But Plunkett's fairy tale life came to a screeching halt in New England. The Patriots were football's worst team in 1970, finishing with a 2-12 record. The offensive line offered quarterbacks little protection.

It got no better in 1971. Plunkett spent the first year of his professional career running for his life. He finished the season with 19 touchdown passes, second-best in history by a rookie, and was named Rookie of the Year. But a pattern had been set. Plunkett was taking enormous punishment.

In 1973, the situation came to a head when Chuck Fairbanks took over the Patriots' coaching job. Fairbanks had been successful at Oklahoma running the option. He thought Plunkett was the right man to execute it in the NFL. By 1975 Plunkett was a physical wreck. During a preseason game that season, he separated his shoulder and had a pin inserted. Six weeks later he was back in action against the San Francisco 49ers. During a short yardage situation, Fairbanks called for the option play. Plunkett was hit from the blind side and the pin in his shoulder popped loose. He was lost to the team for another four weeks.

Plunkett's five years

at New England were a disaster. He was sacked on average of 3.5 times a game, went through three knee operations and separated a shoulder. By the end of the 1975 season, Plunkett was ready to move on. He asked to be traded. New England obliged by sending him to the 49ers for three first-round draft choices, a second rounder and backup quarterback Tom Owens.

Plunkett was eager to return home to the San Francisco Bay Area. It was the site of his greatest triumphs. The Bay Area fans knew and loved him. They remembered his accomplishments as a collegiate star at Stanford and were certain Plunkett would be a savior for the struggling 49er franchise.

Everything went as planned during the first half of the 1976 season. The 49ers started with a 6-1 record. Plunkett was the toast of the town. Then the club lost five of its last six games and Plunkett was booed unmercifully. Things got worse the next season when San Francisco went 5-9. In the 1978 preseason the unthinkable happened. Plunkett was unceremoniously cut by San Francisco, the worst team in football. He was ready to look for a new line of work.

Several days later Plunkett got a reprieve. The Oakland Raiders, the final stop for football's wandering gypsies, gave Plunkett a call. Raider owner Al Davis wanted to give

Plunkett a look. After running the 30-year-old quarterback through a degrading rookie-style tryout, Davis signed him to three one-year contracts. There was one catch, his pay was reduced from $200,000 per year to $150,000.

Plunkett's role with the Raiders was simple—sit on the bench, recover from the seven-year beating he took in the NFL and learn the Raider system. Plunkett waited patiently for two years. During the 1978-79 seasons, he threw just 15 passes, completing seven. In 1980, things quickly changed.

The Raiders started the 1980 season with Dan Pastorini at quarterback. Pastorini was obtained from Houston in a trade for Ken Stabler and was handed the starting job in training camp. He guided the Raiders to a 2-2 record. Then, in the club's fifth game, Pastorini's season suddenly ended when a pair of Kansas City linemen converged at his right leg and shattered it. Coach Tom Flores had Plunkett and rookie quarterback Marc Wilson on the bench. He called on Plunkett to relieve Pastorini.

It was a perfect situation for Plunkett to make his comeback. The fans, writers and coaches did not expect miracles from the veteran quarterback. If he won a few games, that's all they could ask. Moreover, Plunkett finally found himself with a team that played football the way he like it—drop back and wing

the football to one of several talented receivers.

Oakland's offense was perfectly suited to Plunkett's abilities. He could work behind a big, sturdy offensive line that took great pride in its ability to protect the passer. And he was gifted with three excellent receivers—Cliff Branch, Raymond Chester and Bob Chandler.

Plunkett made the most of it. In his first game as a starter in over 2½ years, he completed 11 of 14 passes as Oakland defeated San Diego, 38-24. It was just the start. Plunkett guided the Raiders to five straight wins and 12 victories in its final 14 games.

On January 25, 1981 Plunkett found himself on top of the world when he led Oakland to victory in Super Bowl XV. Plunkett was flawless that day. He completed 13 of 21 passes for 261 yards and three touchdowns. He was a unanimous choice as the game's Most Valuable Player.

Plunkett's football career had run full circle—from Heisman Trophy winner to NFL castoff to Super Bowl MVP. He had gone from hero to goat to hero. Plunkett had risen from the NFL trash pile to capture America's ultimate athletic spectacle. His performance earned him the NFL Comeback Player of the Year award.

Super Bowl XV turned out to be a catalyst for Plunkett. Since that game he has performed

with the kind of consistency that was predicted for him when he graduated from Stanford in 1970. Indeed, in 1983, at the age of 35, Plunkett put together his best season as a pro. He had all-time highs in every statistical category, completing 230 of 379 passes for 2,935 yards and 20 touchdowns. For the first time in his career, he completed over 60 percent of his passes.

Moreover, he guided the Raiders to a 12-4 regular season record and another Super Bowl win. As always, when the chips were down Plunkett was ready. In Super Bowl XVIII, he completed 16 of 25 passes for 172 yards and one touchdown. Los Angeles' 38-9 victory over the Washington Redskins was the largest Super Bowl margin in history.

After the win Plunkett was asked what he had done differently since his days at New England and San Francisco to become such an effective quarterback.

"Nothing," he said. "I didn't go from being a bad quarterback to being a good quarterback. I always felt I could get the job done. I'm just with a better team here. If I'd played with the Raiders my whole career, I'd have always been with a winner."

But it took seven years of Plunkett's professional career to find the Raiders. And once the gun-shy signal caller found a home, he finally became the winner that everyone expected.

Marcus Allen (32) is hemmed in by the San Francisco 49er defense. Allen was college football's Heisman Trophy winner in 1981, gaining 2,342 yards that season at USC.

on for a 17-14 victory.

The loss buried Los Angeles in third place in the AFC west behind Seattle, with a 9-2 record, and Denver at 10-1. More importantly, the offensive line began to crumble. Tackle Shelby Jordan hobbled out of the Seattle game with an ankle injury. A week earlier, guard Don Mosebar was lost for the season with a back injury.

Despite the injuries the Raiders stayed in contention by beating their next four opponents and clinching a wild card spot in the playoffs. In the process they sustained two more key injuries. Center Dave Dalby suffered a badly sprained ankle and Charley Hannah, another offensive lineman, twisted his knee. The trainer had one bit of good news. Jim Plunkett recovered from his abdominal injury and was ready to play against Seattle in the wild card game.

Seattle ended the season with a 12-4 record. The Raiders were 11-5. The two clubs had split their earlier season confrontations. Los Angeles won the first game, 28-14, but Seattle took the second one, 17-14.

The Seahawks dominated Los Angeles for nearly four quarters in the wild card game. Seattle controlled the line of scrimmage and with 10 minutes to play held a 13-0 lead. The defensive line, led by nose guard Joe Nash, sacked Plunkett six times. The Raiders were able to cross the 50-yard line just once during three and a half quarters of play.

Meanwhile, Seattle's offensive line blew out the Raiders. Running back Dan Doornick gained 126 yards on the ground, his best day as a pro. Quarterback Dave Krieg threw just 10 times and completed four passes for 70 yards and one touchdown.

Plunkett, who was making his first start in 10 weeks, began to move the club midway through the fourth quarter. He started a drive at his 23-yard line by completing a nine-yard pass to Marcus Allen, then hit Allen on a 20-yard pass over the middle. After two running plays went nowhere, Plunkett hit Allen again down the middle for a 46-yard touchdown. Suddenly, with over five minutes to play, the Raiders were within six points at 13-7.

The Raiders needed the football, but Seattle picked up two first downs before they were stopped and forced to punt. The Raiders took over at their six-yard line with just 45 seconds to play and no timeouts. They couldn't score and Seattle held on to win, 13-7.

1985 The Raiders used their first two draft choices in 1985 to select a pair of highly acclaimed receivers. The club's first-round pick was Florida State's Jessie Hester. On the third round Los Angeles chose Mississippi's Tim Moffett.

Los Angeles started the season with gusto, whipping the New York Jets in the home opener, 31-0. It was the first Raider shutout since 1977. More importantly, the 37-year-old Jim Plunkett showed he could still wing the football. He completed 14 of 21 passes for 242 yards. He threw one touchdown pass, a 41-yarder to Dokie Williams.

The Raider defense was impressive in its first outing of the season. New York's All-Pro running back Freeman McNeil was held to just 44 yards in 17 carries. In addition, quarterback Ken O'Brien was sacked 10 times. Oakland defensive end Sean Jones had three sacks, while Lyle Alzado, Rod Martin and Brad Van Pelt were in on two. Defensive end Greg Townsend contributed one sack.

Marcus Allen was largely responsible for the Raiders' first score. He completed a 16-yard option pass on a third down play, caught a 17-yard pass from Plunkett two plays later and then scored on a one-yard run.

On the Raiders' next possession it took just seven plays to go 80 yards. Dokie Williams came up with the big plays. He caught two passes to cover 74 yards.

The Raider defense was not as effective in its next two games. Los Angeles was beaten by the Kansas City Chiefs, 36-20, and the San Francisco 49ers, 34-10.

The offense suffered a big blow in the 49er game. Quarterback Jim Plunkett separated a shoulder after taking a vicious hit and was lost for the remainder of the season. Plunkett was off to one of the best starts in his career. In less than three games he passed for 803 yards and three touchdowns, and completed 68.9 percent of his passes.

The quarterback situation began to look even worse a week later at New England when backup Marc Wilson was forced to leave the game with a sprained ankle. He was replaced by rookie Rusty Hilger.

The Raiders held on to win the game, 35-20, but the defense deserves most of the credit for the victory. Defensive back Lester Hayes returned an intercepted pass for the first Raider touchdown, then defensive end Lyle Alzado picked up a fumble and ran it into the end zone to put the Raiders ahead, 21-20. Defensive back Sammy Seale iced the game in the fourth quarter when he picked off a pass and returned it 38 yards to score in the 35-20 victory.

The Raider passing game was virtually nonexistent against New England. Wilson completed nine of 19 passes before leaving the game with an ankle injury. Rusty Hilger connected on just one of seven attempts. Again, Marcus Allen carried the offense. He gained 98 yards on 21 carries.

Wilson was back in the lineup a week later against Kansas City and completed 18 of 29 passes in the club's 19-10 victory. It was the start of a five-game win streak that included victories over the dangerous San Diego Chargers and division rival Kansas City.

Against San Diego, the defense came to life again and sacked quarterback Dan Fouts six times. After the contest, Fouts called the Raider pass rush, "the best I've ever seen." Linebacker Matt Millen added, "This is the best our defense has played in my six years here."

Marcus Allen continued his impressive offensive output. He scored three touchdowns and rushed for 111 yards.

After a midseason slump that saw the Raiders lose to Seattle and San Diego, the club got back on track and finished the season with six straight victories. Most important were two overtime wins over the Denver Broncos that moved the Raiders into first place in the AFC west. The club's second victory over Denver was especially dramatic.

After spotting the Broncos a 14-point advantage, the Raiders scored two third quarter touchdowns to tie the game. Neither team scored in the final period forcing the game into overtime.

The Broncos won the coin toss to start the overtime period, but honorary team captain Barney Chavous mixed-up the signals from head coach

Gene Upshaw 1967-82

If Gene Upshaw had played a glamour position, like quarterback or running back, he would have found himself on more magazine covers than Henry Kissinger.

Upshaw played 16 exceptional seasons with the Oakland and Los Angeles Raiders. He was a starter from the first game of his rookie season. He was named All-AFL three times before the AFL-NFL merger, and All-AFC five times afterward. He was four times All-Pro. He appeared in three Super Bowls, two on the winning side. So how many big-time magazine covers did he grace?

"None," says Upshaw without hesitation.

The reason, of course, is that he played guard, and the role of a guard, while important, is nearly anonymous. With the Raiders during

Upshaw's tenure, it was even more so. Because a standout lineman on a standout offensive line doesn't stand out, he blends.

Gene Upshaw understood his role. The Raider running game was straight ahead and brutal, drive blocking for four quarters, strength against resistance. The demands were heavy but the internal rewards were worth it.

"We were big and strong," Upshaw remembered, "and we liked to pop people. We did some finesse blocking, but never on the first move. Ollie (then line coach Ollie Spencer) always taught us to knock the guy off the line first, then move him with finesse if we had to."

Run blocking for Raider linemen was all grunt work. It involved slamming forearms and

facemasks into heaving chests, ploughing defensive ends and tackles, sometimes linebackers, off the line of scrimmage and opening holes for consistent gains of four and five yards a crack.

"Nothing we liked better than going one-on-one and knocking the defense off the ball," Upshaw said.

Pass blocking, if anything, was more physically demanding, with linemen receiving no help at all from the design of the Raider passing game. In Upshaw's 16 years, a good 90 percent of the Raider air attack involved the quarterback dropping back and surveying the field, always looking for the deepest option before releasing. There were no sprint outs, waggles, or dump offs to take pressure off the

blockers.

"Our offensive linemen used to drool when we watched game films of teams like San Francisco and San Diego that threw the ball up so quickly," Upshaw said.

Raider linemen were expected to pass protect for however long the quarterback needed to find a receiver. The idea was sophisticated but demanding.

It all rested on the premise of time, the time necessary to execute complex patterns or improvise developing routes. Stabler was one quarterback with excellent parabolic field vision. He was always looking across unraveling patterns for longer gains. The Raiders placed so high a premium on time that Ollie Spencer invented drills to lengthen the

instincts.

"We didn't put a clock on our pass protection," Spencer said. "Some teams do. They teach pass blocking with a stopwatch. They pick some time, say three and a half or four seconds, then they blow the whistle. They figure the pass should be thrown by then. But we never looked at it that way."

Upshaw would attest. "There we were scrimmaging in that 90-degree heat in Santa Rosa," he said. "The quarterback dropped to throw. He maybe found an open receiver right away, but the coaches wouldn't let him release. We're getting our brains beat in. The receivers were waving their hands, but the coaches were yelling at the quarterback to hold the ball. We had to go on blocking, not knowing when or if it was going to be thrown. It was something."

Gene Upshaw didn't start out to be a pass blocker, not even a football player. Growing up in Robstown, Texas, he preferred baseball—he was an all-district pitcher four years in high school—and track, where he competed in the shot put, discus and broad jump.

Of course, he hadn't reached his full growth by then. He was only 5'10", 180 when he graduated from high school. But he filled out in college at Texas A&I where his destiny began to emerge. He played three positions on the offensive line, and in his senior year he was named NAIA All-American.

Al Davis had scouted him personally. Davis wanted to break new ground on his offensive line, and someone like Upshaw was the key. Davis believed in taking full measure of divisional opposition. He said you don't win the Super Bowl until you win your own division.

From 1963 when he first took over, Davis saw Hank Stram's Kansas City Chiefs fast becoming his strongest intradivisional opponent. In competing with and beating the Chiefs, Davis had to deal with the mountainous (6'9", 290) defensive right tackle, Junius "Buck" Buchanan.

In those days, the prototypical guard in pro football was Jerry Kramer, 6'2", 250, muscular and compact. Davis broke the mold when he drafted Upshaw, 6'5", 255, as a guard in the first round of the 1967 college draft.

Upshaw was fast—he could run a 4.7 forty—and he was as big as most tackles. But Davis pencilled him in at left guard, primarily to offset Buchanan.

"Some thought we were crazy," Davis said, "but look who was on the other side of the line. I wanted to go to sleep at that position for about 10 years."

Davis didn't get his 10, he got 16. Upshaw started from day one. In fact, he gained a rather gilded view of life in professional football that first year. He was a rookie starter. His team won the season opener against Denver, 51-0.

They went 13-1 in the regular season. They beat Houston in the AFL Championship Game 40-7, and they went on to meet Green Bay in Super Bowl II, losing 33-14.

"My only worry in those days," Upshaw said, "was whether I'd have enough fingers to hold all the Super Bowl rings we were going to earn over the years."

Reality hit the ensuing nine seasons, when yearly the Raiders finished runner-up to a succession of Super Bowl champions—the New York Jets, Kansas City Chiefs, Miami Dolphins and Pittsburgh Steelers.

It wasn't until 1976 that the Raiders had their turn. And when they took it, against Minnesota in Super Bowl XI, the offensive line had perhaps the most visible day a group of blockers has ever known. The Raiders gained a record 429 yards of total offense while failing to break a single individual mark in the process. The blockers took center stage that day.

Twenty seven of the first 33 runs went over the left side behind Upshaw and big Art Shell. By then the game was Oakland's, and action in the pit had accounted for victory. For his part, Upshaw had negated Jim Marshall, Vikings' right defensive end, to the point Marshall didn't make a single tackle. Not one.

The cliche is universal. Control the line of scrimmage, and victory follows. In Super Bowl XI, the Raiders didn't control the line of scrimmage as much as they invaded and conquered it. Referring to Upshaw and Art Shell, Vikings left defensive tackle Doug Southerland said, "Those two guys block out the sun."

Upshaw eclipsed defenders five more years after that first Super Bowl victory. But when the Raider offense bogged down five games into the 1981 season, he was replaced somewhat unsentimentally by a big rookie from the University of Washington, Curt Marsh.

To that point, Upshaw had played in 207 consecutive regular season games, three games short of Jim Otto's record. Typically, he understood.

"We weren't scoring points," he said at the time. "Let's make the change."

Upshaw played his last season as a backup in Los Angeles during the strike shortened season of 1982. He had long been active in players union affairs, so a transition was natural. He retired as a player and became full-time executive director of the National Football League Players Association.

In that capacity, Upshaw no doubt generates more news and makes more headlines than he ever did as one of the best offensive linemen of his time.

That's the way it is for an All-Pro guard.

Dan Reeves. Reeves wanted to kick off and force the Raiders to move the ball into the bitter wind at Mile High Stadium. Instead, Chavous chose to receive and Los Angeles had the wind at its back.

After the kickoff, the Raiders pinned the Broncos within their own 20. They got another break when Howie Long and Greg Townsend sacked quarterback John Elway and forced a fumble. The Raiders recovered and on first down Chris Bahr kicked a 26-yard field goal for the Raider win. It gave Los Angeles undisputed first place in the western division.

The Raiders ended the season with a 12-4 mark and found themselves facing the New England Patriots in the playoffs. Earlier in the season Los Angeles clobbered the Patriots, 35-20.

The key to this game was turnovers and they started early. The Raiders fumbled away a punt in the opening minutes of the game and the Patriots recovered. New England capitalized by going just 21 yards for their first touchdown.

Los Angeles battled back, scoring 17 straight points to take a 17-7 lead early in the second period. Then the turnovers started all over again. The Patriots turned two of them into scores and went into the dressing room at halftime trailing just, 20-17.

The Patriots tied the game early in the third quarter on a field goal, then took the lead for good on yet another turnover.

Sammy Seale was deep to receive the kickoff for Los Angeles. He fumbled it, picked it up, then dropped it again in the end zone where New England's Jim Bowman pounced on it. It proved to be the winning touchdown.

The Raiders weren't about to let the season end without one last battle. On the sideline after the game, Raiders Howie Long and Matt Millen accused New England general manager Pat Sullivan of taunting them during the game. Words were exchanged and fists flew but nobody was hurt. It was a fitting end to a frustrating game.

1986 Despite having one of the toughest defensive units in the league in 1985, Los Angeles attempted to add depth to its defense by drafting University of Pittsburgh's standout defensive tackle, Bob Buczkowski on the first round of the 1986 draft. The 6-5, 270-pound Buczkowski earned All-East honors as a senior and was the Panthers defensive player of the year. Unfortunately, he was injured early in the 1986 season and sat out most of the year with back problems.

Michigan cornerback Brad Cochran was the club's third-round choice and Cal-Davis defensive end Mike Wise was selected on the fourth round. The biggest surprise of the draft was Navy's Napolean McCallum. McCallum, a fourth-round pick, became the first Annapolis graduate ever allowed to play professional football while serving in the Navy. He reported to Raider practices each afternoon after serving his eight hours of duty with the Navy. McCallum proved to be an essential part of the Los Angeles offense when Marcus Allen was sidelined with an ankle injury early in the season.

The Raiders began 1986 with a wild game at Mile High Stadium in Denver. Marc Wilson earned the starting quarterback job over Jim Plunkett and put together an excellent passing attack. He threw for 315 yards and the Raiders gained 431 yards of total offense. Nevertheless, three Raider turnovers were the key as Denver came out on top, 38-36.

The Raiders then lost their next two contests against a pair of the NFC's toughest teams. The Washington Redskins downed Los Angeles, 10-6, in a defensive battle at the nation's capital, then, in week three, the eventual Super Bowl champion New York Giants handed Los Angeles a 14-9 loss. In both games the Los Angeles offense looked stagnant as Wilson failed to move the club.

In the fourth week of the season, the Raiders' luck began to change. They defeated archrival San Diego, 17-13, as Wilson threw touchdown passes to Dokie Williams and Jesse Hester. The victory began a streak in which Los Angeles won eight of its next nine games. Included in that string were wins over two eventual layoff teams, the Cleveland Browns and Kansas City Chiefs, as well as wins at Miami, Dallas and San Diego. The Raiders also defeated the Seattle Seahawks at Los Angeles, 14-10, when Jim Plunkett threw two first half touchdown passes. The club's only loss during that time was at the hands of the Denver Broncos, 21-10.

With four games left to play, the Raiders had an 8-4 record and an excellent shot at the playoffs.

Philadelphia was next on the Raider schedule. It turned out to be one of the most exciting games of the season. It also became one of the most devastating losses in Raider history.

The stage was set in the first quarter of the game when the Raiders' Fulton Walker returned a punt 70 yards to give Los Angeles a 7-3 lead. Several minutes later Philadelphia's Gregg Garrity got into the act when he returned a Ray Guy punt 76 yards for a touchdown. It was only the third time in NFL history that each team returned a punt for a touchdown. The lead changed hands several times but Jim Plunkett kept the Raiders in the contest with his pinpoint passing. He completed 16 passes for 366 yards, an average of 23 yards per catch, and two touchdowns.

With just under two minutes to play, Philadelphia held a 27-24 lead and was in position to run out the clock. On a critical third down play, Eagle quarterback Randall Cunningham, who had been harassed all day by the Raider defense and was sacked 10 times, dropped back to pass in an effort to get the first down. Raider defensive back Lester Hayes played the ball perfectly. He intercepted the pass and returned it to the midfield stripe. Plunkett quickly regrouped his offense and led the Raiders to the 27-yard line. Chris Bahr kicked a field goal from there with just 11 seconds remaining to tie the game at 27-27 and send it into overtime.

The excitement wasn't over yet. Six minutes into the overtime period Cunningham lost a fumble in Philadelphia territory and the Raiders recovered. Sensing victory, Plunkett moved the ball into field goal range at the 25-yard line. On second down, coach Tom Flores decided to run another play before sending Bahr in to kick the potential winning field goal. Marcus Allen took Plunkett's handoff and gained four yards before the ball squirted loose and was recovered on a bounce by Eagle cornerback Andre Waters. Waters quickly headed for the end zone and 81 yards later was dragged down at the Raider four-yard line. It was a stunning turnaround for the Raiders. Cunningham scored from there to hand the Raiders their most heartbreaking loss since the Immaculate Reception.

The Raiders never recovered from that loss. A week later they were destroyed by the Seattle Seahawks before a national television audience. Seattle downed the Raiders on Monday Night

Football, 37-0. It was the club's worst defeat in nearly 25 years when they were trounced in 1962 by Denver, 44-7.

Los Angeles closed out the disappointing season with losses to the Kansas City Chiefs and the Indianapolis Colts, one of the laughingstocks of the NFL. The four straight season-ending defeats gave the Raiders an 8-8 record and ruined what had been a promising year.

The offense turned out to be a trouble spot for the Raiders in 1986. Los Angeles scored the least amount of points in the AFC's Western Division. Plunkett, who took the starting quarterback job from Wilson at midseason, was the club's leading passer. He finished the year with 133 completions in 252 tries for 1986 yards. He was ranked eighth among AFC passers. Marcus Allen gained just 759 yards rushing, exactly 1,000 yards less than his rushing total in 1985. He averaged 3.6 yards per carry. Napolean McCallum ended the year with 536 yards rushing.

Tight end Todd Christensen was one of the bright spots on offense. He led the NFL in receiving with 95 catches for 1,153 yards. Christensen became the first player in NFL history to catch 80 or more passes in four consecutive seasons.

Although the Raider offense was disappointing, the defense was once again the class of the league. Los Angeles allowed an average of only 300 yards a game. It was ranked first in the AFC and third in the NFL behind the Chicago Bears and New York Giants. Defensive end Sean Jones led the league in sacks with 15.5. Bill Pickel and Greg Townsend were right behind him with 11.5.

RECORDS

All-Time Raider Roster

NOTE: Players listed below (name, position, college, years with Raiders) are those who have appeared in at least one regular season game (or on active roster) for the Raiders between 1960-85.

A

Ackerman, Rick (DT), Memphis State, 1984
Adams, Stanley (LB), Memphis State, 1984
Agajanian, Ben (K), New Mexico, 1962
Allen, Dalva (DE), Houston, 1962-64
Allen, Jackie (DB), Baylor, 1969
Allen, Marcus (RB), Southern California, 1982-85
Alzado, Lyle (DE), Yankton, 1982-85
Archer, Dan (T), Oregon, 1967
Armstrong, Ramon (T), Texas Christian, 1960
Asad, Doug (TE), Northwestern, 1960-61
Atkins, Pervis (WR), New Mexico State, 1965-66
Atkinson, George (DB), Morris Brown, 1968-77

B

Bahr, Chris (K), Penn State, 1980-85
Banaszak, Pete (RB), Miami (Fla.), 1966-78
Bankes, Estes (RB), Colorado, 1967
Bankston, Warren (TE), Tulane, 1973-78
Bansavage, Al (LB), Southern California, 1961
Barbee, Joe (T), Kent State, 1960
Barnes, Jeff (LB), California, 1977-85
Barnes, Larry (LB), Colorado State, 1960
Barnes, Rodrigo (LB), Rice, 1976
Barnwell, Malcolm (WR), Virginia Union, 1981-84
Barrett, Jan (TE), Fresno State, 1963-64
Belcher, Kevin (T), Wisconsin, 1985
Bell, Joe (DE), Norfolk State, 1979
Benson, Duane (LB), Hamline, 1967-71
Berns, Rick (RB), Nebraska, 1982-83
Bess, Rufus (DB) South Carolina State, 1979
Bessillieu, Don (DB), Georgia Tech, 1983, 85
Biletnikoff, Fred (R), Florida State, 1965-78
Bird, Rodger (DB), Kentucky, 1967-71
Birdwell, Dan (DT), Houston, 1962-69
Bishop, Sonny (G), Fresno State, 1963
Blanda, George (QB-K), Kentucky, 1967-75
Blankenship, Greg (LB), Cal State-Hayward, 1976
Bonness, Rik (LB), Nebraska, 1976
Boyd, Greg (DT), San Diego State, 1984
Bodyston, Max (TE), Oklahoma, 1962
Boynton, George (LB), East Texas State, 1962
Bracelin, Greg (LB), California, 1981
Bradshaw, Morris (WR), Ohio State, 1974-81
Branch, Cliff (WR), Colorado, 1972-85

Bravo, Alex (DB), California Poly, SLO, 1960-61
Breech, Jim (K), California, 1978-79
Brewington, Jim (T), North Carolina College, 1961
Brown, Bob (T), Nebraska, 1971-73
Brown, Charles (T), Houston, 1962
Brown, Doug (DT), Fresno State, 1964
Brown, Willie (DB), Grambling, 1967-78
Browning, Dave (DE-DT), Washington, 1978-82
Brunson, Larry (WR), Colorado, 1978-79
Budness, Bill (LB), Boston University, 1964-70
Buehler, George (G), Stanford, 1969-78
Buie, Drew (WR), Catawba, 1969-71
Burch, Gerald (TE), Georgia Tech, 1961
Bryant, Warren (T), Kentucky, 1984
Byrd, Darryl (LB), Illinois, 1983-84

C

Caldwell, Tony (LB), Washington, 1983-85
Campbell, Joe (DE), Maryland, 1980-81
Campbell, Stan (G), Iowa State, 1962
Cannavino, Joe (DB), Ohio State, 1960-61
Cannon, Billy (TE), Louisiana State, 1964-69
Carroll, Joe (LB), Pittsburgh, 1972-73
Carter, Louis (RB), Maryland, 1975
Casper, Dave (TE), Notre Dame, 1974-80, 84
Cavalli, Carmen (DE), Richmond, 1960
Celotto, Mario (LB), Southern California, 1980-81
Chandler, Bob (WR), Southern California, 1980-82
Chester, Raymond (TE), Morgan State, 1970-72, 78-81
Christensen, Todd (RB-TE), Brigham Young, 1979-85
Churchwell, Hansen (DT), Mississippi, 1960
Cline, Tony (DE), Miami (Fla.), 1970-75
Colzie, Neal (DB), Ohio State, 1975-78
Conners, Dan (LB), Miami (Fla.), 1964-74
Coolbaugh, Bob (WR), Richmond, 1961
Costa, Dave (DT), Utah, 1963-65
Craig, Dobie (WR), Howard Payne, 1962-63
Crow, Wayne (RB-DB), California, 1960-61

D

Dalby, Dave (C-G), UCLA, 1972-85
Daniels, Clemon (RB), Prairie View, 1961-67
Daniels, David (DT), Florida A&M, 1966
Davidson, Ben (DE), Washington, 1964-71
Davidson, Cotton (QB), Baylor, 1962-69
Davis, Bruce (T), UCLA, 1979-85
Davis, Clarence (RB), Southern California, 1971-78
Davis, James (DB), Southern, 1982-85
Davis, Mike (DB), Colorado, 1978-85

Dennery, Mike (LB), Southern Mississippi, 1974-75
DePoyster, Jerry (K), Wyoming, 1971-72
Deskins, Don (G), Michigan, 1960
Dickey, Eldridge (WR), Tennessee State, 1968-71
Dickinson, Bo (RB), Southern Mississippi, 1974-75
Diehl, John (DT), Virginia, 1965
Dittrich, John (G), Wisconsin, 1960
Dixon, Hewritt (RB), Florida A&M, 1966-70
Dorsey, Dick (WR), Southern California, 1962
Dotson, Al (DT), Grambling, 1968-70
Dougherty, Bob (LB), Kentucky, 1960-63

E

Eason, John (TE), Florida A&M, 1968
Edwards, Lloyd (TE), San Diego State, 1969
Eischeid, Mike (K), Upper Iowa, 1966-71
Ellison, Glenn (RB), Arkansas, 1971
Enis, Hunter (QB), Texas Christian, 1962
Enyart, Bill (LB), Oregon State, 1971

F

Fairband, Bill (LB), Colorado, 1967-68
Ficca, Dan (G), Southern California, 1962
Fields, George (DT), Bakersfield J.C., 1960-61
Finerman, Garry (DT), Southern California, 1961
Fleming, George (RB), Washington, 1961
Flores, Tom (QB), Pacific, 1960-61, 63-66
Frank, Elvis (DE), Morgan State, 1985
Fuller, Charles (RB), San Francisco State, 1961-62

G

Gallegos, Chon (QB), San Jose State, 1962
Garner, Bob (DB), Fresno State, 1961-62
Garrett, Carl (RB), New Mexico Highlands, 1976-77
Gipson, Tom (DT), North Texas State, 1971
Goldstein, Alan (WR), North Carolina, 1980
Golsteyn, Jerry (QB), Northern Illinois, 1984
Grayson, David (DB), Oregon, 1965-70
Green, Charley (QB), Wittenberg, 1966
Grossart, Kyle (QB), Oregon State, 1980
Guy, Louie (DB), Mississippi, 1964
Guy, Ray (K), Southern Mississippi, 1973-85

H

Hagberg, Roger (RB), Minnesota, 1965-69
Hall, Willie (LB), Southern California, 1975-78
Hannah, Charley (G), Alabama, 1983-85
Hardman, Cedrick (DE), North Texas State, 1980-81
Hardy, Charles (WR), San Jose State, 1960-62
Harris, John (DB), Santa Monica J.C., 1960-61

Harrison, Dwight (DB), Texas A&I, 1980
Hart, Harold (RB), Texas Southern, 1974-75, 78
Harvey, James (G), Mississippi, 1966-71
Hasselbeck, Don (TE), Colorado, 1983
Hawkins, Clarence (RB), Florida A&M, 1979
Hawkins, Frank (RB) Nevada, Reno, 1981-85
Hawkins, Mike (LB), Texas A&I, 1982
Hawkins, Wayne (G), Pacific, 1960-70
Hayes, Lester (DB), Texas A&M, 1977-85
Haynes, Mike (DB), Arizona State, 1983-85
Heinrich, Don (QB), Washington, 1962
Hendricks, Ted (LB), Miami (Fla.), 1975-83
Hermann, Dick (LB), Florida State, 1965
Herock, Ken (TE), West Virginia, 1963-65, 67
Hester, Jessie (WR), Florida State, 1985
Highsmith, Don (RB), Michigan State, 1970-72
Hilger, Rusty (QB), Oklahoma State, 1985
Hill, Kenny (DB), Yale, 1981-83
Hipp, I.M. (RB), Nebraska, 1980
Hoisington, Al (WR), Pasadena J.C., 1960
Hopkins, Jerry (LB), Texas A&M, 1968
Hubbard, Marv (RB), Colgate, 1969-75
Hudson, Bob (RB), Northeast Oklahoma, 1973-74
Huddleston, John (LB), Utah, 1978-79
Humm, David (QB), Nebraska, 1975-79, 83-84

I

Irons, Gerald (LB), Maryland State, 1970-75

J

Jackson, Bobby (RB), New Mexico State, 1964
Jackson, Monte (DB), San Diego State, 1978-82
Jackson, Richard (LB), Southern, 1966
Jackson, Steve (DB), Louisiana State, 1977
Jacobs, Proverb (T), California, 1963-64
Jagielski, Harry (DT), Indiana, 1961
Jakowenko, George (K), Syracuse, 1974
Jelacic, Jon (DE), Minnesota, 1961-64
Jennings, Rick (WR), Maryland, 1976-77
Jensen, Derrick (RB-TE), Texas Arlington, 1979-85
Jensen, Russ (QB) Cal Lutheran, 1985
Johnson, Monte (LB), Nebraska, 1973-80
Jones, Horace (DE), Louisville, 1971-75
Jones, Jim (LB), Washington, 1961
Jones, Sean (DE), Northeastern, 1984-85
Jones, Willie (DE), Florida State, 1979-82
Jordan, Shelby (T), Washington (Mo.), 1983-85
Joyner, L.C. (DB), Diablo Valley J.C., 1960
Junkin, Trey (TE), Louisiana Tech, 1985

All-Time Raider Roster

K

Keating, Tom (DT), Michigan, 1966-72
Kent, Greg (T), Utah, 1966
Keyes, Bob (RB), San Diego University, 1960
King, Kenny (RB), Oklahoma, 1980-85
Kinlaw, Reggie (DT), Oklahoma, 1979-84
Klein, Dick (T), Iowa, 1963-64
Kocourek, Dave (TE), Wisconsin, 1967-68
Koegel, Warren (C), Penn State, 1971
Korver, Kelvin (DT), Northwestern (Iowa), 1973-77
Kowalczyk, Walt (RB), Michigan State, 1961
Koy, Ted (TE), Texas, 1970
Krakoski, Joe (DB), Illinois, 1963-66
Kruse, Bob (G), Wayne State, 1967-68
Kunz, Terry (RB), Colorado, 1976-77
Kwalick, Ted (TE), Penn State, 1975-77

L

Lamonica, Daryle (QB), Notre Dame, 1967-74
Larschied, Jack (RB), Pacific, 1960-61
Larson, Paul (QB), California, 1960
Laskey, Bill (LB), Michigan, 1966-70
Lassiter, Issac (DE), St. Augustine, 1965-69
Lawrence, Henry (T), Florida A&M, 1974-85
Lawrence, Larry (QB), Iowa, 1974-75
Lewis, Harold (RB), Houston, 1962
Liles, Alva (DT), Boise State, 1980
Locklin, Billy Ray (G), New Mexico State, 1960
Long, Howie (DE-DT), Villanova, 1981-85
Lott, Billy (RB), Mississippi, 1960
Louderback, Tom (LB), San Jose State, 1960-61

M

Macon, Ed (DB), Pacific, 1960
MacKinnon, Jacque (TE), Colgate, 1970
Mann, Errol (K), North Dakota, 1976-78
Manoukian, Don (G), Stanford, 1960
Marinovich, Marv (G), Southern California, 1965
Marsh, Curt (G), Washington, 1981-85
Martin, Rod (LB), Southern California, 1977-85
Martini, Rich (WR), California-Davis, 1979-80
Marvin, Mickey (G), Tennessee, 1977-85
Mason, Lindsey (T), Kansas, 1978-81
Matsos, Arch (LB), Michigan State, 1963-65
Mathews, Ira (RB-WR), Wisconsin, 1979-81
Matuszak, John (DE-DT), Tampa, 1976-82
Maxwell, Tom (DB), Texas A&M, 1971-73
Mayberry, Doug (RB), Utah State, 1963
McCall, Joe (RB), Pittsburgh, 1984
McClanahan, Randy (LB), Southwestern Louisiana, 1977, 80-82

McCloughan, Kent (DB), Nebraska, 1965-70
McCoy, Larry (LB), Lamar, 1984
McCoy, Mike (DT), Notre Dame, 1977-78
McElroy, Vann (DB), Baylor, 1982-85
McFarlan, Nyle (DB), Brigham Young, 1960
McKenzie, Reggie (LB), Tennessee, 1985
McKinney, Odis (DB), Colorado, 1980-85
McMath, Herb (DT), Morningside, 1976
McMillin, Jim (DB), Colorado State, 1963-64
McMurtry, Chuck (DT), Whittier, 1962-63
Medlin, Dan (G), North Carolina State, 1974-76
Mendenhall, Terry (B), San Diego State, 1971-72
Mercer, Mike (K), Northern Arizona, 1963-65
Merrill, Mark (LB), Minnesota, 1984
Millen, Matt (LB), Penn State, 1980-85
Miller, Alan (RB), Boston College, 1961-63, 65
Miller, Bill (WR), Miami (Fla.), 1964, 66-68
Mingo, Gene (K), None, 1964-65
Mirich, Rex (DT), Northern Arizona, 1964-66
Mischak, Bob (TE-G), U.S. Military Academy, 1963-65
Mitchell, Tom (TE), Bucknell, 1966
Mix, Ron (T), Southern California, 1971
Moffett, Tim (WR), Mississippi, 1985
Montalbo, Mel (DB), Utah State, 1962
Montgomery, Cle (RB-WR), Abilene Christian, 1981-85
Moody, Keith (DB), Syracuse, 1980
Moore, Bob (TE), Stanford, 1971-75
Moore, Manfred (RB), Southern California, 1976
Morris, Riley (DE), Florida A&M, 1960-62
Morrison, Dave (DB), Southwest Texas State, 1968
Morrow, Tom (DB), Southern Mississippi, 1962-64
Mosebar, Don (C-G), Southern California, 1983-85
Mostardi, Rich (DB), Kent State, 1962
Muhammad, Calvin (WR), Texas Southern, 1982-83
Muransky, Ed (G-T), Michigan, 1982-84
Murdock, Jesse (RB), California Western, 1963

N

Nelson, Bob (LB), Nebraska, 1980-85
Nicklas, Pete (T), Baylor, 1962
Norris, Jim (DT), Houston, 1962-63
Novsek, Joe (DE), Tulsa, 1962

O

Oats, Carleton (DT), Florida A&M, 1965-72

Ogas, Dave (LB), San Diego State, 1968
Oglesby, Paul (T), UCLA, 1960
Oliver, Ralph (LB), Southern California, 1968-69
Osborne, Clancy (LB), Arizona State, 1963-64
O'Steen, Dwayne (DB), San Jose State, 1980-81
Otto, Gus (LB), Missouri, 1965-72
Otto, Jim (C), Miami (Fla.), 1960-74
Ownes, Burgess (DB), Miami (Fla.), 1980-82

P

Papac, Nick (QB), Fresno State, 1961
Parilli, Babe (QB), Kentucky, 1960
Parker, Andy (TE), Utah, 1984-85
Pastorini, Dan (QB), Santa Clara, 1980
Pear, Dave (DT), Washington, 1979-80
Peters, Volney, (DT), Southern California, 1961
Peterson, Calvin (LB), UCLA, 1982
Phillips, Charles (DB), Southern California, 1975-80
Phillips, Irvin (DB), Arkansas Tech, 1983
Phillips, Jess (RB), Michigan State, 1975
Philyaw, Charles (DE), Texas Southern, 1976-79
Pickel, Bill (DT-DE), Rutgers, 1983-85
Pitts, Frank (WR), Southern, 1974
Plunkett, Jim (QB), Stanford, 1978-85
Powell, Art (WR), San Jose State, 1963-66
Powell, Charlie (DE), None, 1960-61
Powers, Warren (DB), Nebraska, 1963-68
Prebola, Gene (TE), Boston University, 1960
Prout, Bob (DB), Knox, 1974
Pruitt, Greg (RB), Oklahoma, 1982-84
Pyle, Palmer (G), Michigan State, 1966

Q

Queen, Jeff (RB-TE), Morgan State, 1973

R

Rae, Mike (QB), Southern California, 1976-78
Ramsey, Derrick (TE), Kentucky, 1978-83
Reese, Archie (DT), Clemson, 1982-83
Reinfeldt, Mike (DB), Wisconsin, Milwaukee, 1976
Reynolds, Billy (QB), Pittsburgh, 1960
Reynolds, M.D. (QB), Louisiana State, 1961
Rice, Floyd (LB), Alcorn A&M, 1976-77
Rice, Harold (DE), Tennessee State, 1971
Rice, Ken (T), Auburn, 1964-65
Rich, Randy (DB), New Mexico, 1978
Ridlehuber, Preston (RB), Georgia, 1968
Rieves, Charles (LB), Houston, 1962-63
Rivera, Hank (DB), Oregon State, 1962
Roberson, Bo (WR), Cornell, 1962-65
Roberts, Cliff (DT), Illinois, 1961
Robinson, Jerry (LB), UCLA, 1985
Robinson, Johnny (DT-DE), Louisiana Tech, 1981-83
Robiskie, Terry (RB), Louisiana State, 1977-79
Roderick, John (WR), Southern Methodist, 1968

Roedel, Herb (G), Marquette, 1961
Romano, Jim (C), Penn State, 1982-84
Rowe, Dave (DT), Penn State, 1975-78
Rubke, Karl (DE), Southern California, 1968
Russell, Booker (RB), Southwest Texas State, 1978-79

S

Sabal, Ron (T), Purdue, 1960-61
Schmautz, Ray (LB), San Diego State, 1966
Schuh, Harry (T), Memphis State, 1965-70
Seale, Sam (WR), Western State (Colorado), 1984-85
Seiler, Paul (T), Notre Dame, 1971-73
Shaw, Glenn (RB), Kentucky, 1963-64
Shell, Arthur (T), Maryland State, 1968-82
Sherman, Rod (WR), Southern California, 1967, 69-71
Shirkey, George (DT), Stephen F. Austin, 1962
Siani, Mike (WR), Villanova, 1972-77
Simpson, Jack (LB), Mississippi, 1962-64
Simpson, Willie (RB), San Francisco State, 1962
Sistrunk, Otis (DE-DT), None, 1972-79
Sligh, Richard (T), North Carolina College, 1967
Slough, Greg (LB), Southern California, 1971-72
Smith, Bubba (DE), Michigan State, 1973-74
Smith, Charles (RB), Utah, 1968-74
Smith, Hal (DT), UCLA, 1961
Smith, James (RB), Compton JC, 1960
Smith, Jim (WR), Michigan, 1985
Smith, Jimmy (RB), Elon, 1984
Smith, Ron (DB), Wisconsin, 1974
Smith, Willie (RB), Michigan, 1961
Somer, Mike (RB), George Washington, 1963
Spencer, Ollie (G), Kansas, 1963
Spivey, Mike (DB), Colorado, 1980
Squirek, Jack (LB), Illinois, 1982-85
Stabler, Ken (QB), Alabama, 1970-79
Stalls, Dave (DT), Northern Colorado, 1983, 85
Steinfort, Fred (K), Boston College, 1976
Stewart, Joe (WR), Missouri, 1978-79
Stone, Jack (T), Oregon, 1961-62
Strachan, Steve (RB), Boston College, 1985
Streigel, Bill (LB), Pacific, 1960
Svihus, Bob (T), Southern California, 1965-70
Sweeney, Steve (WR), California, 1973
Sylvester, Steve (C-G-T), Notre Dame, 1975-83

T

Tatum, Jack (DB), Ohio State, 1971-79
Taylor, Billy (RB), Texas Tech, 1982
Teresa, Tony (RB), San Jose State, 1960
Thomas, Skip (DB), Southern California, 1972-78
Thoms, Art (DT), Syracuse, 1969-76
Todd, Larry (RB), Arizona State, 1965-70
Toomay, Pat (DE), Vanderbilt, 1977-79
Toran, Stacey (DB), Notre Dame, 1984-85

All-Time Raider Roster

Townsend, Greg (DF), Texas Christian, 1983-85
Trask, Orville (DT), Rice, 1962
Truax, Dalton (DT), Tulane, 1960
Tyson, Richard (G), Tulsa, 1966

U

Upshaw, Gene (G), Texas A&I, 1967-82
Urenda, Herman (WR), Pacific, 1963

V

Valdez, Vernon (DB), San Diego University, 1962
Ven Divier, Randy (G), Washington, 1982
van Eeghen, Mark (RB), Colgate, 1974-81

Van Pelt, Brad (LB), Michigan State, 1984-85
Vaughan, Ruben (DT-DE), Colorado, 1982
Vella, John (G-T), Southern California, 1972-79
Villapiano, Phil (LB), Bowling Green, 1971-79
Voight, Bob (DE), Los Angeles State, 1961

W

Walker, Fulton (DB-KR), West Virginia, 1985
Warren, Jimmy (DB), Illinois, 1970-74, 77
Warzeka, Ron (DE), Montana State, 1960

Watts, Robert (LB), Boston College, 1978
Watts, Ted (DB), Texas Tech, 1981-84
Weathers, Carl (LB), San Diego State, 1970-71
Weaver, Gary (LB), Fresno State, 1973
Wells, Warren (WR), Texas Southern, 1967-70
Westbrooks, Greg (LB), Colorado, 1978-81
Wheeler, Dwight (C-T), Tennessee State, 1984
White, Eugene (RB), Florida A&M, 1962
Whittington, Arthur (RB), Southern Methodist, 1978-81
Williams, Dokie (WR), UCLA, 1983-85
William, Henry (DB), San Diego State, 1979
Williams, Howie (DB), Howard, 1964-69
Williams, Ricky (DB), Langston, 1985
Williams, Willie (DB), Grambling, 1966
Williamson, Fred (DB), Northwestern, 1961-64

Williamson, J.R. (LB), Louisiana Tech, 1964-67
Willis, Chester (RB), Auburn, 1981-84
Willis, Mitch (DT), Southern Methodist, 1985
Wilson, Marc (QB), Brigham Young, 1980-85
Wilson, Nemiah (DB), Grambling, 1968-74
Winans, Jeff (G-DT), Southern California, 1976
Wood, Dick (QB), Auburn, 1965
Wyatt, Alvin (DB), Bethune-Cookman, 1970

Y

Youso, Frank (T), Minnesota, 1963-65

Z

Zecher, Rich (T), Utah State, 1965

Raider Individual Records
1960-1985

SERVICE

SEASONS ACTIVE
15	Jim Otto: 1960-74
15	Art Shell: 1968-82
15	Gene Upshaw: 1967-81
14	Fred Biletnikoff: 1965-78
14	Cliff Branch: 1972-85
14	Dave Dalby: 1972-85
13	Pete Banaszak: 1966-78
13	Ray Guy: 1973-85

CONSECUTIVE SEASONS ACTIVE
15	Jim Otto: 1960-74
15	Art Shell: 1968-82
15	Gene Upshaw: 1967-81
14	Fred Biletnikoff: 1965-78
14	Cliff Branch: 1972-85
14	Dave Dalby: 1972-85
13	Pete Banaszak: 1966-78
13	Ray Guy: 1973-85

GAMES (Career)
217	Gene Upshaw: 1967-81
210	Jim Otto: 1960-74
207	Art Shell: 1968-81
205	Dave Dalby: 1972-85
191	Ray Guy: 1973-85

CONSECUTIVE GAMES (Career)
210	Jim Otto: 1960-74
207	Gene Upshaw: 1967-81
205	Dave Dalby: 1972-85
191	Ray Guy: 1973-85

CONSECUTIVE STARTS (Career)
210	Jim Otto: 1960-74
207	Gene Upshaw: 1967-81

SCORING

MOST POINTS (Career)
863	George Blanda: 1967-75, (395 PAT, 156 FG)
543	Chris Bahr: 1980-85 (231 PAT, 104 FG)

MOST POINTS (Season)
117	George Blanda: 1968
116	George Blanda: 1967
114	Chris Bahr: 1983

MOST POINTS (Game)
24	Art Powell: 12-22-63 vs. Houston
24	Marcus Allen: 9-24-84 vs. San Diego

MOST TOUCHDOWNS (Career)
77	Fred Biletnikoff: 1965-78
67	Cliff Branch: 1972-85

MOST TOUCHDOWNS (Season)
18	Marcus Allen: 1984
16	Art Powell: 1963
16	Pete Banaszak: 1975

MOST TOUCHDOWNS (Game)
4	Art Powell: 12-22-63 vs. Houston
4	Marcus Allen: 9-24-84 vs. San Diego

MOST EXTRA POINTS (Career)
395	George Blanda: 1967-75
231	Chris Bahr: 1980-85

MOST EXTRA POINTS (Season)
56	George Blanda: 1967
54	George Blanda: 1968

MOST EXTRA POINTS (Game)
7	Mike Mercer: 10-22-63 vs. New York
7	Mike Mercer: 12-22-63 vs. Houston
7	Errol Mann: 11-28-76 vs. Tampa Bay

MOST CONSECUTIVE EXTRA POINTS (Career)
201	George Blanda: 1967-71

MOST FIELD GOALS (Career)
156	George Blanda: 1967-75
104	Chris Bahr: 1980-85

MOST FIELD GOALS (Season)
23	George Blanda: 1973
21	George Blanda: 1968
21	Chris Bahr: 1983

MOST FIELD GOALS (Game)
4	Mike Mercer: 11-7-65 at Houston
4	George Blanda: 12-10-67 at Houston
4	George Blanda: 12-8-68 vs. Denver
4	George Blanda: 9-23-73 vs. Miami
4	Errol Mann: 10-9-77 at Cleveland
4	Errol Mann: 10-1-78 at Chicago
4	Jim Breech: 12-9-79 vs. Cleveland
4	Chris Bahr: 10-26-80 vs. Seattle
4	Chris Bahr: 10-23-83 at Dallas
4	Chris Bahr: 10-6-85 vs. Kansas City

MOST FIELD GOAL ATTEMPTS (Career)
249	George Blanda: 1967-75
163	Chris Bahr: 1980-85

MOST FIELD GOAL ATTEMPTS (Season)
37	George Blanda: 1969
37	Chris Bahr: 1980

LONGEST FIELD GOAL (Game)
54	George Fleming: 10-2-61 vs. Denver
52	George Blanda: 11-8-70 vs. Cleveland

PASSING

MOST PASSES ATTEMPTED (Career)
2,481	Ken Stabler: 1970-79
2,248	Daryle Lamonica: 1967-74
1,640	Tom Flores: 1960-66

MOST PASSES ATTEMPTED (Season)
498	Ken Stabler: 1979
426	Daryle Lamonica: 1969

MOST PASSES ATTEMPTED (Game)
52	Jim Plunkett: 10-5-80 vs. Kansas City
48	Jim Plunkett: 9-12-85 at Kansas City

Raider Individual Records

**MOST TOUCHDOWN PASSES
(Career)**
150 Ken Stabler: 1970-79
148 Daryle Lamonica: 1967-74
92 Tom Flores: 1960-66

**MOST TOUCHDOWN PASSES
(Season)**
34 Daryle Lamonica: 1969
30 Daryle Lamonica: 1967

**MOST TOUCHDOWN PASSES
(Game)**
6 Tom Flores: 12-22-63 vs. Houston
6 Daryle Lamonica: 10-19-69 vs.
  Buffalo

**MOST PASSES COMPLETED
(Career)**
1,486 Ken Stabler: 1970-79
1,138 Daryle Lamonica: 1967-74
810 Tom Flores: 1960-66

**MOST PASSES COMPLETED
(Season)**
304 Ken Stabler: 1979
237 Ken Stabler: 1978

**MOST PASSES COMPLETED
(Game)**
34 Jim Plunkett: 9-12-85 at Kansas
  City
31 Ken Stabler: 12-16-79 vs. Seattle

**MOST YARDS GAINED PASSING
(Career)**
19,078 Ken Stabler: 1970-79
16,655 Daryle Lamonica: 1967-74
11,635 Tom Flores: 1960-66

**MOST YARDS GAINED PASSING
(Season)**
3,615 Ken Stabler: 1979
3,302 Daryle Lamonica: 1969

**MOST YARDS GAINED PASSING
(Game)**
427 Cotton Davidson: 10-25-64 vs.
  Denver
407 Tom Flores: 12-22-63 vs. Houston

MOST INTERCEPTIONS (Career)
143 Ken Stabler: 1970-79
115 Daryle Lamonica: 1967-74
83 Tom Flores: 1960-66

MOST INTERCEPTIONS (Season)
30 Ken Stabler: 1978
25 Ken Stabler: 1969

MOST INTERCEPTIONS (Game)
7 Ken Stabler: 10-16-77 vs. Denver
6 Cotton Davidson: 11-1-64 at San
  Diego

**BEST PERCENTAGE (200 or more
attempts) (Career)**
59.9 Ken Stabler: 1970-79
56.8 Jim Plunkett: 1978-85

BEST PERCENTAGE (Season)
66.7 Ken Stabler: 1976
62.7 Ken Stabler: 1973

BEST PERCENTAGE (Game)
91.7 Ken Stabler: 12-21-75 vs. Kansas
  City
90.9 Ken Stabler: 12-17-72 vs. Chicago

**MOST CONSECUTIVE GAMES, 300
or More Yards Passing**
3 Cotton Davidson: 1964

**MOST CONSECUTIVE GAMES,
Touchdown Passes**
25 Daryle Lamonica: 1968-70

LONGEST PASS PLAY (Game)
99 Jim Plunkett to Cliff Branch,
  TD: 10-2-83 at Washington
94 George Blanda to Warren Wells,
  TD: 11-10-68 at Denver

RUSHING

**MOST RUSHING ATTEMPTS
(Career)**
1,475 Mark van Eeghen: 1974-81
1,133 Clem Daniels: 1961-67
1,071 Marcus Allen: 1982-85

**MOST RUSHING ATTEMPTS
(Season)**
380 Marcus Allen: 1985
324 Mark van Eeghen: 1977
275 Marcus Allen: 1984

**MOST RUSHING ATTEMPTS
(Game)**
36 Mark van Eeghen: 10-23-77 at
  N.Y. Jets
31 Mark van Eeghen: 10-30-77 at
  Denver
31 Clem Daniels: 11-8-63 at Kansas
  City
31 Marcus Allen: 11-17-85 vs.
  Cincinnati

MOST YARDS RUSHING (Career)
5,907 Mark van Eeghen: 1974-81
5,103 Clem Daniels: 1961-67
4,638 Marcus Allen: 1982-85

MOST YARDS RUSHING (Season)
1,759 Marcus Allen: 1985
1,273 Mark van Eeghen: 1977
1,168 Marcus Allen: 1984

MOST YARDS RUSHING (Game)
200 Clem Daniels: 10-20-63 vs. New
  York
187 Clem Daniels: 12-9-62 at Houston
187 Hewritt Dixon: 9-29-68 at
  Houston

**MOST TOUCHDOWNS RUSHING
(Career)**
47 Pete Banaszak: 1966-78
44 Marcus Allen: 1982-85
35 Mark van Eeghen: 1974-81

**MOST TOUCHDOWNS RUSHING
(Season)**
16 Pete Banaszak: 1975
13 Marcus Allen: 1984
11 Marcus Allen: 1982, 1985

**MOST TOUCHDOWNS RUSHING
(Game)**
3 Tony Teresa: 11-4-60 vs. Boston
3 Pete Banaszak: 11-23-75 at
  Washington, 12-21-75 vs. Kansas
  City
3 Mark van Eeghen: 10-14-79 vs.
  Atlanta
3 Booker Russell: 10-25-79 vs. San
  Diego
3 Marcus Allen: 12-10-82 vs. L.A.
  Rams, 9-24-84 vs. San Diego, 12-
  2-84 at Miami, 10-28-85 vs. San
  Diego

**BEST AVERAGE PER RUSH (150 or
more attempts) (Career)**
4.8 Marv Hubbard: 1969-70
4.5 Clarence Davis: 1971-78
4.5 Clem Daniels: 1961-67

**BEST AVERAGE PER RUSH
(Season)**
6.0 Charlie Smith: 1968
5.9 Clarence Davis: 1971

BEST AVERAGE PER RUSH (Game)
13.0 Charlie Smith: 12-8-68 vs. Denver
11.8 Tony Teresa: 11-30-60 vs. Buffalo

**LONGEST RUN FROM
SCRIMMAGE**
89 Kenny King: 10-12-80 vs. San
  Diego
87 Jack Larscheid: 10-16-60 vs.
  Boston

PASS RECEIVING

MOST PASS RECEPTIONS (Career)
589 Fred Biletnikoff: (1965-78
501 Cliff Branch: 1972-84
304 Todd Christensen: 1979-85

**MOST PASS RECEPTIONS
(Season)**
92 Todd Christensen: 1983
82 Todd Christensen: 1985

MOST PASS RECEPTIONS (Game)
12 Dave Casper: 10-3-76 at New
  England
11 Art Powell: 10-8-65 at Boston
11 Todd Christensen: 10-16-83 at
  Seattle, 9-12-85 at Kansas City

MOST YARDS GAINED (Career)
8,974 Fred Biletnikoff: 1965-78
8,685 Cliff Branch: 1972-85
4,491 Art Powell: 1963-66

MOST YARDS GAINED (Season)
1,361 Art Powell: 1964
1,304 Art Powell: 1963

MOST YARDS GAINED (Game)
247 Art Powell: 12-22-63 vs. Houston
206 Art Powell: 10-8-65 at Boston

**MOST TOUCHDOWN RECEPTIONS
(Career)**
76 Fred Biletnikoff: 1965-78
67 Cliff Branch: 1972-85
50 Art Powell: 1963-66

**MOST TOUCHDOWN RECEPTIONS
(Season)**
16 Art Powell: 1963
14 Warren Wells: 1969

**MOST TOUCHDOWN RECEPTIONS
(Game)**
4 Art Powell: 12-2-63 vs. Houston
3 Art Powell: 12-8-63 vs. San Diego
3 Fred Biletnikoff: 11-10-68 at
  Denver
3 Warren Wells: 12-7-69 vs.
  Cincinnati
3 Warren Wells: 10-11-70 vs.
  Denver
3 Raymond Chester: 10-25-70 vs.
  Pittsburgh
3 Cliff Branch: 11-30-75 vs. Atlanta
3 Bob Chandler: 10-26-80 vs.
  Seattle
3 Todd Christensen: 11-16-83 at
  Seattle
3 Todd Christensen: 12-1-83 at San
  Diego

**BEST AVERAGE GAIN PER CATCH
(50 or more receptions) (Career)**
23.3 Warren Wells: 1967-70
20.2 Dokie Williams: 1983-85
17.7 Art Powell: 1963-66

**BEST AVERAGE PER CATCH (14 or
more receptions) (Season)**
26.8 Warren Wells: 1969
24.2 Cliff Branch: 1976

Marcus Allen

Raider Individual Records

BEST AVERAGE GAIN PER CATCH (3 or more receptions) (Game)
57.3   Clem Daniels: (3 for 172) 9-15-63 vs. Buffalo
43.3   Marcus Allen: (4 for 173) 10-7-84 vs. Seattle

PUNT RETURNS

MOST PUNT RETURNS (Career)
168   Neal Colzie: 1975-78
148   George Atkinson: 1968-77

MOST PUNT RETURNS (Season)
62   Fulton Walker: 1985
58   Greg Pruitt: 1983

MOST PUNT RETURNS (Game)
9   Rodger Bird: 9-10-67 vs. Denver
9   Cle Montgomery: 12-10-84 at Detroit
8   Neal Colzie: 10-5-75 at San Diego

BEST AVERAGE PER RETURN (20 or more returns) (Career)
12.6   Claude Gibson: 1963-65
11.9   Ron Smith: 1974

BEST AVERAGE PER RETURN (14 or more returns) (Season)
14.4   Claude Gibson: (1964
13.9   Cle Montgomery: 1984

BEST AVERAGE PER RETURN (3 or more returns) (Game)
42.3   Neal Colzie: 11-2-75 at Denver
41.0   George Atkinson: 9-15-68 at Buffalo

MOST YARDS RETURNED (Career)
1,747   Neal Colzie: 1975-78
1,350   Greg Pruitt: 1982-84

MOST YARDS RETURNED (Season)
692   Fulton Walker: 1985
666   Greg Pruitt: 1983

MOST YARDS RETURNED (Game)
205   George Atkinson: 7-15-68 at Buffalo
152   Cle Montgomery: 12-10-84 at Detroit

MOST TOUCHDOWNS (Career)
3   Claude Gibson: 1963-65
3   George Atkinson: 1968-77

MOST TOUCHDOWNS (Season)
2   Claude Gibson: 1963
2   George Atkinson: 1968

MOST TOUCHDOWNS (Game)
1   Claude Gibson: 11-3-63 vs. Kansas City
1   Claude Gibson: 12-22-63 vs. Houston
1   Claude Gibson: 9-12-65 vs. Kansas City
1   George Atkinson: 9-15-68 at Buffalo
1   George Atkinson: 10-13-68 vs. San Diego
1   Alvin Wyatt: 9-20-70 at Cincinnati
1   George Atkinson: 9-16-73 at Minnesota
1   Ted Watts: 12-7-81 vs. Pittsburgh
1   Greg Pruitt: 10-2-83 at Washington
1   Cle Montgomery: 12-10-84 at Detroit

LONGEST PUNT RETURN (Game)
97   Greg Pruitt: 10-2-83 at Washington
86   George Atkinson: 9-15-68 at Buffalo

KICKOFF RETURNS

MOST KICKOFF RETURNS (Career)
113   Bo Roberson: 1962-65
79   Clarence Davis: 1971-78

MOST KICKOFF RETURNS (Season)
38   Bo Roberson: 1963
36   Bo Roberson: 1964

MOST KICKOFF RETURNS (Game)
7   Bo Roberson: 10-27-63 at San Diego
7   Bo Roberson: 12-22-63 vs. Houston

MOST YARDS RETURNED (Career)
2,791   Bo Roberson: 1962-65
2,140   Clarence Davis: 1971-78

MOST YARDS RETURNED (Season)
975   Bo Roberson: 1964
873   Ira Matthews: 1979

MOST YARDS RETURNED (Game)
180   Ira Matthews: 10-25-79 vs. San Diego
171   Bo Roberson: 10-27-63 at San Diego

MOST TOUCHDOWNS (Career)
1   Bo Roberson: 1962-65
1   Jim Smith: 1960
1   Harold Hart: 1974-75, 1978
1   Ira Matthews: 1979-80
1   Arthur Whittington: 1978-80
1   Derrick Jensen: 1979-85

MOST TOUCHDOWNS (Season)
1   Jim Smith: 1960
1   Bo Roberson: 1962
1   Harold Hart: 1975
1   Ira Matthews: 1979
1   Arthur Whittington: 1980
1   Derrick Jensen: 1980

MOST TOUCHDOWNS (Game)
1   Jim Smith: 10-9-60 at Dallas Texans
1   Bo Roberson: 9-30-62 vs. San Diego
1   Harold Hart: 9-22-75 at Miami
1   Ira Matthews: 10-25-79 vs. San Diego
1   Arthur Whittington: 11-9-80 vs. Cincinnati
1   Derrick Jensen: 12-21-80 at N.Y. Giants

BEST AVERAGE PER RETURN (20 or more returns) (Career)
28.4   Jack Larscheid: 1960-61
27.1   Clarence Davis: 1971-78

BEST AVERAGE PER RETURN (Season)
30.5   Harold Hart: 1975
28.4   Jack Larscheid: 1960

BEST AVERAGE PER RETURN (3 or more returns) (Game)
53.0   Harold Hart: 9-22-75 at Miami
45.0   Ira Matthews: 10-25-79 vs. San Diego

LONGEST KICKOFF RETURN (Game)
104   Ira Matthews: 10-25-79 vs. San Diego
102   Harold Hart: 9-22-75 at Miami

INTERCEPTIONS

MOST INTERCEPTIONS (Career)
39   Willie Brown: 1967-78
37   Lester Hayes: 1977-85

MOST INTERCEPTIONS (Season)
13   Lester Hayes: 1980
10   Tommy Morrow: 1962
10   Dave Grayson: 1968

MOST INTERCEPTIONS (Game)
3   Tommy Morrow: 9-7-63 at Houston
3   Dave Grayson: 10-26-69 at San Diego
3   Willie Brown: 10-29-72 vs. Los Angeles
3   George Atkinson: 19-6-74 at Cleveland
3   Charles Phillips: 12-8-75 vs. Denver

MOST YARDS RETURNED (Career)
636   Jack Tatum: 1971-79
624   Dave Grayson: 1965-70

MOST YARDS RETURNED (Season)
273   Lester Hayes: 1980
220   Mike Haynes: 1984

MOST YARDS RETURNED (Game)
151   Mike Haynes: 12-2-84 at Miami
96   Tommy Morrow: 10-3-64 at Buffalo

MOST TOUCHDOWNS (Career)
4   Dave Grayson: 1965-70
4   Rod Martin: 1977-85
4   Lester Hayes: 1977-86

MOST TOUCHDOWNS (Season)
2   Dave Grayson: 1965
2   Gus Otto: 1965
2   Warren Powers: 1967
2   Jimmy Warren: 1971
2   Lester Hayes: 1979
2   Rod Martin: 1983

MOST TOUCHDOWNS (Game)
1   By 25 players:

MOST CONSECUTIVE GAMES, PASSES INTECEPTED
8   Tommy Morrow: 1962-63
6   Lester Hayes: 1980

LONGEST INTERCEPTION RETURN
97   Mike Haynes: 12-2-84 at Miami
91   Fred Williamson: 9-30-62 vs. San Diego

PUNTING

MOST PUNTS (Career)
960   Ray Guy: 1973-85
364   Mike Eischeid: 1966-71

MOST PUNTS (Season)
96   Ray Guy: 1981
91   Ray Guy: 1984

MOST PUNTS (Game)
11   Wayne Crow: 9-11-60 vs. Houston
11   Mike Mercer: 9-12-63 vs. Boston
11   Mike Eischeid: 11-20-66 at Denver
11   Ray Guy: 11-18-73 vs. Cleveland

MOST YARDS PUNTING (Career)
40,921   Ray Guy: 1973-85
15,380   Mike Eischeid: 1966-71

MOST YARDS PUNTING (Season)
4,195   Ray Guy: 1981
3,809   Ray Guy: 1984

BEST AVERAGE PER PUNT (Career)
42.6   Ray Guy: 1973-85
42.3   Mike Eischeid: 1966-71

BEST AVERAGE PER PUNT (Season)
45.3   Ray Guy: 1973
44.3   Mike Eischeid: 1967

BEST AVERAGE PER PUNT (3 or more punts) (Game)
57.6   Ray Guy: 9-6-81 at Denver
55.6   Ray Guy: 9-27-81 at Detroit

LONGEST PUNT (Game)
77   Wayne Crow: (10-29-61 vs. New York
74   Ray Guy: 10-30-77 at Denver

Raider Yearly Leaders

PASSING

		Atts.	Comp.	Yds.	Pct.	TD	Int.
1960	Tom Flores	252	136	1738	54.0	12	12
1961	Tom Flores	366	190	2176	51.9	15	19
1962	Cotton Davidson	321	119	1977	37.0	7	23
1963	Tom Flores	247	113	2101	45.7	20	13
1964	Cotton Davidson	320	155	2497	48.4	21	19
1965	Tom Flores	269	122	1593	45.3	14	11
1966	Tom Flores	306	151	2638	49.4	24	14
1967	Daryle Lamonica	425	220	3227	51.8	30	23
1968	Daryle Lamonica	416	206	3245	49.5	25	15
1969	Daryle Lamonica	426	221	3302	51.9	34	25
1970	Daryle Lamonica	356	179	2516	50.3	22	15
1971	Daryle Lamonica	242	118	1717	48.8	16	16
1972	Daryle Lamonica	281	149	1998	53.0	18	12
1973	Ken Stabler	260	163	1997	62.7	14	10
1974	Ken Stabler	310	178	2469	57.4	26	12
1975	Ken Stabler	293	171	2296	58.4	16	24
1976	Ken Stabler	291	194	2737	66.7	27	17
1977	Ken Stabler	294	169	2176	57.5	20	20
1978	Ken Stabler	406	237	2944	58.4	16	30
1979	Ken Stabler	498	304	3615	61.0	26	22
1980	Jim Plunkett	320	165	2299	51.6	18	16
1981	Marc Wilson	366	173	2311	47.3	14	19
1982	Jim Plunkett	261	152	2035	58.2	14	15
1983	Jim Plunkett	379	230	2935	60.7	20	18
1984	Marc Wilson	282	153	2151	54.3	15	17
1985	Marc Wilson	388	193	2608	49.7	16	21

PASS INTERCEPTIONS

		No.	Yds.	Avg.	TD	LR
1960	Eddie Macon	9	105	11.7	1	42
1961	Joe Cannavino	5	14	2.8	0	9
1962	Tom Morrow	10	141	14.1	0	36
1963	Tom Morrow	9	104	11.5	0	35
1964	Fred Williamson	6	40	6.7	0	28
1965	Warren Powers	5	56	11.2	0	12
1966	Warren Powers	5	88	17.6	0	35
1967	Willie Brown	7	33	4.7	0	25
1968	Dave Grayson	10	195	19.5	1	54
1969	Dave Grayson	8	132	16.5	1	76
1970	Kent McCloughan	5	5	1.0	0	5
1971	Nemiah Wilson	5	70	14.0	0	22
1972	Jack Tatum	4	91	22.8	0	56
1973	George Atkinson	3	48	16.0	0	36
1974	Alonzo Thomas	6	70	11.7	1	34
1975	Alonzo Thomas	6	86	14.3	0	48
1976	Monte Johnson	4	40	10.0	0	22
1977	Jack Tatum	6	146	24.3	0	41
1978	Charles Phillips	6	121	20.2	1	42
1979	Lester Hayes	7	100	14.3	2	52
1980	Lester Hayes	13	273	21.0	1	62
1981	Odis McKinney	3	38	12.7	0	34
1982	Burgess Owens	4	56	14.0	0	35
1983	Vann McElroy	8	68	8.5	0	28
1984	Mike Haynes	6	220	36.7	1	97
1985	Lester Hayes	4	27	6.8	1	27

RUSHING

		No.	Yds.	Avg.	TD	LR
1960	Tony Teresa	139	608	4.4	6	83
1961	Wayne Crow	119	490	4.1	2	62
1962	Clem Daniels	161	766	4.7	7	72
1963	Clem Daniels	215	1099	5.1	3	74
1964	Clem Daniels	173	824	4.7	2	42
1965	Clem Daniels	219	953	4.0	5	57
1966	Clem Daniels	204	801	3.9	7	64
1967	Clem Daniels	130	575	4.4	4	52
1968	Hewritt Dixon	206	865	4.2	2	28
1969	Charlie Smith	177	600	3.4	2	23
1970	Hewritt Dixon	197	861	4.4	1	39
1971	Marv Hubbard	181	867	4.8	5	20
1972	Marv Hubbard	219	1100	5.0	4	39
1973	Marv Hubbard	193	903	4.7	6	50
1974	Marv Hubbard	188	865	4.6	4	32
1975	Pete Banaszak	187	672	3.6	16	27
1976	Mark van Eeghen	233	1012	4.3	3	21
1977	Mark van Eeghen	324	1273	3.9	7	27
1978	Mark van Eeghen	270	1080	4.0	9	34
1979	Mark van Eeghen	223	818	3.7	7	19
1980	Mark van Eeghen	222	838	3.8	5	34
1981	Kenny King	170	828	4.9	0	60
1982	Marcus Allen	160	697	4.4	11	53
1983	Marcus Allen	266	1014	3.8	9	19
1984	Marcus Allen	275	1168	4.2	13	52
1985	Marcus Allen	380	1759	4.6	11	61

PUNTING

		No.	Yds.	Avg.	LP
1960	Wayne Crow	76	2958	38.9	72
1961	Wayne Crow	61	2613	42.8	77
1962	Cotton Davidson	40	1569	39.2	64
1963	Mike Mercer	75	3007	40.0	53
1964	Mike Mercer	58	2446	42.1	67
1965	Mike Mercer	75	3079	41.1	70
1966	Mike Eischeid	64	2703	42.2	56
1967	Mike Eischeid	76	3364	44.3	62
1968	Mike Eischeid	64	2788	43.6	72
1969	Mike Eischeid	69	2944	42.7	58
1970	Mike Eischeid	79	3121	39.5	57
1971	Jerry DePoyster	57	2013	39.4	56
1972	Jerry DePoyster	55	2031	36.9	57
1973	Ray Guy	69	3127	45.3	72
1974	Ray Guy	74	3124	42.2	66
1975	Ray Guy	68	2979	43.8	64
1976	Ray Guy	67	2785	41.6	66
1977	Ray Guy	59	2552	43.3	74
1978	Ray Guy	81	3462	42.7	69
1979	Ray Guy	69	2939	42.6	71
1980	Ray Guy	71	3099	43.6	66
1981	Ray Guy	96	4195	43.7	69
1982	Ray Guy	47	1839	39.1	57
1983	Ray Guy	79	3384	42.8	67
1984	Ray Guy	91	3809	41.9	63
1985	Ray Guy	89	3627	40.8	68

Raider Yearly Leaders

SCORING

		TD	PAT	FG	Total
1960	Tony Teresa	10	0	0	60
1961	George Fleming	1	24	11	63
1962	Clem Dnaiels	8	0	0	48
1963	Art Powell	16	0	0	96
1964	Mike Mercer	0	34	15	79
1965	Clem Daniels	12	0	0	72
	Art Powell	12	0	0	72
1966	Mike Eischeid	0	37	11	70
1967	George Blanda	0	56	20	116
1968	George Blanda	0	54	21	117
1969	George Blanda	0	45	20	105
1970	George Blanda	0	36	16	84
1971	George Blanda	0	41	15	86
1972	George Blanda	0	44	17	95
1973	George Blanda	0	31	23	100
1974	Cliff Branch	13	0	0	78
1975	Pete Banaszak	16	0	0	96
1976	Cliff Branch	12	0	0	72
1977	Errol Mann	0	39	20	99
1978	Errol Mann	0	33	12	66
1979	Jim Breech	0	41	18	95
1980	Chris Bahr	0	41	19	98
1981	Chris Bahr	0	27	14	69
1982	Marcus Allen	14	0	0	84
1983	Chris Bahr	0	51	21	114
1984	Marcus Allen	18	0	0	108
1985	Chris Bahr	0	40	20	100

PUNT RETURNS

		No.	Yds.	Avg.	TD	LR
1960	Jack Larscheid	12	106	8.8	0	41
1961	Charles Fuller	4	52	13.8	0	25
1962	Bob Garner	20	162	8.1	0	25
1963	Claude Gibson	26	307	11.8	2	85
1964	Claude Gibson	29	419	14.4	0	58
1965	Claude Gibson	31	357	11.8	1	58
1966	Rodger Bird	37	323	8.7	0	42
1967	Rodger Bird	46	612	13.3	0	78
1968	George Atkintson	36	490	13.6	2	86
1969	George Atkinson	25	153	6.1	0	30
1970	Alvin Wyatt	25	231	9.2	1	63
1971	George Atkinson	20	159	8.0	0	34
1972	George Atkinson	10	33	3.3	0	8
1973	George Atkinson	41	336	8.2	1	63
1974	Ron Smith	41	486	11.9	0	55
1975	Neal Colzie	48	655	13.6	0	64
1976	Neal Colzie	41	448	10.9	0	32
1977	Neal Colzie	32	334	10.4	0	23
1978	Neal Colzie	47	310	6.6	0	24
1979	Ira Matthews	32	165	5.2	0	20
1980	Ira Matthews	48	421	8.8	0	34
1981	Ted Watts	35	284	8.1	1	52
1982	Greg Pruitt	26	209	8.0	0	25
1983	Greg Pruitt	58	668	11.5	1	97
1984	Greg Pruitt	53	473	8.9	0	38
1985	Fulton Walker	62	692	11.2	0	32

RECEIVING

		No.	Yds.	Avg.	TD	LR
1960	Billy Lott	49	524	10.7	1	28
1961	Doug Asad	36	501	13.0	2	51
1962	Max Boydston	30	374	12.4	0	58
1963	Art Powell	73	1304	17.8	16	85
1964	Art Powell	76	1361	17.9	11	77
1965	Art Powell	52	800	15.4	12	66
1966	Art Powell	53	1026	19.4	11	46
1967	Hewritt Dixon	59	563	9.5	2	48
1968	Fred Biletnikoff	61	1037	17.0	6	82
1969	Fred Biletnikoff	54	837	15.3	12	53
1970	Fred Biletnikoff	45	768	17.1	7	51
1971	Fred Biletnikoff	61	929	15.2	9	49
1972	Fred Biletnikoff	58	802	13.8	7	39
1973	Fred Biletnikoff	48	660	13.8	4	32
1974	Cliff Branch	60	1092	18.2	13	67
1975	Cliff Branch	51	893	17.5	9	53
1976	Dave Casper	53	691	13.0	10	30
1977	Dave Casper	48	584	12.2	6	27
1978	Dave Casper	62	852	13.7	9	44
1979	Cliff Branch	59	844	14.3	6	66
1980	Bob Chandler	49	786	16.0	10	56
1981	Derrick Ramsey	52	674	13.0	4	66
1982	Todd Christensen	42	510	12.1	4	50
1983	Todd Christensen	92	1247	13.6	12	45
1984	Todd Christensen	80	1007	12.6	7	38
1985	Todd Christensen	82	987	12.0	6	48

KICKOFF RETURNS

		No.	Yds.	Avg.	TD	LR
1960	Jack Larscheid	30	852	28.4	0	78
1961	George Fleming	29	588	20.3	0	36
1962	Bo Roberson	27	748	27.7	1	87
1963	Bo Roberson	38	809	21.2	0	58
1964	Bo Roberson	36	975	27.0	0	59
1965	Larry Todd	20	461	23.1	0	50
1966	Pervis Atkins	29	608	21.0	0	35
1967	Dave Grayson	19	405	21.3	0	29
1968	George Atkinson	32	802	25.1	0	60
1969	George Atkinson	16	382	23.9	0	39
1970	George Atkinson	23	574	25.0	0	62
1971	Clarence Davis	27	734	27.2	0	44
1972	Clarence Davis	18	464	25.8	0	49
1973	Clarence Davis	19	504	26.5	0	76
1974	Harold Hart	18	466	25.9	0	67
1975	Harold Hart	17	518	30.5	1	102
1976	Rick Jennings	16	417	26.1	0	55
1977	Carl Garrett	21	420	20.0	0	31
1978	Arthur Whittington	23	473	20.6	0	34
1979	Ira Matthews	35	873	24.9	1	104
1980	Ira Matthews	29	585	20.2	0	45
1981	Arthur Whittington	25	563	22.5	0	47
1982	Greg Pruitt	14	371	28.4	0	55
1983	Cle Montgomery	21	464	22.1	0	48
1984	Dokie Williams	24	621	25.9	0	62
1985	Fulton Walker	21	467	22.2	0	57

All-Time Raider Coaches Roster

NOTE: Coaches listed below (name, college, years with Raiders) are those who have been either head or assistant coaches of the Raiders.

Boghosian, Sam, UCLA, 1979-86
Brown, Willie, Grambling, 1979-86
Cody, Ed, Purdue, 1960
Conkright, Red, Oklahoma, 1962
Dahms, Tom, San Diego State, 1963-78
Davis, Al, Syracuse, 1963-65
Dickson, Genrge, Notre Dame, 1961

Engleberg, Buggsy, East Tennessee State, 1968
Erber, Lew, Montclair State, 1976-81
Erdelatz, Eddie, St. Mary's, 1960-61
Feldman, Marty, Stanford, 1960-62
Flores, Tom, Pacific, 1972-86
Franklin, Chet, Utah, 1980-86
George, Ernie, St. Mary's, 1960
Hall, Sid, Pacific, 1969-70
Holovak, Mike, Boston College, 1971
Kalminar, Tom, Nevada, 1960-62
Kennan, Larry, La Verne, 1982-86
Leggett, Earl, LSU, 1979-86

Madden, John, California Poly, SLO, 1967-78
Maddock, Bob, Notre Dame, 1963
Madro, Joe, Ohio State. 1977-82
Malavasi, Ray, Mississippi State, 1971-72
Marinovich, Marv, Southern Californi. 1968-70
McCabe, Richard, Pittsburgh, 1969-70
Michaels, Walt, Washington & Lee, 1962
Mischak, Bob, West Point, 1973-74,1979-86
Moore, Myrel, California-Davis, 1978-79
Ortmayer, Steve, LaVerne, 1978-86
Polonchek, John, Michigan State, 1967-71

Rauch, John, Georgia, 1963-68
Roach, Paul, Black Hills State, 1972-74
Robinson, John, Oregon, 1975
Scannella, Joe, Lehigh, 1972-77
Shell, Art, Maryland State, 1983-86
Shinnick, Don, UCLA, 1973-77
Spencer, Oliver, Kansas, 1962-79
Sumner, Charles, William & Mary, 1963-68,1979-83
Seeeney, Jim, Portland State, 1978
Walsh, Bill, San Jose State, 1966
Walsh, Tom, U.C. Santa Barbara, 1982-86
Willsey, Ray, California, 1978-85
Wood, Dick, Auurn, 1969-70
Zeman, Bob, Wisconsin, 1971-77, 1984-86

Year-By-Year Raider Scores

Below, Raider scores are listed first, followed by opponent's scores and opponent name (H-home or A-away).

1960 (6-8)
22-37 Houston (H)
16-34 Dallas (H)
14-13 Houston (A)
14-31 Denver (A)
20-19 Dallas Texans (A)
27-14 Boston (H)
9-38 Buffalo (A)
28-27 New York Titans (A)
28-34 Boston (A)
20-7 Buffalo (A)
28-52 Los Angeles Chargers (A)
17-41 Los Angeles Chargers (H)
28-31 New York Titans (H)
48-10 Denver (H)

1961 (2-12)
0-55 Houston (A)
0-44 San Diego (A)
35-42 Dallas Texans (H)
33-19 Denver (H)
24-27 Denver (A)
10-41 San Diego (H)
6-14 New York Titans (H)
31-22 Buffalo (A)
12-23 New York Titans (A)
17-20 Boston (H)
11-43 Dallas Texans (A)
21-26 Buffalo (H)
21-35 Boston (H)
16-47 Houston (H)

1962 (1-13)
17-28 New York Titans (H)
16-26 Dallas Texans (H)
33-42 San Diego (H)
7-44 Denver (A)
6-23 Denver (H)
6-14 Buffalo (A)

16-26 Boston (A)
21-31 New York Titans (A)
20-28 Houston (H)
6-10 Buffalo (H)
7-35 Dallas Texans (A)
21-31 San Diego (A)
17-32 Houston (A)
20-0 Boston (H)

1963 (10-4)
24-13 Houston (A)
35-17 Buffalo (H)
14-20 Boston (H)
7-10 New York Jets (A)
0-12 Buffalo (A)
14-20 Boston (A)
49-26 New York Jets (H)
34-33 San Diego (A)
10-7 Kansas City (H)
22-7 Kansas City (A)
26-10 Denver (A)
41-27 San Diego (H)
35-31 Denver (H)
52-49 Houston (H)

1964 (5-7-2)
14-17 Boston (H)
28-42 Houston (A)
9-21 Kansas City (H)
20-23 Buffalo (A)
13-35 New York (A)
43-43 Boston (A)
40-7 Denver (H)
17-31 San Diego (A)
7-42 Kansas City (A)
20-10 Houston (H)
35-26 New York (H)
20-20 Denver (H)
16-13 Buffalo (H)
21-20 San Diego (H)

1965 (8-5-1)
37-10 Kansas City (H)
6-17 San Diego (H)

21-17 Houston (H)
12-17 Buffalo (A)
24-10 Boston (A)
24-24 New York (A)
30-21 Boston (H)
7-14 Kansas City (A)
33-21 Houston (A)
14-17 Buffalo (H)
28-20 Denver (A)
24-13 Denver (H)
24-14 New York (H)
14-24 San Diego (A)

1966 (8-5-1)
23-14 Miami (A)
0-31 Houston (A)
10-32 Kansas City (H)
20-29 San Diego (H)
21-10 Miami (H)
34-13 Kansas City (A)
24-21 New York (A)
21-24 Boston (A)
38-23 Houston (H)
41-19 San Diego (H)
17-3 Denver (A)
10-31 Buffalo (H)
28-28 New York (H)
28-10 Denver (H)

1967 (13-1)
51-0 Denver (H)
35-7 Boston (H)
23-21 Kansas City (H)
14-27 New York (A)
24-20 Buffalo (A)
48-14 Boston (A)
51-10 San Diego (H)
21-17 Denver (A)
31-17 Miami (H)
44-22 Kansas City (A)
41-21 San Diego (A)
19-7 Houston (A)
38-29 New York (H)
28-21 Buffalo (H)

- **POST-SEASON GAMES**
40-7 Houston
14-33 Green Bay (SUPER BOWL II at Miami)

1968 (12-2)
48-6 Buffalo (A)
47-21 Miami (A)
24-15 Houston (A)
41-10 Boston (A)
14-23 San Diego (H)
10-24 Kansas City (A)
31-10 Cincinnati (H)
38-21 Kansas City (H)
43-7 Denver (A)
43-32 New York (H)
34-0 Cincinnati (A)
13-10 Buffalo (H)
33-27 Denver (H)
34-27 San Diego (A)
- **POST-SEASON GAMES**
41-6 Kansas City (AFL Playoff)
23-27 New York (AFL Championship)

1969 (12-1-1)
21-17 Houston (H)
20-17 Miami (H)
38-23 Boston (A)
20-20 Miami (A)
24-14 Denver (A)
50-21 Buffalo (H)
24-12 San Diego (A)
17-31 Cincinnati (A)
41-10 Denver (H)
21-16 San Diego (H)
27-24 Kansas City (A)
27-14 New York (A)
37-17 Cincinnati (H)
10-6 Kansas City (H)
- **POST-SEASON GAMES**
56-7 Houston (AFL Playoff)
7-17 Kansas City (AFL Championship)

Year-By-Year Raider Scores

1970 (8-4-2)
21-31 Cincinnati (A)
27-27 San Diego (A)
13-20 Miami (A)
35-23 Denver (H)
34-20 Washington (H)
31-14 Pittsburgh (H)
17-17 Kansas City (A)
23-20 Cleveland (H)
24-19 Denver (A)
20-17 San Diego (H)
14-28 Detroit (A)
14-13 New York Jets (A)
20-6 Kansas City (H)
7-38 San Francisco (H)
- **POST-SEASON GAMES**
21-14 Miami (AFC Playoff)
17-27 Baltimore (AFC Championship)

1971 (8-4-2)
6-20 New England (A)
34-0 San Diego (A)
34-20 Cleveland (A)
27-16 Denver (A)
34-10 Philadelphia (H)
31-27 Cincinnati (H)
20-20 Kansas City (H)
21-21 New Orleans (A)
41-21 Houston (H)
34-33 San Diego (H)
14-37 Baltimore (H)
14-23 Atlanta (A)
14-16 Kansas City (A)
21-13 Denver (H)

1972 (10-3-1)
28-34 Pittsburgh (A)
20-14 Green Bay (A)
17-17 San Diego (H)
34-0 Houston (A)
28-16 Buffalo (H)
23-30 Denver (H)
45-17 Los Angeles (H)
14-27 Kansas City (A)
20-14 Cincinnati (A)
37-20 Denver (A)
26-3 Kansas City (H)
21-19 San Diego (A)
24-16 New York Jets (H)
28-21 Chicago (H)
- **POST-SEASON GAMES**
7-13 Pittsburgh (A)

1973 (9-4-1)
16-24 Minnesota (A)
12-7 Miami (H)
3-16 Kansas City (A)
17-10 St. Louis (A)
27-17 San Diego (A)
23-23 Denver (A)
34-21 Baltimore (A)
42-0 New York Giants (H)
9-17 Pittsburgh (A)
3-7 Cleveland (H)
31-3 San Diego (H)
17-6 Houston (A)

37-7 Kansas City (H)
21-17 Denver (H)
- **POST-SEASON GAMES**
33-14 Pittsburgh (AFC Playoff)
10-27 Miami (AFC Championship)

1974 (12-2)
20-21 Buffalo (A)
27-7 Kansas City (H)
17-0 Pittsburgh (A)
40-24 Cleveland (A)
14-10 San Diego (A)
30-27 Cincinnati (H)
35-24 San Francisco (A)
28-17 Denver (A)
35-13 Detroit (H)
17-10 San Diego (H)
17-20 Denver (H)
41-26 New England (H)
7-6 Kansas City (A)
27-23 Dallas (H)
- **POST-SEASON GAMES**
28-26 Miami (AFC Playoff)
13-24 Pittsburgh (AFC Championship)

1975 (11-3)
31-21 Miami (A)
31-20 Baltimore (A)
6-0 San Diego (A)
10-42 Kansas City (A)
10-14 Cincinnati (A)
25-0 San Diego (H)
42-17 Denver (A)
48-10 New Orleans (H)
38-17 Cleveland (H)
26-23 Washington (A) (OT)
37-34 Atlanta (H) (OT)
17-10 Denver (H)
26-27 Houston (H)
28-20 Kansas City (H)
- **POST-SEASON GAMES**
31-28 Cincinnati (AFC Playoff)
10-16 Pittsburgh (AFC Championship)

1976 (13-1)
31-28 Pittsburgh (H)
24-21 Kansas City (A)
14-13 Houston (A)
17-48 New England (A)
27-17 San Diego (A)
17-10 Denver (A)
18-14 Green Bay (H)
19-6 Denver (H)
28-27 Chicago (A)
21-10 Kansas City (H)
26-7 Philadelphia (A)
49-16 Tampa Bay (H)
35-20 Cincinnati (H)
24-0 San Diego (H)
- **POST-SEASON GAMES**
24-21 New England (AFC Playoff)
24-7 Pittsburgh (AFC Championship)
32-14 Minnesota (SUPER BOWL XI, Pasadena)

1977 (11-3)
24-0 San Diego (H)
16-7 Pittsburgh (A)
37-28 Kansas City (A)
26-10 Cleveland (A)
7-30 Denver (H)
28-27 New York Jets (A)
24-14 Denver (A)
44-7 Seattle (H)
34-29 Houston (H)
7-12 San Diego (A)
34-13 Buffalo (H)
14-20 Los Angeles (H)
35-13 Minnesota (H)
21-20 Kansas City (H)
- **POST-SEASON GAMES**
37-31 Baltimore (AFC Playoff) (OT)
17-20 Denver (AFC Champtionship)

1978 (9-7)
6-14 Denver (A)
21-20 San Diego (A)
28-3 Green Bay (A)
14-21 New England (H)
25-19 Chicago (A) (OT)
21-17 Houston (H)
28-6 Kansas City (H)
7-27 Seattle (A)
23-27 San Diego (H)
20-10 Kansas City (A)
34-21 Cincinnati (A)
29-17 Detroit (H)
16-17 Seattle (H)
6-21 Denver (H)
6-23 Miami (A)
27-20 Minnesota (H)

1979 (9-7)
24-17 Los Angeles (A)
10-30 San Diego (A)
10-27 Seattle (A)
7-35 Kansas City (A)
27-3 Denver (H)
13-3 Miami (H)
50-19 Atlanta (H)
19-28 New York Jets (A)
45-22 San Diego (H)
23-10 San Francisco (H)
17-31 Houston (A)
21-24 Kansas City (H)
14-10 Denver (A)
42-35 New Orleans (A)
19-14 Cleveland (H)
24-29 Seattle (H)

1980 (11-5)
27-14 Kansas City (A)
24-30 San Diego (A) (OT)
24-21 Washington (H)
7-24 Buffalo (A)
17-31 Kansas City (H)
38-24 San Diego (H)
45-34 Pittsburgh (A)
33-14 Seattle (H)
16-10 Miami (H)
28-17 Cincinnati (H)

19-17 Seattle (A)
7-10 Philadelphia (A)
9-3 Denver (H)
13-19 Dallas (H)
24-21 Denver (A)
33-17 New York Giants (A)
- **POST-SEASON GAMES**
27-7 Houston (AFL Wildcard Playoff)
14-12 Cleveland (AFC Playoff)
34-27 San Diego (AFC Championship)
27-10 Philadelphia (SUPER BOWL XV, New Orleans)

1981 (7-9)
7-9 Denver (A)
36-10 Minnesota (A)
20-10 Seattle (A)
0-16 Detroit (A)
0-17 Denver (H)
0-27 Kansas City (A)
18-16 Tampa Bay (H)
17-28 Kansas City (H)
27-17 New England (H)
16-17 Houston (A)
33-17 Miami (A)
21-55 San Diego (H)
32-31 Seattle (A)
30-27 Pittsburgh (H)
6-23 Chicago (H)
10-23 San Diego (A)

Howie Long

1982 (8-1)
23–17 San Francisco (A)
38–14 Atlanta (A)
28–24 San Diego (H)
17–31 Cincinnati (A)
28–23 Seattle (H)
21–16 Kansas City (A)
37–31 LA Rams (H)
27–10 Denver (H)
41–34 San Diego (A)
- **POST-SEASON GAMES**
27–10 Cleveland (AFC Playoff Round 1)
14–17 NY Jets (AFC Playoff Round 2)

1983 (12-4)
20–10 Cincinnati (A)
20–6 Houston (H)
27–14 Miami (H)
22–7 Denver (A)
35–37 Washington (A)
21–20 Kansas City (H)
36–38 Seattle (A)
40–38 Dallas (A)
21–34 Seattle (H)
28–20 Kansas City (A)
22–20 Denver (H)
27–24 Buffalo (A)
27–12 NY Giants (H)
42–10 San Diego (A)
24–34 St. Louis (H)
30–14 San Diego (H)
- **POST-SEASON GAMES**
38–10 Pittsburgh (Divisional Playoff)
30–14 Seattle (AFC Championship)
38–9 Washington (SUPER BOWL XVIII, Tampa)

1984 (11-5)
24–14 Houston (A)
28–7 Green Bay (H)
22–20 Kansas City (A)
33–30 San Diego (H)
13–16 Denver (A)
28–14 Seattle (H)
23–20 Minnesota (H)
44–37 San Diego (A)
19–22 Denver (H) (OT)
6–17 Chicago (A)
14–17 Seattle (A)
17–7 Kansas City (H)
21–7 Indianapolis (H)
45–34 Miami (A)
24–3 Detroit (A)
7–13 Pittsburgh (H)
- **POST-SEASON GAME**
7–13 Seattle (AFC Wild Card Playoff)

1985 (12-4)
31–0 New York Jets (H)
20–36 Kansas City (A)
10–34 San Francisco (H)
35–20 New England (A)
19–10 Kansas City (H)
23–13 New Orleans (H)
21–20 Cleveland (A)
34–21 San Diego (H)
3–33 Seattle (A)
34–40 San Diego (A)
13–6 Cincinnati (H)
31–28 Denver (H) (OT)
34–24 Atlanta (H)
17–14 Denver (A) (OT)
13–3 Seattle (H)
16–6 Los Angeles Rams (A)
- **POST-SEASON GAME**
20–27 New England (AFC Playoff)

Raider Preseason Game Results

The following preseason game results are listed by Raiders' score first, then opponent's score, opponent name (site of game).

1960
13–20 Dallas (Kezar)
23–17 New York (Sacramento)
17–24 Los Angeles (Kezar)
26–21 Buffalo (Buffalo)
14–28 Boston (Amherst)

1961
17–35 Houston (Honolulu)
21–48 Denver (Spokane)
7–35 San Diego (San Diego)
49–12 Denver (Candlestick)

1962
3–13 Dallas (Atlanta)
21–20 Boston (Providence)
6–22 Dallas (Midland, TX)
27–33 San Diego (Youell)
12–41 Denver (Stockton)

1963
24–17 Boston (Youell)
35–19 Denver (Youell)
21–35 Kansas City (Seattle)
43–16 New York (Youell)
3–13 San Diego (San Diego)

1964
14–21 Kansas City (Youell)
20–7 Denver (Denver)
34–31 Buffalo (Youell)
34–20 Houston (Las Vegas)
10–24 San Diego (San Diego)

1965
10–3 San Diego (San Diego)
17–27 Denver (Salt Lake City)
23–6 Kansas City (Youell)
17–46 San Diego (Portland, Oregon)
30–20 Denver (Sacramento)

1966
17–26 Houston (Houston)
17–7 San Diego (San Diego)
10–21 Boston (Anaheim)
52–21 Denver (Denver)

1967
24–23 San Diego (Oakland)
24–7 Houston (Oakland)
0–48 Kansas City (Portland, Oregon)
17–21 Denver (North Platte, Neb.)
10–13 San Francisco (Oakland)

1968
12–14 Baltimore (Oakland)
37–7 San Diego (Oakland)
21–31 Kansas City (Kansas City)
26–19 San Francisco (Kezar)
23–7 Denver (Portland, Oregon)

1969
33–0 Dallas Cowboys (Oakland)
17–23 Kansas City (Birmingham, Ala.)
30–34 Baltimore (Oakland)
7–10 San Diego (San Diego)
24–6 New York Jets (Oakland)
42–28 San Francisco (Oakland)

1970
21–33 Baltimore (Oakland)
30–19 Philadelphia (Philadelphia)
23–34 Los Angeles (Los Angeles)
7–37 Green Bay (Oakland)
31–17 San Francisco (San Francisco)
6–20 Pittsburgh (Oakland)

1971
24–25 Philadelphia (Oakland)
41–20 New York Jets (Oakland)
20–7 Los Angeles (Berkeley)
17–13 Green Bay (Green Bay)
34–28 San Francisco (Oakland)
24–3 Baltimore (Jacksonville, Fla.)

1972
31–24 New England (Oakland)
16–0 Baltimore (Oakland)
34–9 Los Angeles (Los Angeles)
31–13 Buffalo (Berkeley)
21–34 San Francisco (San Francisco)
10–16 Dallas (Dallas)

1973
17–17 New England (New England)
27–26 Dallas (Oakland)
16–3 Los Angeles (Berkeley)
10–34 Minnesota (Berkeley)
23–17 San Francisco (Oakland)
17–7 Buffalo (Buffalo)

1974
27–7 Dallas (Oakland)
28–16 Atlanta (Berkeley)
41–10 Detroit (Detroit)
14–25 Philadelphia (Oakland)
20–19 San Francisco (San Francisco)
31–6 New York Jets (Berkeley)

1975
34–0 Detroit (Berkeley)
24–21 Pittsburgh (Berkeley)
22–7 Atlanta (Atlanta)
40–21 San Francisco (Oakland)
31–20 Dallas (Dallas)
0–6 Los Angeles (Los Angeles)

Raider Preseason Game Results

1980
14–33 San Francisco (San Francisco)
31–29 New England (Oakland)
17–34 Washington (Washington)
24–23 Philadelphia (Oakland)

1983
26–23 San Francisco (Los Angeles) (OT)
17–20 New York Jets (Giants' Stadium)
21–27 Chicago (Los Angeles)
17–20 Cleveland (Cleveland)

1976
27–14 Dallas (Oakland)
20–9 St. Louis (Phoenix, Ariz.)
41–17 New York Jets (Yankee Stadium)
14–23 Los Angeles (Oakland)
14–9 San Francisco (San Francisco)
15–28 Seattle (Oakland)

1979
20–13 Dallas (Canton, Ohio)
14–20 Los Angeles (Los Angeles)
41–10 San Francisco (Oakland)
14–35 New England (New England)
48–21 Buffalo (Oakland)

1981
17–16 Atlanta (Oakland)
14–34 Green Bay (Green Bay)
21–23 New England (New England)
21–7 San Francisco (Oakland)

1984
10–13 San Francisco (San Francisco)
21–20 Washington (Washington)
23–29 Miami (Los Angeles)
14–20 New York Jets (Los Angeles)

1977
40–0 Houston (Oakland)
13–20 Chicago (Oakland)
10–12 Seattle (Seattle)
35–7 San Diego (Oakland)
33–0 San Francisco (Oakland)
21–0 Los Angeles (Los Angeles)

1978
14–13 Chicago (Chicago)
7–21 New England (Oakland)
31–14 San Francisco (San Francisco)
3–28 Los Angeles (Oakland)

1982
17–14 San Francisco (San Francisco)
16–30 Detroit (Detroit)
24–3 Green Bay (Los Angeles)
10–37 Cleveland (Los Angeles)

1985
21–28 San Francisco (Los Angeles)
9–14 Washington (Los Angeles)
17–23 Miami (Los Angeles)
26–7 Cleveland (Cleveland)

Raiders vs. All Opponents (1960-85)

Opponent (First met)	W	L	T	Win %
Atlanta Falcons (1971)	4	1	0	.800
Buffalo Bills (1960)	12	11	0	.522
Chicago Bears (1972)	3	2	0	.600
Cincinnati Bengals (1968)	11	4	0	.733
Cleveland Browns (1970)	7	1	0	.875
Dallas Cowboys (1974)	2	1	0	.667
Denver Broncos (1960)	36	13	2	.735
Detroit Lions (1970	3	2	0	.600
Green Bay Packers (1972)	4	0	0	1.000
Houston Oilers (1960)	18	10	0	.643
Indianapolis Colts (1971)	3	1	0	.750
Kansas City Chiefs (1960)	29	20	2	.592
Los Angeles Rams (1972)	4	1	0	.800
Miami Dolphins (1966)	12	2	1	.853
Minnesota Vikings (1973)	4	1	0	.800
New England Patriots (1960)	11	11	1	.500
New Orleans Saints (1971)	3	0	1	1.000
New York Giants (1973)	3	0	0	1.000
New York Jets (1960)	12	9	2	.571
Philadelphia Eagles (1971)	2	1	0	.667
Pittsburgh Steelers (1970)	6	3	0	.667
St. Louis Cardinals (1973)	1	1	0	.500
San Diego Chargers (1960)	32	18	2	.640
San Francisco 49ers (1970)	3	2	0	.600
Seattle Seahawks (1977)	8	8	0	.500
Tampa Bay Buccaneers (1976)	2	0	0	1.000
Washington Redskins (1970)	3	1	0	.750
TOTALS	238	124	11	.657

Jesse Hester

NFL Yearly Standings

The Raiders played in the American Football League from 1960 through 1969. In 1970, with the assimilation of all AFL teams into the National Football League, the Raiders began playing as members of the American Football Conference (AFC), Western Division.

1970

AFC WEST

Team	W	L	T	Pts	Opp
Oakland	8	4	2	300	293
Kansas City	7	5	2	272	244
San Diego	5	6	3	282	278
Denver	5	8	1	253	264

AFC CENTRAL

Team	W	L	T	Pts	Opp
Cincinnati	8	6	0	312	255
Cleveland	7	7	0	286	265
Pittsburgh	5	9	0	210	272
Houston	3	10	1	217	352

AFC EAST

Team	W	L	T	Pts	Opp
Baltimore	11	2	1	312	234
Miami	10	4	0	297	228
NY Jets	4	10	0	255	286
Buffalo	3	10	1	204	337
Boston	2	12	0	149	361

NFC WEST

Team	W	L	T	Pts	Opp
San Francisco	10	3	1	352	267
Los Angeles	9	4	1	325	202
Atlanta	4	8	2	206	261
New Orleans	2	11	1	172	347

NFC CENTRAL

Team	W	L	T	Pts	Opp
Minnesota	12	2	0	299	221
Detroit	10	2	0	347	202
Chicago	6	8	0	256	261
Green Bay	6	8	0	196	293

NFC EAST

Team	W	L	T	Pts	Opp
Dallas	10	4	0	299	221
N.Y. Giants	9	5	0	301	270
St. Louis	8	5	1	325	228
Washington	6	8	0	297	314
Philadelphia	3	10	1	241	332

AFC PLAYOFFS: Oakland 21, Miami 14; Baltimore 17, Cincinnati 0
AFC CHAMPIONSHIP: Baltimore 27, Oakland 17
NFC PLAYOFFS: Dallas 5, Detroit 0; San Francisco 17, Minnesota 14
NFC CHAMPIONSHIP: Dallas 17, San Francisco 10
SUPER BOWL: Baltimore 16, Dallas 13

1971

AFC WEST

Team	W	L	T	Pts	Opp
Kansas City	10	3	1	302	208
Oakland	8	4	2	344	278
San Diego	6	8	0	311	341
Denver	4	9	1	203	275

AFC CENTRAL

Team	W	L	T	Pts	Opp
Cleveland	9	5	0	285	273
Pittsburgh	6	8	0	246	292
Houston	4	9	1	251	330
Cincinnati	4	10	0	284	265

AFC EAST

Team	W	L	T	Pts	Opp
Miami	10	3	1	315	174
Baltimore	10	4	0	313	140
New England	6	8	0	238	325
NY Jets	6	8	0	212	299
Buffalo	1	13	0	184	394

NFC WEST

Team	W	L	T	Pts	Opp
San Francisco	9	5	0	300	216
Los Angeles	8	5	1	313	260
Atlanta	7	6	1	274	277
New Orleans	4	8	2	266	347

NFL CENTRAL

Team	W	L	T	Pts	Opp
Minnesota	11	3	0	245	139
Detroit	7	6	1	341	286
Chicago	6	8	0	185	276
Green Bay	4	8	2	274	298

NFC EAST

Team	W	L	T	Pts	Opp
Dallas	11	3	0	406	222
Washington	9	4	1	276	190
Philadelphia	6	7	1	221	302
St. Louis	4	9	1	231	279
NY Giants	4	10	0	228	362

AFC PLAYOFFS: Miami 27, Kansas City 24 (2 OT); Baltimore 20, Cleveland 3
AFC CHAMPIONSHIP: Miami 21, Baltimore 0
NFC PLAYOFFS: San Francisco 24, Washington 20; Dallas 20, Minnesota 12
NFC CHAMPIONSHIP: Dallas 14, San Francisco 3
SUPER BOWL: Dallas 24, Miami 3

1972

AFC WEST

Team	W	L	T	Pct	Pts	Opp
Oakland	10	3	1	.750	365	248
Kansas City	8	6	0	.571	287	254
Denver	5	9	0	.429	325	350
San Diego	4	9	1	.321	264	344

AFC CENTRAL

Team	W	L	T	Pct	Pts	Opp
Pittsburgh	11	3	0	.786	343	175
Cleveland	10	4	0	.714	268	249
Cincinnati	8	6	0	.571	299	229
Houston	1	13	0	.071	164	380

AFC EAST

Team	W	L	T	Pct	Pts	Opp
Miami	14	0	0	1.000	385	171
NY Jets	7	7	0	.500	367	324
Baltimore	5	9	0	.429	235	252
Buffalo	4	9	1	.321	257	377
New England	3	11	0	.214	192	446

NFC WEST

Team	W	L	T	Pct	Pts	Opp
San Francisco	8	5	1	.607	353	249
Atlanta	7	7	0	.500	269	274
Los Angeles	6	7	1	.464	291	286
New Orleans	2	11	1	.179	215	261

NFC CENTRAL

Team	W	L	T	Pct	Pts	Opp
Green Bay	10	4	0	.714	304	226
Detroit	8	5	1	.607	339	290
Minnesota	7	7	0	.500	301	252
Chicago	4	9	1	.321	225	275

NFC EAST

Team	W	L	T	Pct	Pts	Opp
Washington	11	3	0	.786	336	218
Dallas	10	4	0	.714	319	240
NY Giants	8	6	0	.571	331	247
St. Louis	4	9	1	.321	193	303
Philadelphia	2	11	1	.179	145	352

AFC PLAYOFFS: Pittsburgh 13, Oakland 7; Miami 20, Cleveland 14
AFC CHAMPIONSHIP: Miami 21, Pittsburgh 17
NFC PLAYOFFS: Dallas 30, San Francisco 28; Washington 16, Green Bay 3
NFC CHAMPIONSHIP: Washington 26, Dallas 3
SUPER BOWL: Miami 14, Washington 7

1973

AFC WEST

Team	W	L	T	Pct	Pts	Opp
Oakland	9	4	1	.679	292	175
Denver	7	5	2	.571	354	296
Kansas City	7	5	2	.571	231	192
San Diego	2	11	1	.179	188	386

AFC CENTRAL

Team	W	L	T	Pct	Pts	Opp
Cincinnati	10	4	0	.714	286	231
Pittsburgh	10	4	0	.714	347	210
Cleveland	7	5	2	.571	234	255
Houston	1	13	0	.071	199	447

AFC EAST

Team	W	L	T	Pct	Pts	Opp
Miami	12	2	0	.857	343	150
Buffalo	9	5	0	.643	259	230
New England	5	9	0	.357	258	300
Baltimore	4	10	0	.286	226	341
NY Jets	4	10	0	.286	240	306

NFC WEST

Team	W	L	T	Pct	Pts	Opp
Los Angeles	12	2	0	.857	388	178
Atlanta	9	5	0	.643	318	224
New Orleans	5	9	0	.357	163	312
San Francisco	5	9	0	.357	262	319

NFC CENTRAL

Team	W	L	T	Pct	Pts	Opp
Minnesota	12	2	0	.857	296	168
Detroit	6	7	1	.464	271	247
Green Bay	5	7	2	.429	202	259
Chicago	3	11	0	.241	195	334

NFC EAST

Team	W	L	T	Pct	Pts	Opp
Dallas	10	4	0	.714	382	203
Washington	10	4	0	.714	325	198
Philadelphia	5	8	1	.393	310	393
St. Louis	4	9	1	.321	286	365
NY Giants	2	11	1	.179	226	362

AFC PLAYOFFS: Oakland 33, Pittsburgh 14; Miami 34, Cincinnati 16
AFC CHAMPIONSHIP: Miami 27, Oakland 10
NFC PLAYOFFS. Minnesota 27, Washington 20; Dallas 27, Los Angeles 16
NFC CHAMPIONSHIP: Minnesota 27, Dallas 10
SUPER BOWL: Miami 24, Minnesota 7

NFL Yearly Standings

1974

AFC WEST

Team	W	L	T	Pct	Pts	Opp
Oakland	12	2	0	.857	355	228
Denver	7	6	1	.536	302	294
Kansas City	5	9	0	.357	233	293
San Diego	5	9	0	.357	212	285

AFC CENTRAL

Team	W	L	T	Pct	Pts	Opp
Pittsburgh	10	3	1	.750	305	189
Cincinnati	7	7	0	.500	283	259
Houston	7	7	0	.500	236	282
Cleveland	4	10	0	.286	251	344

AFC EAST

Team	W	L	T	Pct	Pts	Opp
Miami	11	3	0	.786	327	216
Buffalo	9	5	0	.643	348	289
New England	7	7	0	.500	264	244
NY Jets	7	7	0	.500	279	300
Baltimore	2	12	0	.143	190	329

NFC WEST

Team	W	L	T	Pct	Pts	Opp
Los Angeles	10	4	0	.714	263	181
San Francisco	6	8	0	.429	226	236
New Orleans	5	9	0	.357	166	263
Atlanta	3	11	0	.214	111	271

NFC CENTRAL

Team	W	L	T	Pct	Pts	Opp
Minnesota	10	4	0	.714	310	195
Detroit	7	7	0	.500	256	270
Green Bay	6	8	0	.429	210	206
Chicago	4	10	0	.286	152	279

NFC EAST

Team	W	L	T	Pct	Pts	Opp
St. Louis	10	4	0	.714	285	218
Washington	10	4	0	.714	320	196
Dallas	8	6	0	.571	297	235
Philadelphia	7	7	0	.500	242	217
NY Giants	2	12	0	.143	195	299

AFC PLAYOFFS: Oakland 28, Miami 26; Pittsburgh 32, Buffalo 14
AFC CHAMPIONSHIP:
Pittsburgh 24, Oakland 13
NFC PLAYOFFS: Minnesota 30, St. Louis 14; Los Angeles 19, Washington 10
NFC CHAMPIONSHIP:
Minnesota 14, Los Angeles 10
SUPER BOWL: Pittsburgh 16, Minnesota 6

1975

AFC WEST

Team	W	L	T	Pct	Pts	Opp
Oakland	11	3	0	.786	375	255
Denver	6	8	0	.429	254	307
Kansas City	5	9	0	.357	282	341
San Diego	2	12	0	.143	189	345

AFC CENTRAL

Team	W	L	T	Pct	Pts	Opp
Pittsburgh	12	2	0	.587	373	162
Cincinnati	11	3	0	.786	340	246
Houston	10	4	0	.714	293	226
Cleveland	3	11	0	.214	218	372

AFL EAST

Team	W	L	T	Pct	Pts	Opp
Baltimore	10	4	0	.714	395	269
Miami	10	4	0	.714	357	222
Buffalo	8	6	0	.571	420	355
New England	3	11	0	.214	258	358
NY Jets	3	11	0	.214	258	433

NFC WEST

Team	W	L	T	Pct	Pts	Opp
Los Angeles	12	2	0	.857	312	135
San Francisco	5	9	0	.357	255	286
Atlanta	4	10	0	.286	240	289
New Orleans	2	12	0	.143	165	360

NFC CENTRAL

Team	W	L	T	Pct	Pts	Opp
Minnesota	12	2	0	.857	377	180
Detroit	7	7	0	.500	245	262
Chicago	4	10	0	.286	191	379
Green Bay	4	10	0	.286	226	285

NFC EAST

Team	W	L	T	Pct	Pts	Opp
St. Louis	11	3	0	.786	356	276
Dallas	10	4	0	.714	350	268
Washington	8	6	0	.571	325	276
NY Giants	5	9	0	.357	216	306
Philadelphia	4	10	0	.286	225	302

AFC PLAYOFFS: Oakland 31, Cincinnati 28; Pittsburgh 28, Baltimore 10
AFC CHAMPIONSHIP:
Pittsburgh 16, Oakland 10
NFC PLAYOFFS: Dallas 17, Minnesota 14; Los Angeles 35, St. Louis 23
NFC CHAMPIONSHIP:
Dallas 37, Los Angeles 7
SUPER BOWL: Pittsburgh 21, Dallas 17

1976

AFC WEST

Team	W	L	T	Pct	Pts	Opp
Oakland	13	1	0	.929	350	237
Denver	9	5	0	.643	315	206
San Diego	6	8	0	.429	248	285
Kansas City	5	9	0	.357	290	376
Tampa Bay	0	14	0	.000	125	412

AFC CENTRAL

Team	W	L	T	Pct	Pts	Opp
Pittsburgh	10	4	0	.714	342	138
Cincinnati	10	4	0	.714	335	210
Cleveland	9	5	0	.643	267	287
Houston	5	9	0	.357	222	273

AFC EAST

Team	W	L	T	Pct	Pts	Opp
Baltimore	11	3	0	.786	417	246
New England	11	3	0	.786	376	236
Miami	6	8	0	.429	263	264
NY Jets	3	11	0	.214	169	383
Buffalo	2	12	0	.143	245	363

NFC WEST

Team	W	L	T	Pct	Pts	Opp
Los Angeles	10	3	1	.750	351	190
San Francisco	8	6	0	.571	270	190
Atlanta	4	10	0	.286	172	312
New Orleans	4	10	0	.286	253	346
Seattle	2	12	0	.143	229	429

NFC CENTRAL

Team	W	L	T	Pct	Pts	Opp
Minnesota	11	2	1	.821	305	176
Chicago	7	7	0	.500	253	216
Detroit	6	8	0	.429	262	220
Green Bay	5	9	0	.357	218	299

NFC EAST

Team	W	L	T	Pct	Pts	Opp
Dallas	11	3	0	.786	296	194
Washington	10	4	0	.714	291	217
St. Louis	10	4	0	.714	309	267
Philadelphia	4	10	0	.286	165	286
NY Giants	3	11	0	.214	170	250

AFC PLAYOFFS: Oakland 24, New England 21; Pittsburgh 40, Baltimore 14
AFC CHAMPIONSHIP:
Oakland 24, Pittsburgh 7
NFC PLAYOFFS: Minnesota 35, Washington 20; Los Angeles 14, Dallas 12
NFC CHAMPIONSHIP:
Minnesota 24, Los Angeles 13
SUPER BOWL: Oakland 32, Minnesota 14

1977

AFC WEST

Team	W	L	T	Pct	Pts	Opp
Denver	12	2	0	.857	274	148
Oakland	11	3	0	.786	351	230
San Diego	7	7	0	.500	222	205
Seattle	5	9	0	.357	282	373
Kansas City	2	12	0	.143	225	349

AFC CENTRAL

Team	W	L	T	Pct	Pts	Opp
Pittsburgh	9	5	0	.643	283	243
Houston	8	6	0	.571	299	230
Cincinnati	8	6	0	.571	238	235
Cleveland	6	8	0	.429	269	267

AFC EAST

Team	W	L	T	Pct	Pts	Opp
Baltimore	10	4	0	.714	295	221
Miami	10	4	0	.714	313	197
New England	9	5	0	.643	278	217
New York	3	11	0	.214	191	300
Buffalo	3	11	0	.214	160	313

NFC WEST

Team	W	L	T	Pct	Pts	Opp
Los Angeles	10	4	0	.714	302	146
Atlanta	7	7	0	.500	179	129
San Francisco	5	9	0	.357	220	260
New Orleans	3	11	0	.214	232	336

NFC WEST

Team	W	L	T	Pct	Pts	Opp
Minnesota	9	5	0	.643	231	227
Chicago	9	5	0	.643	255	253
Detroit	6	8	0	.429	183	252
Green Bay	4	10	0	.286	134	219
Tampa Bay	2	12	0	.143	103	223

NFC EAST

Team	W	L	T	Pct	Pts	Opp
Dallas	12	2	0	.857	345	212
Washington	9	5	0	.643	196	189
St. Louis	7	7	0	.500	272	287
Philadelphia	5	9	0	.357	220	207
NY Giants	5	9	0	.357	181	265

AFC PLAYOFFS: Oakland 37, Baltimore 31; Denver 34, Pittsburgh 21
AFC CHAMPIONSHIP:
Denver 20, Oakland 17
NFC PLAYOFFS: Dallas 37, Chicago 7; Minnesota 14, Los Angeles 7
NFC CHAMPIONSHIP:
Dallas 23, Minnesota 6
SUPER BOWL: Dallas 27, Denver 10

NFL Yearly Standings

1978

AFC WEST
Team	W	L	T	Pct	Pts	Opp
Denver	10	6	0	.625	282	198
Oakland	9	7	0	.563	311	283
Seattle	9	7	0	.563	345	358
San Diego	9	7	0	.563	355	309
Kansas City	4	12	0	.250	243	327

AFC CENTRAL
Team	W	L	T	Pct	Pts	Opp
Pittsburgh	14	2	0	.875	356	195
Houston	10	6	0	.625	283	298
Cleveland	8	8	0	.500	334	356
Cincinnati	4	12	0	.250	252	284

AFC EAST
Team	W	L	T	Pct	Pts	Opp
New England	11	5	0	.688	358	286
Miami	11	5	0	.688	372	254
NY Jets	8	8	0	.500	359	364
Buffalo	5	11	0	.313	302	354
Baltimore	5	11	0	.313	239	421

NFC WEST
Team	W	L	T	Pct	Pts	Opp
Los Angeles	12	4	0	.750	316	245
Atlanta	9	7	0	.563	240	290
New Orleans	7	9	0	.438	281	298
San Francisco	2	14	0	.125	219	350

NFC CENTRAL
Team	W	L	T	Pct	Pts	Opp
Minnesota	8	7	1	.531	294	306
Green Bay	8	7	1	.531	249	269
Detroit	7	9	0	.438	290	300
Chicago	7	9	0	.438	253	274
Tampa Bay	5	11	0	.313	241	259

NFC EAST
Team	W	L	T	Pct	Pts	Opp
Dallas	12	4	0	.750	384	208
Philadelphia	9	7	0	.563	270	250
Washington	8	8	0	.500	273	283
St. Louis	6	10	0	.375	248	296
NY Giants	6	10	0	.375	264	298

AFC WILDCARD PLAYOFF:
Houston 17, Miami 9
AFC PLAYOFFS: Pittsburgh 33, Denver 10;
Houston 31, New England 14
AFC CHAMPIONSHIP:
Pittsburgh 34, Houston 5
NFC WILDCARD PLAYOFF:
Atlanta 14, Philadelphia 13
NFC PLAYOFFS: Dallas 27, Atlanta 20;
Los Angeles 34, Minnesota 10
NFC CHAMPIONSHIP:
Dallas 28, Los Angeles 0
SUPER BOWL: Pittsburgh 35, Dallas 31

1979

AFC WEST
Team	W	L	T	Pct	Pts	Opp
San Diego	12	4	0	.750	411	246
Denver	10	6	0	.625	289	262
Seattle	9	7	0	.563	378	372
Oakland	9	7	0	.563	365	337
Kansas City	7	9	0	.438	238	262

AFC CENTRAL
Team	W	L	T	Pct	Pts	Opp
Pittsburgh	12	4	0	.750	416	262
Houston	11	5	0	.688	362	331
Cleveland	9	7	0	.563	359	352
Cincinnati	4	12	0	.250	337	421

AFC EAST
Team	W	L	T	Pct	Pts	Opp
Miami	10	6	0	.625	341	257
New England	9	7	0	.563	411	326
NY Jets	8	8	0	.500	337	383
Buffalo	7	9	0	.438	268	279
Baltimore	5	11	0	.313	271	351

NFC WEST
Team	W	L	T	Pct	Pts	Opp
Los Angeles	9	7	0	.563	323	309
New Orleans	8	8	0	.500	370	360
Atlanta	6	10	0	.375	300	388
San Francisco	2	14	0	.125	308	416

NFC CENTRAL
Team	W	L	T	Pct	Pts	Opp
Tampa Bay	10	6	0	.625	273	237
Chicago	10	6	0	.625	306	249
Minnesota	7	9	0	.438	259	337
Green Bay	5	11	0	.313	246	316
Detroit	2	14	0	.125	219	365

NFC EAST
Team	W	L	T	Pct	Pts	Opp
Dallas	11	5	0	.688	371	313
Philadelphia	11	5	0	.688	339	282
Washington	10	6	0	.625	348	295
NY Giants	6	10	0	.375	237	323
St. Louis	5	11	0	.313	307	358

AFC WILDCARD PLAYOFF:
Houston 13, Denver 7
AFC PLAYOFFS: Houston 17, San Diego
14; Pittsburgh 34, Miami 14
AFC CHAMPIONSHIP:
Pittsburgh 27, Houston 13
NFC WILDCARD PLAYOFF:
Philadelphia 27, Chicago 17
NFC PLAYOFFS: Tampa Bay 24,
Phillladelphia 17;
Los Angeles 21, Dallas 19
NFC CHAMPIONSHIP:
Los Angeles 9, Tampa Bay 0
SUPER BOWL: Pittsburgh 31,
Los Angeles 19

1980

AFC WEST
Team	W	L	T	Pct	Pts	Opp
San Diego	11	5	0	.688	418	327
Oakland	11	5	0	.688	364	306
Kansas City	8	8	0	.500	319	336
Denver	8	8	0	.500	310	323
Seattle	4	12	0	.250	291	408

AFC CENTRAL
Team	W	L	T	Pct	Pts	Opp
Cleveland	11	5	0	.688	357	310
Houston	11	5	0	.688	295	251
Pittsburgh	9	7	0	.563	352	313
Cincinnati	6	10	0	.375	244	312

AFC EAST
Team	W	L	T	Pct	Pts	Opp
Buffalo	11	5	0	.688	320	260
New England	10	6	0	.625	441	325
Miami	8	8	0	.500	266	305
Baltimore	7	9	0	.438	355	387
NY Jets	4	12	0	.250	302	395

NFC WEST
Team	W	L	T	Pct	Pts	Opp
Atlanta	12	4	0	.750	305	272
Los Angeles	11	5	0	.688	424	289
San Francisco	6	10	0	.375	320	415
New Orleans	1	15	0	.063	291	487

NFC CENTRAL
Team	W	L	T	Pct	Pts	Opp
Minnesota	9	7	0	.563	317	308
Detroit	9	7	0	.563	334	272
Chicago	7	9	0	.438	304	264
Tampa Bay	5	10	1	.344	271	341
Green Bay	5	10	1	.344	231	371

NFC EAST
Team	W	L	T	Pct	Pts	Opp
Philadelphia	12	4	0	.750	384	222
Dallas	12	4	0	.750	454	311
Washington	6	10	0	.375	261	293
St. Louis	5	11	0	.313	299	350
NY Giants	4	12	0	.250	249	425

AFC WILDCARD PLAYOFF:
Oakland 27, Houston 7
AFC PLAYOFFS: Oakland 14, Cleveland 12;
San Diego 20, Buffalo 14
AFC CHAMPIONSHIP:
Oakland 34, San Diego 27
NFC WILDCARD PLAYOFF:
Dallas 34, Los Angeles 13
NFC PLAYOFFS: Philadelphia 31, Minnesota
16; Dallas 30, Atlanta 27
NFC CHAMPIONSHIP:
Philadelphia 20, Dallas 7
SUPER BOWL: Oakland 27, Philadelphia 10

1981

AFC WEST
Team	W	L	T	Pct	Pts	Opp
San Diego	10	6	0	.625	478	390
Denver	10	6	0	.625	321	289
Kansas City	9	7	0	.563	343	290
Oakland	7	9	0	.438	273	343
Seattle	6	10	0	.375	322	388

AFC CENTRAL
Team	W	L	T	Pct	Pts	Opp
Cincinnati	12	4	0	.750	421	304
Pittsburgh	8	8	0	.500	356	297
Houston	7	9	0	.438	281	355
Cleveland	5	11	0	.313	276	375

AFC EAST
Team	W	L	T	Pct	Pts	Opp
Miami	11	4	1	.719	345	275
NY Jets	10	5	1	.656	355	287
Buffalo	10	6	0	.625	311	276
Baltimore	2	14	0	.125	259	533
New England	2	14	0	.125	322	370

NFC WEST
Team	W	L	T	Pct	Pts	Opp
San Francisco	13	3	0	.813	357	250
Atlanta	7	9	0	.438	426	355
Los Angeles	6	10	0	.375	303	351
New Orleans	4	12	0	.250	207	378

NFC CENTRAL
Team	W	L	T	Pct	Pts	Opp
Tampa Bay	9	7	0	.563	315	268
Detroit	8	8	0	.500	397	322
Green Bay	8	8	0	.500	324	361
Minnesota	7	9	0	.438	325	369
Chicago	6	10	0	.375	253	324

NFC EAST
Team	W	L	T	Pct	Pts	Opp
Dallas	12	4	0	.750	367	277
Philadelphia	10	6	0	.625	368	221
NY Giants	9	7	0	.563	295	257
Washington	8	8	0	.500	347	349
St. Louis	7	9	0	.438	315	408

AFC WILDCARD PLAYOFF:
Buffalo 31, New York Jets 27
AFC PLAYOFFS: Cincinnati 28, Buffalo 21;
San Diego 41, Miami 38
AFC CHAMPIONSHIP:
Cincinnati 27, San Diego 7
NFC WILDCARD PLAYOFF:
New York Giants 27, Philadelphia 21
NFC PLAYOFFS: San Francisco 38, New
York Giants 24; Dallas 38, Tampa Bay 0
NFC CHAMPIONSHIP:
San Francisco 28, Dallas 27
SUPER BOWL: San Francisco 26,
Cincinnati 21

NFL Yearly Standings

1982

AFC WEST

Team	W	L	T	Pct	Pts	Opp
LA Raiders	8	1	0	.889	260	200
San Diego	6	3	0	.667	288	221
Seattle	4	5	0	.444	108	154
Kansas City	3	6	0	.333	176	184
Denver	2	7	0	.222	148	126

AFC CENTRAL

Team	W	L	T	Pct	Pts	Opp
Cincinnati	7	2	0	.778	232	177
Pittsburgh	6	3	0	.667	204	146
Cleveland	4	5	0	.444	140	154
Houston	1	8	0	.111	136	245

AFC EAST

Team	W	L	T	Pct	Pts	Opp
Miami	7	2	0	.778	188	132
NY Jets	6	3	0	.667	241	166
New England	5	4	0	.556	243	157
Buffalo	4	5	0	.444	150	154
Baltimore	0	8	1	.063	113	236

NFC WEST

Team	W	L	T	Pct	Pts	Opp
Atlanta	5	4	0	.556	183	199
New Orleans	4	5	0	.444	129	166
San Francisco	3	6	0	.333	209	206
LA Rams	2	7	0	.222	200	250

NFC CENTRAL

Team	W	L	T	Pct	Pts	Opp
Green Bay	5	3	1	.602	226	169
Tampa Bay	5	4	0	.556	158	178
Minnesota	5	4	0	.556	187	198
Detroit	4	5	0	.444	196	161
Chicago	3	6	0	.333	141	174

NFC EAST

Team	W	L	T	Pct	Pts	Opp
Washington	8	1	0	.889	190	128
Dallas	6	3	0	.667	226	145
St. Louis	5	3	0	.556	135	170
NY Giants	4	5	0	.444	155	171
Philadelphia	3	6	0	.333	199	186

AFC FIRST ROUND PLAYOFFS:
Los Angeles Raiders 27, Cleveland 10;
Miami 28, New England 13; San Diego 31,
Pittsburgh 28; New York Jets 44,
Cincinnati 17
AFC SECOND ROUND PLAYOFFS:
New York Jets 17, Los Angeles Raiders 14;
Miami 34, San Diego 13
AFC CHAMPIONSHIP:
Miami 17, New York Jets 0
NFC FIRST ROUND PLAYOFFS:
Washington 31, Detroit 7; Green Bay 41,
St. Louis 16; Dallas 30, Tampa Bay 17;
Minnesota 30, Atlanta 24
NFC SECOND ROUND PLAYOFFS:
Dallas 37, Green Bay 26; Washington 21,
Minnesota 7
NFC CHAMPIONSHIP:
Washington 31, Dallas 17
SUPER BOWL: Washington 27, Miami 17

1983

AFC WEST

Team	W	L	T	Pct	Pts	Opp
LA Raiders	12	4	0	.750	442	338
Seattle†	9	7	0	.563	403	397
Denver†	9	7	0	.563	302	327
Kansas City	6	10	0	.375	386	367
San Diego	6	10	0	.375	358	462

AFC CENTRAL

Team	W	L	T	Pct	Pts	Opp
Pittsburgh	10	6	0	.625	355	303
Cleveland	9	7	0	.563	356	342
Cincinnati	7	9	0	.438	346	302
Houston	2	14	0	.125	288	460

AFC EAST

Team	W	L	T	Pct	Pts	Opp
Miami	12	4	0	.750	389	250
Buffalo	8	8	0	.500	283	351
New England	8	8	0	.500	274	289
Baltimore	7	9	0	.438	264	354
NY Jets	7	9	0	.438	313	331

NFC WEST

Team	W	L	T	Pct	Pts	Opp
San Francisco	10	6	0	.625	432	293
LA Rams†	9	7	0	.563	361	344
New Orleans	8	8	0	.500	319	337
Atlanta	7	9	0	.438	370	389

NFC CENTRAL

Team	W	L	T	Pct	Pts	Opp
Detroit	9	7	0	.563	347	286
Chicago	8	8	0	.500	311	301
Green Bay	8	8	0	.500	429	439
Minnesota	8	8	0	.500	316	348
Tampa Bay	2	14	0	.125	241	380

NFC EAST

Team	W	L	T	Pct	Pts	Opp
Washington	14	2	0	.875	541	333
Dallas†	12	4	0	.750	479	360
St. Louis	8	7	1	.533	374	428
Philadelphia	5	11	0	.313	233	322
NY Giants	3	12	1	.200	267	347

† Wild Card for Playoffs

AFC FIRST ROUND:
Seattle 31, Denver 7
AFC DIVISIONAL PLAYOFFS: Seattle 27,
Miami 20; Los Angeles Raiders 38,
Pittsburgh 10
AFC CHAMPIONSHIP:
Los Angeles Raiders 30, Seattle 14
NFC FIRST ROUND:
Los Angeles Rams 24, Dallas 17
NFC DIVISIONAL PLAYOFFS: Washington
51, Los Angeles Rams 7; San Francisco
24, Detroit 23
NFC CHAMPIONSHIP:
Washington 24, San Francisco 21
SUPER BOWL: Los Angeles Raiders 38,
Washington 9

1984

AFC WEST

Team	W	L	T	Pct	Pts	Opp
Denver	13	3	0	.813	353	241
Seattle†	12	4	0	.750	418	282
LA Raiders†	11	5	0	.688	368	278
Kansas City	8	8	0	.500	314	324
San Diego	7	9	0	.438	394	413

AFC CENTRAL

Team	W	L	T	Pct	Pts	Opp
Pittsburgh	9	7	0	.563	387	310
Cincinnati	8	8	0	.500	339	339
Cleveland	5	11	0	.313	250	297
Houston	3	13	0	.188	240	437

AFC EAST

Team	W	L	T	Pct	Pts	Opp
Miami	14	2	0	.857	513	298
New England	9	7	0	.563	362	352
NY Jets	7	9	0	.438	332	364
Indianapolis	4	12	0	.250	239	414
Buffalo	2	14	0	.125	250	454

NFC WEST

Team	W	L	T	Pct	Pts	Opp
San Francisco	15	1	0	.938	475	227
LA Rams†	10	6	0	.625	346	316
New Orleans	7	9	0	.438	298	361
Atlanta	4	12	0	.250	281	382

NFC CENTRAL

Team	W	L	T	Pct	Pts	Opp
Chicago	10	6	0	.625	325	248
Green Bay	8	8	0	.500	390	309
Tampa Bay	6	10	0	.375	335	380
Detroit	4	11	1	.281	283	408
Minnesota	3	13	0	.188	276	484

NFC EAST

Team	W	L	T	Pct	Pts	Opp
Washington	11	5	0	.688	426	310
NY Giants†	9	7	0	.563	299	301
St. Louis	9	7	0	.563	423	345
Dallas	9	7	0	.563	308	308
Philadelphia	6	9	1	.406	278	320

† Wild Card for Playoffs

AFC WILD CARD PLAYOFF:
Seattle 13, Los Angeles Raiders 7
AFC DIVISIONAL PLAYOFFS: Miami 31,
Seattle 10; Pittsburgh 24 Denver 17
AFC CHAMPIONSHIP:
Miami 45, Pittsburgh 28
NFC WILD CARD PLAYOFF: New York
Giants 16, Los Angeles Rams 13
NFC DIVISIONAL PLAYOFFS: San Francisco
21, New York Giants 10; Chicago 23,
Washington 19
NFC CHAMPIONSHIP:
San Francisco 23, Chicago 0
SUPER BOWL:
San Francisco 38, Miami 16

1985

AFC WEST

Team	W	L	T	Pct	Pts	Opp
LA Raiders	12	4	0	.750	354	308
Denver	11	5	0	.688	380	329
Seattle	8	8	0	.500	349	303
San Diego	8	8	0	.500	467	435
Kansas City	6	10	0	.375	317	360

AFC CENTRAL

Team	W	L	T	Pct	Pts	Opp
Cleveland	8	8	0	.500	287	294
Cincinnati	7	9	0	.438	441	437
Pittsburgh	7	9	0	.438	379	355
Houston	5	11	0	.313	284	412

AFC EAST

Team	W	L	T	Pct	Pts	Opp
Miami	12	4	0	.750	428	320
NY Jets†	11	5	0	.688	393	264
New England†	11	5	0	.688	362	290
Indianapolis	5	11	0	.313	320	386
Buffalo	2	14	0	.125	200	381

NFC WEST

Team	W	L	T	Pct	Pts	Opp
LA Rams	11	5	0	.688	340	277
San Francisco†	10	6	0	.625	411	263
New Orleans	5	11	0	.313	294	401
Atlanta	4	12	0	.250	282	452

NFC CENTRAL

Team	W	L	T	Pct	Pts	Opp
Chicago	15	1	0	.938	456	198
Green Bay	8	8	0	.500	337	355
Minnesota	7	9	0	.438	346	359
Detroit	7	9	0	.438	307	366
Tampa Bay	2	14	0	.125	294	448

NFC EAST

Team	W	L	T	Pct	Pts	Opp
Dallas	10	6	0	.625	357	333
NY Giants†	10	6	0	.625	399	283
Washington	10	6	0	.625	297	221
Philadelphia	7	9	0	.438	286	310
St. Louis	5	11	0	.313	278	414

† Wild Card for Playoffs

AFC WILD CARD PLAYOFF:
New England 26, New York Jets 14
AFC DIVISIONAL PLAYOFFS: Miami 24,
Cleveland 21; New England 27, Los
Angeles Raiders 20
AFC CHAMPIONSHIP:
New England 31, Miami 14
NFC WILD CARD PLAYOFF: New York
Giants 21, San Francisco 3
NFC DIVISIONAL PLAYOFFS: Chicago 21,
New York Giants 0; Los Angeles Rams 20,
Dallas 0
NFC CHAMPIONSHIP:
Chicago 24, Los Angeles Rams 0
SUPER BOWL:
Chicago 46, New England 10

AFL Yearly Standings

1960

WESTERN DIVISION

Team	W	L	T	Pts	Opp
Los Angeles	10	4	0	373	336
Dallas	8	6	0	362	253
Oakland	6	8	0	319	399
Denver	4	9	1	309	393

EASTERN DIVISION

Team	W	L	T	Pts	Opp
Houston	10	4	0	379	285
New York	7	7	0	382	399
Buffalo	5	8	1	296	303
Boston	5	9	0	286	349

CHAMPIONSHIP GAME:
Houston 24, Los Angeles 16

1961

WESTERN DIVISION

Team	W	L	T	Pts	Opp
San Diego	12	2	0	396	319
Dallas	6	8	0	334	343
Denver	3	11	0	251	432
Oakland	2	12	0	237	458

EASTERN DIVISION

Team	W	L	T	Pts	Opp
Houston	10	3	1	513	242
Boston	9	4	1	413	313
New York	7	7	0	301	390
Buffalo	6	8	0	294	342

CHAMPIONSHIP GAME:
Houston 10, San Diego 3

1962

WESTERN DIVISION

Team	W	L	T	Pts	Opp
Dallas	11	3	0	389	233
Denver	7	7	0	353	334
San Diego	4	10	0	314	392
Oakland	1	13	0	213	370

EASTERN DIVISION

Team	W	L	T	Pts	Opp
Houston	11	3	0	387	270
Boston	9	4	1	346	295
Buffalo	7	6	1	309	272
New York	5	9	0	278	423

CHAMPIONSHIP GAME:
Dallas 20, Houston 17

1963

WESTERN DIVISION

Team	W	L	T	Pts	Opp
San Diego	11	3	0	399	256
Oakland	10	4	0	363	288
Kansas City	5	7	2	347	263
Denver	2	11	1	301	473

EASTERN DIVISION

Team	W	L	T	Pts	Opp
Buffalo*	7	6	1	304	291
Boston*	7	6	1	317	257
Houston	6	8	0	302	372
New York	5	8	1	249	399

*Boston won playoff game 26-8

CHAMPIONSHIP GAME:
San Diego 51, Boston 10

1964

WESTERN DIVISION

Team	W	L	T	Pts	Opp
San Diego	8	5	1	341	300
Kansas City	7	7	0	366	306
Oakland	5	7	2	303	350
Denver	2	11	1	240	438

EASTERN DIVISION

Team	W	L	T	Pts	Opp
Buffalo	12	2	0	400	242
Boston	10	3	1	365	297
New York	5	8	1	278	315
Houston	4	10	0	310	355

CHAMPIONSHIP GAME:
Buffalo 20, San Diego 7

1965

WESTERN DIVISION

Team	W	L	T	Pts	Opp
San Diego	9	2	3	340	227
Oakland	8	5	1	298	239
Kansas City	7	5	2	322	285
Denver	4	10	0	303	392

EASTERN DIVISION

Team	W	L	T	Pts	Opp
Buffalo	10	3	1	313	226
New York	5	8	1	285	303
Boston	4	8	2	244	302
Houston	4	10	0	298	429

CHAMPIONSHIP GAME:
Buffalo 23, San Diego 0

1966

WESTERN DIVISION

Team	W	L	T	Pts	Opp
Kansas City	11	2	1	448	276
Oakland	8	5	1	315	288
San Diego	7	6	1	335	284
Denver	4	10	0	196	381

EASTERN DIVISION

Team	W	L	T	Pts	Opp
Buffalo	9	4	1	358	255
Boston	8	4	2	315	283
New York	6	6	2	322	312
Houston	3	11	0	335	396
Miami	3	11	0	213	362

CHAMPIONSHIP GAME:
Kansas City 31, Buffalo 7
WORLD CHAMPIONSHIP GAME:
Green Bay 35, Kansas City 10

1967

WESTERN DIVISION

Team	W	L	T	Pts	Opp
Oakland	13	1	0	468	233
Kansas City	9	5	0	408	254
San Diego	8	5	1	360	352
Denver	3	11	0	256	409

EASTERN DIVISION

Team	W	L	T	Pts	Opp
Houston	9	4	1	258	196
New York	8	5	1	371	329
Buffalo	4	10	0	237	285
Miami	4	10	0	219	407
Boston	3	10	1	280	389

CHAMPIONSHIP GAME:
Oakland 40, Houston 7
WORLD CHAMPIONSHIP GAME:
Green Bay 33, Oakland 14

1968

WESTERN DIVISION

Team	W	L	T	Pts	Opp
Oakland*	12	2	0	453	233
Kansas City*	12	2	0	371	170
San Diego	9	5	0	382	310
Denver	5	9	0	264	404
Cincinnati	3	11	0	215	329

*Oakland won playoff game 41-6

EASTERN DIVISION

Team	W	L	T	Pts	Opp
New York	11	3	0	419	280
Houston	7	7	0	303	248
Miami	5	8	1	276	355
Boston	4	10	0	229	406
Buffalo	1	12	1	199	367

AFL CHAMPIONSHIP GAME:
New York 27, Oakland 23
WORLD CHAMPIONSHIP GAME:
New York Jets 16, Baltimore 7

1969

WESTERN DIVISION

Team	W	L	T	Pts	Opp
Oakland	12	1	1	377	242
Kansas City	11	3	0	359	177
San Diego	8	6	0	288	276
Denver	5	8	1	297	344
Cincinnati	4	9	1	280	367

PLAYOFF: Oakland 56, Houston 7

EASTERN DIVISION

Team	W	L	T	Pts	Opp
New York	10	4	0	353	269
Houston	6	6	2	278	279
Boston	4	10	0	266	316
Buffalo	4	10	0	230	359
Miami	3	10	1	233	332

PLAYOFF: Kansas City 13, New York 6

CHAMPIONSHIP GAME:
Kansas City 17, Oakland 7
WORLD CHAMPIONSHIP GAME:
Kansas City 23, Minnesota 7

Lyle Alzado

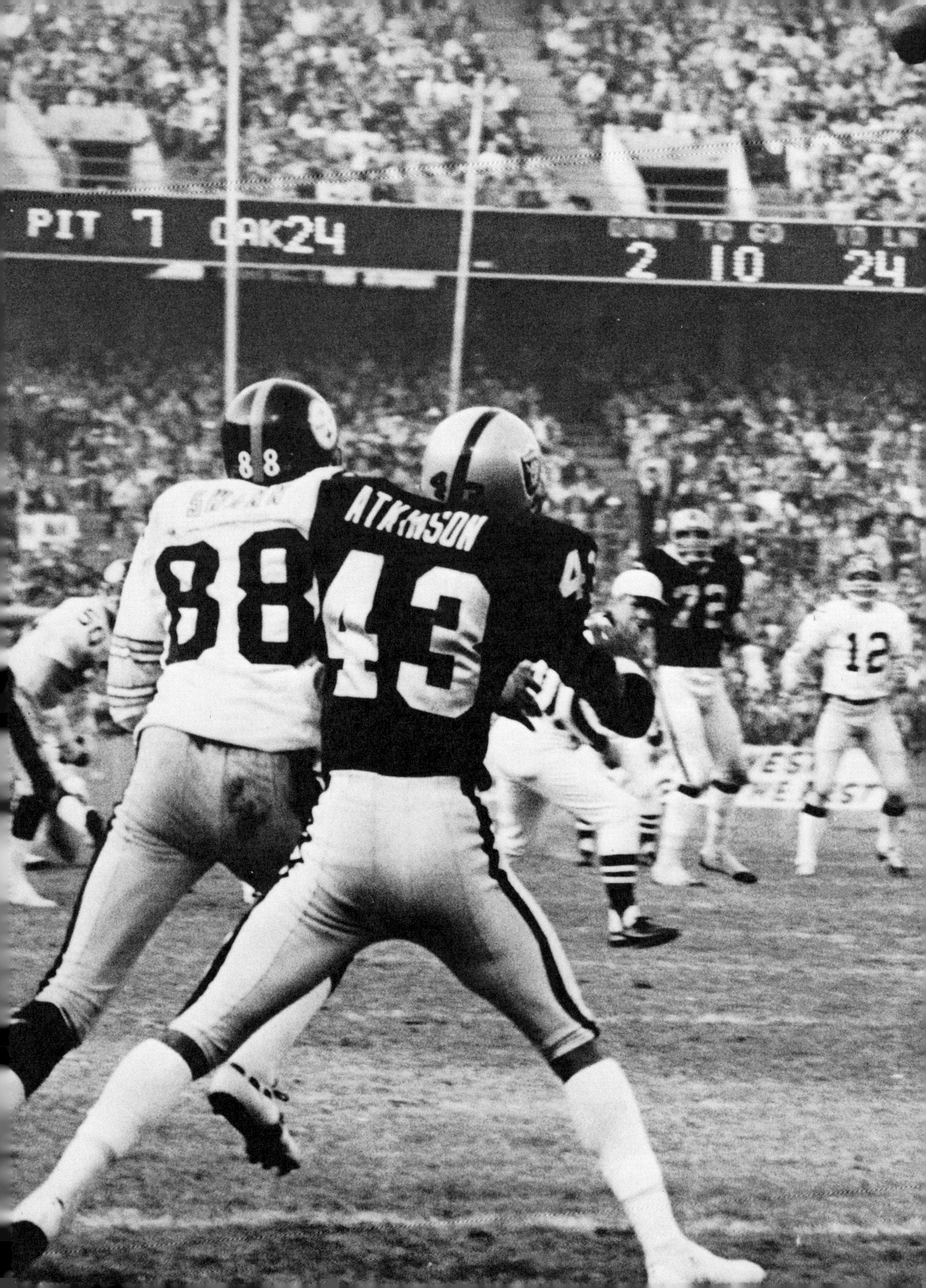
PIT 7 OAK 24
2 10 24
ATKINSON
88
43
72
12

PHOTO CREDITS

AP/Wide World Photos: pages 18, 20, 22, 23, 24 (both), 27, 28-29, 30-31, 35, 36-37, 38-39, 43, 44-45, 51, 53, 54, 55, 59, 61, 68 (top), 71 (bottom)

Glenn Cooper: page 84

Russ Reed: page 104

Michael Zagaris: pages 2-3, 4, 6, 6-7, 8-9, 10-11, 12-13, 14, 25, 33, 41, 46, 49, 57, 64, 66, 67, 68 (bottom), 69, 70, 71 (top), 72-73, 74, 75, 77, 78-79, 80-81, 82, 83 (both), 85, 87, 89, 90-91, 92 (both), 93 (all), 94 (both), 94-95, 96, 98 (both), 99, 100-101, 102-103, 105, 106, 107, 108, 109, 111, 112-113, 114-115, 116, 117 (both), 119, 1212, 122-123, 124, 125 (both), 126, 127, 129, 130, 131, 132 (both), 133, 134, 135 (both), 136 (both), 138, 140, 143, 145, 146-147, 149, 151 (both), 152, 155, 157, 159, 167, 172, 174, 179, 180-181, 182, covers

Pittsburgh Steeler receiver Lynn Swann (88) battles defensive back George Atkinson for position as a pass approaches. **Page 182:** Clarence Davis rambles upfield for a big gain.

INDEX